Against All Odds

Against All Odds

HOW KANSAS WON
THE 1988 NCAA CHAMPIONSHIP

CHUCK WOODLING

PUBLISHED BY THE LAWRENCE JOURNAL-WORLD

DISTRIBUTED BY THE UNIVERSITY PRESS OF KANSAS

Acknowledgments

Journal-World Publisher	Dolph C. Simons, Jr.
"Against All Odds" Editor	Allen Torrey
Editorial Assistant	Bob Nordyke
Photographers	Ben Bigler, Richard Gwin, Brenda Steele, Mike Yoder
Special thanks to	Gary Bedore, Ralph Boylan, Kurt Caywood, Chris Cottrell, Dallas Dolan, Claudia Ericson, Ralph Gage, Lisa Gaumnitz, Tom Hitt, Bill Porter, Butch Porter, Kathy Snyman, Beata Zawadzka

Manufactured by W.A. Krueger in Olathe, Kansas

Distributed by the University Press of Kansas
329 Carruth, Lawrence KS 66045
ISBN O-7006-0387-5

Contents

For Archie Marshall, KU's 1987-88 season held an injury that would end his college career — and an against-all-odds moment of triumph when the Jayhawks netted an NCAA championship in Kemper Arena.

Introduction

All in all, reasoned the members of the Lawrence Cosmopolitan Club, it wasn't a bad idea for a fundraiser.

Why not, a club member suggested, hold a banquet and bring in Bob Knight, coach of Indiana University's men's NCAA champions, as the featured speaker? The controversial Knight was sure to draw a crowd, and the $35 tickets for his talk might be a windfall for the club's charities.

By mid-summer, the deal seemed set. Knight was booked, or so the club thought, to appear on Oct. 12, three days before the opening of preseason basketball practice. But something went wrong. Just days before the banquet, the club members learned that the Indiana coach wasn't coming. It seemed too late to bring in another speaker, and refunding the ticket money already collected seemed like the only alternative.

Enter Larry Brown. On the brink of his fifth season as Kansas head coach, Brown graciously told club officials that he'd bail them out. With four successful seasons at KU behind him, Brown's teams had been filling Allen Fieldhouse, and his own drawing power was con-

In his fifth season at KU, Larry Brown delivered his message to Jayhawk players and to a growing number of fans.

siderable. So from his seat on the dais at the banquet, he listened as master of ceremonies Bob Davis asked the crowd, "Who would you rather have tonight — the coach of last year's national champions, or the coach of next year's NCAA champs?"

Thus with an inadvertent assist from Knight, Davis, play-by-play broadcaster for the Jayhawk Net-

"Who would you rather have tonight — the coach of last year's national champions, or the coach of next year's NCAA champs?"

— BOB DAVIS

Danny Manning had the stuff to stay at KU for his senior year.

Mike Yoder

work, earned an Oscar for prescience. He was telling the Cosmopolitan Club members what they wanted to hear, but he was also stating a fact.

Nearly six months later, at the end of a season of heartbreak, adversity and triumph, Brown's team would indeed capture the men's national basketball championship, KU's first in 36 years. To do it, the Jayhawks would have to overcome an almost overwhelming series of obstacles both on and off the court. It showed in their record. The Jayhawks would go into the championship game against Oklahoma with 11 losses, the most ever for an eventual NCAA champion. Their path to the title would be studded with higher-rated teams and teams that had already beaten KU during the regular season. Their Final Four victories — against all odds — over Duke and Oklahoma ranked among the most memorable upsets in NCAA Tournament history. An irony was that when Knight's Indiana team won the NCAA crown in 1987, the win evoked inevitable comparisons to the movie "Hoosiers," which told the heartwarming story of a small Indiana high school that overcame staggering odds to defeat a big-city school and win the state championship. Yet IU's 1987 team had been highly ranked for most of the season, and the NCAA title was the school's third in 12 years. KU's 1988 win actually reflected more of the "Hoosiers" spirit. Like the movie's tiny high school, the Jayhawks beat adversity and the odds to reach basketball's peak.

But when Brown spoke at the club's banquet, optimism, not obstacles, was on the menu. "We'll be good," he told the audience. "If we're not good, blame it on me. I

feel we'll be great, unless we screw them up."

Enthusiasm for the 1987-88 season had been fueled by an eventful day in May. On May 8, All-American Danny Manning announced he would not apply for the NBA draft; instead he would play his senior season at KU and remain eligible for a place on the 1988 U.S. Olympic basketball team. It was also the day Brown signed a new four-year contract. By then Brown's KU tenure had already outlasted the expectations of many who saw him as a wanderer, a city dweller certain to find Lawrence too limited. But now he would stay.

Actually, Brown's decision had been made a day earlier, when he issued a statement saying: "I'm staying at the University of Kansas. It's final." That announcement was in part prompted by stories that linked Brown to the New York Knicks' head coaching vacancy — as he had been for much of the 1986-87 season. Manning's decision to return no doubt helped Brown make up his own mind.

Also important in Brown's thinking was the signing a couple of days earlier of Otis Livingston, a junior college point guard. Graduation had depleted KU's strength at the position. Gone were Cedric Hunter, the Jayhawks' all-time assist leader, and Mark Turgeon, an experienced back-up. Hunter would go on to play for the Topeka Sizzlers of the CBA, while Turgeon remained with the Jayhawks as student assistant coach. Brown and his staff had been frustrated in their search for immediate help at point guard until they discovered Livingston at El Camino Junior College in California. Livingston didn't score much, but his 12.5 assists per game stood out like a beacon.

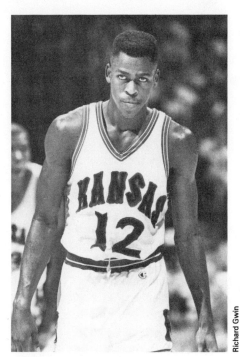

Brown and Otis Livingston would have some glaring problems.

Panthers' 6-10 senior center. Smith had just recanted an earlier decision to turn pro; he would play another year of college ball. "After Charles came back," Branch said, "it was to my advantage to play elsewhere. Kansas was my second choice all along."

Brown saw help ahead for his senior star: With Branch on the floor, Manning, a natural forward whose quickness makes him a threat all over the court, wouldn't have to camp under the basket. "One of the biggest disappointments I had was when he (Branch) said he wasn't

"If we're not good blame it on me. I feel we'll be great, unless we screw them up."

— LARRY BROWN

Marvin Branch would get his lessons at KU, not Pittsburgh.

"He has the skills to step in and contribute immediately," Brown said at the time. "He's an unselfish athlete with excellent quickness and great leadership qualities." At the Cosmopolitan banquet, the coach went further: "By the middle of the year he'll be your favorite player," he said. As it turned out, Livingston was turnover-prone — he would lead the Jayhawks in that category by losing the ball once every 6.7 minutes of playing time — and would also prove prone to confrontations with Brown. But the coach felt better with a promising point guard finally in hand.

Brown was doubly pleased because Marvin Branch, a 6-10 junior college player who had signed with Pittsburgh, had abruptly announced in May that he too was coming to Kansas. Branch's action was spurred by Charles Smith, the

Ben Bigler

Later in the season, Manning would keep Archie Marshall's number close at hand.

Branch's strength, however, wouldn't extend to his first-semester grades, a problem that frustrated Brown, sparked controversy at KU over athletes and academics, and eventually forced Manning back into the middle.

Also stoking preseason optimism was the projected return to health of Archie Marshall — a 6-6 forward and potentially the team's best outside shooter — from a season on the shelf. Marshall had been the sixth man on the Jayhawks' NCAA Final Four team in 1986. Playing perhaps his best game in that year's semifinal clash with Duke in Dallas, he had torn up a knee so badly that he was forced to red-shirt while rehabilitating during the 1986-87 season.

Yet Marshall wouldn't even last as long as Branch. In the last game of 1987, the championship game of the ECAC Holiday Festival in New York's Madison Square Garden, Marshall severely damaged his other knee. His season was history. Brown wept openly on the bench that night. But down the stretch, Marshall would become a force for the Jayhawks, an inspirational force. The KU team used his cheery outlook as a hedge against self-pity. Manning even penned No. 23, Marshall's uniform number, on his wristband. It all helped when times became tough.

They did, too. During one stretch the Jayhawks would lose five of six games, suffer through the end of their record-breaking 55-game homecourt winning streak and feel their hopes sink for earning even a berth in the NCAA Tournament. How they battled back and went on to surprise the nation by fulfilling Bob Davis' Cosmopolitan Club prophecy was to be the stuff of a new Kansas basketball legend.

coming," Brown said. "But we were lucky. He takes the pressure off Danny on the boards and defensively. He's a great, great worker." So Brown had a point guard and a strong inside player to complement his returning All-American. Branch was a scorer and rebounder who would prevent opposing defenses from ganging up on just about everybody's choice as college basketball's player-of-the-year.

Getting started

Chances are, if you were a member of the Kansas team, you spent the summer of 1987 playing basketball in somebody else's backyard. Archie Marshall and Mark Randall went all the way to China with a Big Eight Select team. Kevin Pritchard was on the U.S. Junior World Games team in Bormio, Italy. Danny Manning and Milt Newton, playing for different teams, were both in Indianapolis for the Pan American Games, while junior college transfer Lincoln Minor and freshman recruit Mike Maddox participated in the National Sports Festival in Chapel Hill, N.C. Larry Brown crossed basketball borders too, coaching Pritchard and his fellow Junior World Games teammates on the Italian trip.

None of the traveling Jayhawks, however, played on a championship team during the summer, a fact that may have heightened the Jayhawks' hunger during the NCAA Tournament in the spring. Whatever the implications for KU's season, however, the failure of the U.S. team to win the Pan American Games astonished many Americans. Playing in the Hoosier Dome in Indianapolis, Brazil shocked the U.S. team, coached by Den-

ny Crum of Louisville, 120-115, in the championship game.

"It was tough because everybody just assumed we'd win it," Manning said. "I took it really hard." The senior forward's desire to play on U.S. coach John Thompson's 1988 Olympic team was a factor in his decision not to turn pro after his junior year at KU. Still earlier, as a high school senior, Manning had been one of only two prep players invited to try out for the 1984 Olympic team, but didn't make the squad. He wanted the Americans to win in international competition, and he felt he knew what had gone wrong in Indianapolis.

"We had a lot of talent," he said. "We had a lot of guys who could do a lot of things. But, when I think of it, I think coach Thompson will pick more role players."

Nobody believed in role players more than Brown — the search for effective complements to Manning's talents would mark much of the coming season — but the KU coach also felt that Manning should have played a lead role with the World Games team, and didn't. "He was back into that old mode of his where he lets others step forward," Brown said. "I want him to be assertive.

"I want him (Danny Manning) to be assertive. That doesn't mean he'll be selfish. It's not an equal opportunity sport when you're that talented."

— LARRY BROWN

Larry Brown wanted Danny Manning, fresh from the Pan American Games in Indianapolis, to be more assertive in his senior season at KU.

That doesn't mean he'll be selfish. It's not an equal opportunity sport when you're that talented."

The Virgin Islands' Pan American Games team turned out to be an equal opportunity showcase, however, and a new Jayhawk talent began to emerge over the summer. A little-used reserve during three seasons at Kansas, one as a redshirt, Newton had no hope of making the U.S. squad for the Games. The team from the Virgin Islands embraced him gladly.

"It was kind of a last-minute thing," said Newton, who had been born in the Virgin Islands and whose family had moved to Washington, D.C., not long afterward. Last-minute or not, the arrangement provided a first-rate opportunity. The 6-4 forward averaged 20 points a game for the Virgin Islands, including 32 points against Brazil, the eventual champion.

"Our coach wanted us to take advantage of the three-point line." Newton explained. "Our two biggest guys were 6-8 and 6-6. We'd go inside and they would kick it out. Our coach told the guys to try to get it inside, but if Milt was open, give it to him. He said I was our best shooter. He told me to shoot the three-pointer. Against Brazil, I was seven of 11 (in three-point shots).

"I had a chance to work on my dribbling because I brought the ball up the floor a lot. It really was more physical than college basketball. The Games taught me to deal with physical play. After the Brazil game, my face was swollen. I took an elbow in the face. It was rough."

Overall, Newton felt, "It helped me in terms of confidence, a whole lot of confidence." The added assurance gained in Indianapolis would come in handy when Newton, who had averaged just 3.7

points a game as a sophomore, was thrust into a starting role.

Even though he was playing his summer ball halfway around the world from the Hoosier Dome, Marshall was the Jayhawk under the closest scrutiny. Originally, he wasn't supposed to make the trip to China with a barnstorming Big Eight team. But 15 months after undergoing surgery to repair his knee, Marshall got the stamp of approval from Dr. Ken Wertzberger of Lawrence, the team orthopedist. "I was concerned about him going over there before he was completely healthy," Brown said. "But Dr. Wertzberger cleared him. He said Archie was making tremendous progress."

Marshall needed playing time, even if he had to go to China to find it. He found out, though, that there was no substitute for the court time he'd already missed. "As far as the knee is concerned," he said after getting back to Lawrence, "I had no problems, but I didn't play well on the trip. I was terribly rusty. I didn't play as well as I can. I tried to force a lot of things instead of letting the game come to me." Final statistics for the Chinese trip showed Marshall shot just 24.2 percent (eight of 33) from the field. He was zero for eight from the three-point line. Randall shot better, 56.8 percent (21 of 37).

Pritchard, at the Junior World Games in Italy, soon wondered if he and his teammates would ever get a chance to play in competition. Disastrous floods in northern Italy forced a nine-day postponement of the Bormio tournament and left Brown's U.S. team stranded in West Germany. "We thought we would go straight from Germany and start playing," Pritchard recalled, "but instead we had another week of practice. Actually, we could have used

about another month of practice."

The Junior World Games' team, which had scrimmaged in Allen Fieldhouse before leaving for Europe, played well enough in Italy to make the championship game against Yugoslavia (with Pritchard scoring a team-high 15 points and LaSalle's Lionel Simmons adding 13), but the Yugoslavs won, 86-76. It was no surprise, Brown stressed. "These teams play together a long time and they're used to each other," he said of the European competition. "People don't realize these teams are good. This is a blessing in the long run. People will understand we need to give the kids more time to prepare."

For all his concern about the U.S. effort, international summer basketball isn't the Final Four, and Brown appeared to treat it that way. "Coach Brown was a little different from the way he is during the season," Pritchard noted. "He was more mellow, but all of his concepts were the same."

Once back in Lawrence, Brown's mellow mood ran straight into a series of frustrations over players he'd recruited for KU. He learned that two of his November signees — guard Antoine Lewis and forward Ricky Butler — hadn't qualified academically. So Lewis went off to Hutchinson Community College, and Butler to California-Irvine. And 6-8 center Mark Pellock, who had started 26 games the previous season, wouldn't be a factor in the coming season, either. He was leaving the team, Brown said, in order to resolve personal problems. As it developed, Pellock wouldn't return to school but instead would go to work for a Lawrence T-shirt firm. In early April he was making Jayhawk championship shirts.

For two other freshman recruits,

Milt Newton picked up confidence and his scoring average after starring for the Virgin Islands at the Pan American Games.

"*The keys are how healthy Archie is, and how quick the juco players adjust, and how we replace Ced (Cedric Hunter) and Mark (Turgeon).*"

— LARRY BROWN

the situation was better. Mike Maddox of Putnam City, Okla., who had been the leading high school scorer in Oklahoma during his senior season, was all set, as was 6-10 Mike Masucci of Kansas City, Mo., Grandview. And from the junior college ranks Kansas had recruited Lincoln Minor, Marvin Branch, Otis Livingston and Joe Young.

"I think we have a good mix," Brown said late in the summer. "But I want to keep it real simple and recognize what the kids are capable of doing. I believe the kids we recruited are more suited to what we've done than in the past. The keys are how healthy Archie is, and how quick the juco players adjust, and how we replace Ced (Cedric Hunter) and Mark (Turgeon)."

The junior college transfers' adjustment to life in the Big Eight would challenge Brown to the limit. While other juco transfers like Mookie Blaylock at Oklahoma stepped smoothly into the Division I ranks, Livingston and Minor experienced rough transitions. Branch, after starting several games for the Jayhawks, would be bedeviled by his first-semester grades. And Young never got to play. The 6-6 swingman had averaged 16 points and nine rebounds at Dodge City Community College, but shortly before preseason practice began in mid-October — "that's a helluva time to find out," Brown said — the KU coaching staff learned he didn't have enough credit hours to be eligible under NCAA rules. Young transferred to Washburn University in Topeka for the second semester.

So after a summer on the road, signs of an unstable season loomed. First, though, the levity of Late Night with Larry Brown would offer comic relief, high spirits and a strong

shot of optimism. The midnight show was rapidly establishing itself as a local attraction, especially with KU students. It wasn't exactly New Year's Eve in Times Square or Elvis Presley's birthday in Memphis, but on the night of Oct. 14, Allen Fieldhouse was the place to be in Lawrence. "It's unlike anything else," said Doug Vance, KU's sports information director. "It's a happening."

Two years earlier, Brown decided he'd start KU's preseason practice at the precise moment it became legal under NCAA rules — at 12:01 a.m. on Oct. 15. From a modest beginning, a monster attraction was created. Boosted by an appearance by Larry Melman of the David Letterman Show, Late Night with Larry Brown II in 1986 lured 13,000 fans to Allen Fieldhouse. The size of the throng caught KU officials off guard. But on Oct. 14-15, 1987, they were ready for Late Night III.

It was a good thing they were. An estimated 15,200 fans — only 600 under capacity — squeezed into the 33-year-old fieldhouse. Admission was free, and even without a "name" entertainer, Late Night promised to be something special. It was. By the time the 1987 edition was over, it was clear that never had so many been rewarded so handsomely for coughing up so little loot. There was, for instance, Manning and his teammates singing "My Girl" and that alone was surely worth a bundle more than the non-price of admission. After Manning had crooned the lead vocal on the Temptations' classic, the fans reacted as if he'd just scored his 50th point against Oklahoma on a slam dunk.

Record producers did not, however, come pouring out of the stands, pens and legal paper in hand to offer him a contract. Or as Brown quipped: "Let's put it this way. I'd rather be his agent as a player than as a singer." Added teammate Chris Piper: "From where I was standing, he sounded pretty good, but I think he'd better stick to basketball." Scooter Barry, who teamed with Manning for a rap duo after the "My Girl" rendition, judged Manning's singing "adequate." Then Barry added with a twinkle, "But I don't think he's going into that."

Following the players' vocals, the lights dimmed. When they rekindled, the KU pep band struck up "Goin' to Kansas City" as cheerleaders placed NCAA Final Four logos on the fieldhouse floor. The crowd roared even louder.

Looking on, not by chance, was John Feinstein, a Washington Post sportswriter who had caused a stir the year before by writing "On the Brink," a runaway best-seller that chronicled an Indiana basketball season under Bob Knight. Feinstein was in Lawrence working on a new project, the story of the entire 1987-88 college basketball season. He planned to draw on his experiences at several schools throughout the long campaign, and he decided to use Late Night in Allen Fieldhouse as its beginning.

The Late Night rap on Manning and Scooter Barry was that they'd better stick to basketball.

Ben Bigler

Ben Bigler

On Oct. 15, a No. 1 finish was a cheering possibility.

"Some teams have the goal of just making the NCAAs. Our goal is to go all the way. People are talking about the Final Four already, but that's what they expect."

— CHRIS PIPER

"I couldn't think of a better place to start a book about an entire season than 12:01 a.m. today in Lawrence, Kansas," he said. And why not? There was that electric enthusiasm in the fieldhouse, and Feinstein already knew that his final chapter, with or without the Jayhawks, would unfold in April just 40 miles down the road at Kansas City's Kemper Arena.

Late Night III put the KU players in the singing spotlight and it also highlighted their on-court talent. In the early morning scrimmage that followed the entertainment, the leading scorer was Newton with 21 points. Although not much was expected from the fourth-year junior, he would be heard from later in the season, and loudly, after hard times gave him an opportunity.

"I'm not sure the scrimmage is the attraction," Vance said afterwards. "I'm sure everybody wants to see the team, but they can see them work out every afternoon. The event is the thing."

For the Jayhawks, practice became the thing. After a month of afternoon workouts, KU's annual international exhibition game approached. This year's opponent was the Italian National team, and on Nov. 14 in Allen Fieldhouse the Italians had a better chance of building Rome in a day than they did of stopping Manning that night. The senior forward made 16 of 20 field goal attempts and eight of nine free throws for a 41-point performance in the Jayhawks' 88-82 victory. "He is not a normal player," remarked Sando Dell'Agnello, a guard for the Italian squad. "My teammates," Manning said not for the first and nowhere near the last time in his career, "did a good job of getting me the ball."

That 41-point outing — one under his career high of 42 during the 1987 NCAA Tournament against Southwest Missouri State — didn't count in Manning's career statistics, though, because the game was an exhibition played under international rules. What did count in Brown's mind was the rugged international competition.

"I told our kids they'd be as good as any team we'd play," he said. At the same time, Brown raised a serious concern. He mentioned that the Jayhawks ". . .did not look good in the backcourt when Kevin (Pritchard) was out." Livingston, the junior college transfer, was having difficulties. "He's got a lot of problems with me now," Brown said. "I'm the toughest defensive player he's played against . . . in terms of attitude. He'll be fine, he's a great kid, he's just got to relax." Brown would return to that theme again and again in coming weeks. It would take more than half the season before the coach would discover the elusive solution to KU's problems at guard. But around the time of the

Italian game, Brown was more concerned with recruiting.

The exhibition game took place during the NCAA's early signing period for high school seniors, and Brown struck out, losing such top prospects as Chucky Sproling of Denver to St. John's, and Kansas City, Mo., Paseo's Anthony Peeler to Missouri. The 6-4 Peeler said Brown couldn't assure him that he'd still be in Lawrence next season.

Frustrated by it all, the KU coach lashed out, accusing unnamed rival coaches of harping on rumors that he would leave for you-name-it — another school or an NBA team.. "We've just had a terrible time," Brown said. "Every kid we're involved with hears I'm leaving. It's been awful. More people have hit kids with that. It's a small percentage of schools, but this year it's been really bad.

"It's ironic," Brown continued, that "more than half the kids who say that are being recruited by coaches who haven't been at their institutions half as long as I've been here. I don't like it. I think as a coach you've got a responsibility to sell your program and that's it. To talk negatively like this, I'm surprised and disappointed. I'm not saying we do everything exactly right here, but we never ever talk about other peoples' programs.

"One kid we recruited narrowed it down to five schools. He said, 'Coach I can't come. You won't be there.'" Another, who signed with Kansas State, said he rejected KU and Brown because "I just feel he's going back into the NBA after Manning turns pro." In particular, rumors linked Brown to the Charlotte Hornets, an NBA expansion team. They were based in part on Brown's college days in North Carolina and the fact the Hornets'

general manager, Carl Scheer, was a longtime friend.

Brown, a 47-year-old native of Long Island, N.Y., had started his coaching career with the Carolina Cougars of the old American

"He is not a normal player," Italy's Sando Dell'Agnello observed of Manning.

Mike Yoder

Prognostications

Before the 1987-88 college basketball season started, only one publication — Basketball Times — predicted Kansas would win the NCAA championship. Basketball Times is published in Detroit. Its selections were made by editor Larry Donald.

The Sporting News came in second best. The St. Louis-based publication picked Syracuse to win the national championship, with Kansas second. KU was picked to finish ninth by Dick Vitale, 10th by Game Plan, 14th by Basketball Digest, 17th by Street and Smith and 20th by Inside Sports.

In the Big Eight preseason media poll, the Jayhawks were forecast to finish second to defending champion Missouri. Oklahoma, the team Kansas would defeat in the NCAA title game, was picked for third place.

In the Associated Press poll, compiled from votes by sportswriters and sportscasters all over the country, Kansas was seventh in preseason balloting. Then the Jayhawks, after dropping two of three games at the Maui Classic, fell to 16th in the AP poll the next week. For the next eight weeks, Kansas hovered between the No. 16 and No. 18 positions before eventually dropping out of the poll in late January, after the 80-76 loss to Notre Dame in South Bend, Ind.

Kansas never returned to the AP Top Twenty. During the final seven weeks of the AP poll the Jayhawks received, at most, 17 votes (after their 82-77 win at Missouri), but 27 teams received more votes in that poll. In the final AP poll, taken after Kansas State defeated the Jayhawks, 69-54, in the Big Eight Tournament, KU got only six votes and was ranked No. 33.

Here are some of the preseason polls:

STREET AND SMITH — 1. Purdue. 2. Michigan. 3. North Carolina. 4. Pittsburgh. 5. Duke. 6. Indiana. 7. Louisville. 8. Syracuse. 9. Arizona. 10. Temple. 11. Missouri. 12. DePaul. 13. Georgia Tech. 14. Kentucky. 15. Georgetown. 16. Wyoming. 17. KANSAS. 18. Nevada-Las Vegas. 19. LaSalle. 20. Iowa.

BASKETBALL TIMES — 1. KANSAS. 2. Kentucky. 3. Syracuse. 4. North Carolina. 5. UCLA. 6. Purdue. 7. Memphis State. 8. Iowa. 9. Florida. 10. Pittsburgh. 11. Wyoming. 12. Indiana. 13. Duke. 14. Arizona. 15. LSU. 16. Bradley. 17. Alabama-Birmingham. 18. Missouri. 19. Xavier. 20. Louisville.

GAME PLAN — 1. Pittsburgh. 2. North Carolina. 3. Purdue. 4. Syracuse. 5. Indiana. 6. Louisville. 7. Duke. 8. Georgetown. 9. Kentucky. 10. KANSAS. 11. Michigan. 12. Arizona. 13. North Carolina State. 14. Missouri. 15. Temple. 16. Florida. 17. Arkansas. 18. Georgia Tech. 19. Nevada-Las Vegas. 20. Bradley.

INSIDE SPORTS — 1. Kentucky. 2. Michigan. 3. Pittsburgh. 4. North Carolina. 5. Missouri. 6. Purdue. 7. Temple. 8. Syracuse. 9. Louisville. 10. Wyoming. 11. Indiana. 12. Georgetown. 13. Duke. 14. DePaul. 15. Georgia Tech. 16. Bradley. 17. Notre Dame. 18. Marshall. 19. Florida. 20. KANSAS.

THE SPORTING NEWS — 1. Syracuse. 2. KANSAS. 3. Purdue. 4. Pittsburgh. 5. Temple. 6. Missouri. 7. North Carolina. 8. Iowa. 9. Wyoming. 10. Oklahoma. 11. Indiana. 12. Florida. 13. Louisville. 14. Georgia Tech. 15. Kentucky. 16. Michigan. 17. New Orleans. 18. Arizona. 19. Auburn. 20. Memphis State.

DICK VITALE — 1. Michigan. 2. Kentucky. 3. Indiana. 4. Syracuse. 5. Pittsburgh. 6. Purdue. 7. North Carolina. 8. Missouri. 9. KANSAS. 10. Temple. 11. Arizona. 12. Iowa. 13. Louisville. 14. Duke. 15. Wyoming. 16. Georgia Tech. 17. Georgetown. 18. Notre Dame. 19. Florida. 20. DePaul.

Richard Gwin

Basketball Association during the 1972-73 season. Brown spent two years with the Carolina team, then accompanied the franchise when it moved to Denver. He stayed in the Mile High City for five years, the first three as head coach of the ABA team and the final two as coach of the NBA Nuggets. Actually, he didn't last quite five full years in Denver, resigning in February of 1979 — two months before the season ended — to become head coach at UCLA.

In Brown's first season as a college head coach, he led the Bruins to the 1980 NCAA Final Four, where underdog UCLA lost to Louisville, 59-54, in the championship game. After one more year in Los Angeles, Brown headed cross-country to the New Jersey Nets, where he coached for nearly two seasons. The Nets were six games away from the end of the regular season and on their way to the NBA playoffs with a 47-29 record when Brown abruptly left to become head

coach at Kansas, replacing the fired Ted Owens on April 7, 1983.

Although he had logged five complete seasons at Kansas — his longest coaching stint in one place — Brown's proven ability to win and his reputation for availability continued to focus attention on him whenever a choice coaching job opened.

KU players, with the regular season just around the corner, had more pressing concerns than next year's recruiting class, but they found time to be optimistic. "This is probably the most talented team I've ever been on at KU," Manning said. "It's a lot of fun to come out and play against these guys in practice. I hope all the guys here can make an impact." Fifth-year senior Piper wasn't reluctant to proclaim the team's top priority. "Some teams have the goal of just making the NCAAs," he said. "Our goal is to go all the way. People are talking about the Final Four already, but that's what they expect."

"This is probably the most talented team I've ever been on at KU."

— DANNY MANNING

*"I told our kids
they'd be as good as
any team we'd
play."*

— LARRY BROWN

Mark Randall's season began
and ended with Italy.

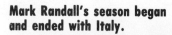

Defense by Lincoln Minor and
Barry helped KU steal the
show against the rugged
Italians.

Branch was counted on for his
defense and rebounding.

For Brown, international competition was a plus, recruiting
woes a recurring headache.

2

Sea cruise?

Haleakala is a huge, dormant volcano that rises more than 10,000 feet and dominates the eastern half of the Hawaiian island of Maui. Among the many diversions for tourists on Maui is an exhilarating bicycle ride from the top of Haleakala — it means House of the Sun — all the way down to the beaches below.

Kansas opened its regular basketball season during Thanksgiving weekend on Maui and, like the Haleakala cyclists, the Jayhawks went downhill in a hurry.

None of the seven other schools in the Maui Classic was ranked any higher in the Associated Press preseason poll than No. 7 Kansas. The Jayhawks quickly affirmed that ranking by punishing host Chaminade, an NAIA school with a reputation as a giant-killer, by a score of 89-62 in the opening round at the Lahaina Civic Center. Kansas seemed determined to make its second straight visit to the Hawaiian Islands more pleasurable than the first. A year earlier, KU had played in the Rainbow Classic in Honolulu and dropped two of three games.

"Last year was kind of a downer and we didn't want that to happen again," said Danny Manning after

NOV. 27 AT LAHAINA, HAWAII

Kansas (89)

	MIN	FG m-a	FT m-a	REB o-t	PF	TP
Archie Marshall	25	5-9	0-0	2-3	2	10
Danny Manning.	33	10-18	4-5	3-9	1	24
Marvin Branch.	16	3-6	5-6	1-3	5	11
Kevin Pritchard	31	3-5	6-6	0-3	2	12
Lincoln Minor	25	2-4	0-0	0-3	2	4
Scooter Barry	11	0-1	0-1	0-2	2	0
Otis Livingston	12	5-5	2-2	0-2	1	12
Mike Maddox.	10	1-2	0-0	0-1	2	3
Jeff Gueldner.	16	1-2	3-4	2-4	1	5
Mike Masucci	21	4-6	0-0	0-3	4	8
Totals		34-58	20-24	8-33	22	89

Three-point goals: 1-2 (Maddox 1-1, Pritchard 0-1). **Assists:** 20 (Minor 5, Livingston 4, Pritchard 3, Manning 3, Barry 2, Marshall 2, Gueldner). **Turnovers:** 15 (Minor 5, Pritchard 3, Barry 2, Marshall, Manning, Gueldner, Branch, Masucci). **Blocked shots:** 4 (Manning 2, Branch, Masucci). **Steals:** 9 (Minor 2, Livingston 2, Pritchard 2, Barry, Manning, Masucci).

Chaminade (62)

	MIN	FG m-a	FT m-a	REB o-t	PF	TP
Sam Trusty	29	4-11	0-3	3-5	3	8
Peter Schomers.	32	0-8	2-2	2-5	.2	2
John Wyatt	28	4-9	2-4	2-5	3	10
Rod McCray.	35	6-20	4-6	3-3	2	18
Walter Carpenter. . . .	28	0-5	0-1	1-2	5	0
Arthur King	30	9-12	3-4	6-10	4	21
Anthony Hall	11	0-1	0-0	0-0	1	0
Bruce Mann	12	0-1	3-3	0-1	0	3
Totals		23-67	14-23	17-31	20	62

Three-point goals: 2-15 (McCray 2-10, Carpenter 0-3, Schomers 0-2). **Assists:** 10 (McCray 4, Mann 3, Carpenter, Schomers, Trusty). **Turnovers:** 18 (McCray 5, King 3, Schomers 3, Carpenter 2, Wyatt 2, Trusty 2, Hall). **Blocked shots:** 1 (King). **Steals:** 2 (McCray, Carpenter).

Kansas	39	50 — 89
Chaminade	28	34 — 62

Technical foul: Pritchard. **Officials:** Jim Burch, Wayne Samford, Donovan Lewis. **Attendance:** 3,000.

"I'm hard on the point guards because I'm spoiled. I just want us to be great yesterday."

— LARRY BROWN

scoring 24 points and pulling down nine rebounds in the Chaminade cruise. Added Archie Marshall, "Last year I didn't think we were ready to play. This year we came in with our heads on straight."

Coach Larry Brown saw a lot to like, especially in the backcourt, where junior college transfer Otis Livingston came off the bench to score a dozen points in a dozen minutes. Livingston, however, never scored that many points in a game again, and the point guard position would remain a Jayhawk problem spot for weeks to come. There were signs of trouble already. A few days before the Hawaiian trip, Brown had complained that ". . . we don't have any direction on the court. We haven't had anybody assume that responsibility." KU's coach hadn't been tender in pushing point guards toward perfection in preseason practices. "I'm hard on the point guards because I'm spoiled," Brown said. "I just want us to be great yesterday." Chaminade coach Merv Lopes thought the Jayhawks were great enough as is. "That's a big-time team," he said. "That's a Final Four team."

Like broadcaster Bob Davis at the Cosmopolitan Club function, Lopes turned out to be a prophet, but the Final Four was a long way off. The Jayhawks wouldn't be great tomorrow or the next day, either. They were, in fact, about to be dotted — emphatically — by a couple of I's. Iowa beat KU handily, 100-81, in the tourney semifinals and Illinois added to the misery by winning 81-75 in a consolation game that wasn't as close as the final score.

The Iowa game was particularly brutal, and not just because of the score. The referees called 52 personal fouls — 30 on Kansas, 22 on Iowa — as well as five technicals

NOV. 28 AT LAHAINA, HAWAII

Kansas (81)

	MIN	FG m-a	FT m-a	REB o-t	PF	TP
Archie Marshall	30	6-13	1-2	0-2	4	16
Danny Manning	33	10-16	3-6	3-7	5	23
Marvin Branch	16	2-3	2-2	1-1	4	6
Kevin Pritchard	28	5-13	0-3	1-2	5	10
Lincoln Minor	26	4-9	1-2	2-3	2	9
Otis Livingston	18	2-3	0-0	1-2	3	4
Milt Newton	9	2-5	2-4	1-2	2	6
Mike Maddox	7	0-1	0-0	0-1	0	0
Jeff Gueldner	10	1-3	0-0	0-0	3	2
Mike Masucci	23	2-5	1-2	2-4	2	5
Totals		34-71	10-21	11-24	30	81

Three-point goals: 3-9 (Marshall 3-5, Gueldner 0-2, Maddox 0-1, Pritchard 0-1). Assists: 23 (Livingston 8, Minor 5, Pritchard 4, Manning 3, Marshall 2, Branch). Turnovers: 21 (Manning 5, Livingston 3, Masucci 3, Minor 2, Branch 2, Gueldner 2, Newton 2, Pritchard, Marshall). Blocked shots: 5 (Manning 2, Pritchard, Maddox, Branch). Steals: 8 (Minor 3, Livingston 2, Manning 2, Masucci).

Iowa (100)

	MIN	FG m-a	FT m-a	REB o-t	PF	TP
Kent Hill	25	4-6	6-6	2-7	4	14
Al Lorenzen	29	2-4	7-7	1-5	2	11
Roy Marble	29	7-10	8-10	1-5	0	22
Bill Jones	28	5-7	5-7	2-4	3	15
B. J. Armstrong	24	2-6	0-0	0-2	3	5
Jeff Moe	24	7-11	3-5	1-3	2	22
Ed Horton	11	1-5	1-2	0-0	5	3
Michael Reaves	15	1-2	6-6	0-2	1	8
Mike Morgan	2	0-0	0-0	0-0	0	0
Mark Jewell	11	0-1	0-0	1-3	2	0
Les Jepsen	2	0-0	0-0	0-0	0	0
Totals		29-52	36-43	8-31	22	100

Three-point goals: 6-10 (Moe 5-7, Armstrong 1-2, Lorenzen 0-1). Assists: 19 (Moe 5, Armstrong 4, Jones 3, Marble 2, Jewell 2, Lorenzen 2, Reaves). Turnovers: 27 (Lorenzen 7, Marble 6, Moe 4, Horton 3, Hill 3, Armstrong, Jones, Morgan, Jewell). Blocked shots: 0. Steals: 7 (Hill 2, Armstrong, Reaves, Moe, Marble, Lorenzen).

Kansas	39 42	— 81
Iowa	54 46	— 100

Technical fouls: Lorenzen, Kansas coach Brown, Manning, Branch (ejected), Kansas bench, Iowa bench. Officials: Jim McDaniels, Joe Shosid, Ryan Suroka. Attendance: 1,500.

(including one on the usually mild-mannered Manning), a flagrant foul and an intentional foul. The flagrant foul was against KU's Marvin Branch, who touched off a bench-clearing incident with 5:26 remaining by taking a swing at Iowa's Michael Reaves. "He elbowed me in the throat," explained Branch, who was ejected from the game. "I just retaliated. I didn't think it was fair, but I guess the ref didn't see it when he cheap-shotted me."

Brown thought the officials didn't

see a lot of things, and was himself the victim of one of the technicals. He was mostly unhappy about Branch picking up two fouls in the first four and a half minutes. KU was leading by seven points when Brown had to sit Branch down. Iowa, led by the three-point shooting of reserve Jeff Moe (five of seven), raced to leads of as many as 23 points in the second half. The Hawkeyes were the only other ranked team in the Maui Classic — No. 11 in the AP poll — but this game was an embarrassment for Kansas.

"I didn't think we were ready to play a team like that at this time," Brown said calmly following a 15-minute, decidedly uncalm postgame debriefing with his players. "Iowa got us into the game they wanted to play and we didn't stop them. I thought they were great. I love their team."

The Iowa postgame session wasn't for the faint of heart. Brown was highly emotional and critical. "It wasn't a very good scene," senior Chris Piper reflected after the season. "He was pretty upset and, you know, it's probably the worst game this KU team played. A lot of nasty things were said. But everybody was upset, coach and all of us."

Piper had seen plenty of Brown's postgame sessions and, he confirmed, this one "would rank up with them. Iowa State is usually the hardest postgame speech when we lose up there, but this one ranked."

Iowa went on to wallop Villanova for the Maui Classic title. Kansas, its island woes continuing for a second year, failed to bounce back against Illinois. Despite 28 points and 12 rebounds from Manning, KU fell behind by as many as 19 points early in the second half. A late rally made the 81-75 score respectable, but the

Jayhawks had clearly lost a lot of self-confidence.

"It's a rude awakening," guard Kevin Pritchard confessed. What had gone wrong? Defense. Iowa shot 55.7 percent; Illinois 50.8 percent. And the two Big Ten teams made a total of 73 trips to the foul line (Iowa 43; Illinois 30). "We're letting people get to the free throw line and that's a sign of not being a good defensive team," Brown said. "When you've got so many young kids, you realize you have a deficiency, and that's defense."

While in Hawaii, Brown made two decisions about red-shirting.

NOV. 29 AT LAHAINA, HAWAII

Kansas (75)

	MIN	FG m-a	FT m-a	REB o-t	PF	TP
Archie Marshall	12	2-4	0-0	1-2	3	5
Danny Manning.	37	13-20	2-4	5-12	5	28
Marvin Branch.	24	4-8	2-2	1-5	5	10
Kevin Pritchard	34	4-8	4-7	2-3	4	12
Lincoln Minor	26	5-10	0-0	1-2	2	10
Otis Livingston	16	0-4	0-0	0-2	3	0
Milt Newton.	7	1-2	0-0	0-2	3	2
Jeff Gueldner.	26	3-3	0-0	0-2	3	6
Mike Masucci	18	1-1	0-1	0-1	3	2
Totals		33-60	8-14	10-31	31	75

Three-point goals: 1-6 (Marshall 1-1, Minor 0-2, Manning 0-2, Livingston 0-1). Assists: 17 (Minor 5, Pritchard 3, Manning 3, Gueldner 2, Masucci 2, Livingston, Marshall, Masucci). Turnovers: 20 (Minor 4, Livingston 4, Gueldner 3, Branch 3, Newton 2, Manning 2, Pritchard, Masucci). Blocked shots: 4 (Branch 3, Manning). Steals: 8 (Minor 2, Pritchard 2, Livingston, Marshall, Manning, Gueldner).

Illinois (81)

	MIN	FG m-a	FT m-a	REB o-t	PF	TP
Nick Anderson.	19	1-4	0-0	1-5	2	2
Ken Battle	39	9-15	3-5	3-6	3	21
Jens Kujawa	30	4-8	0-2	4-7	1	8
Kendall Gill.	29	4-9	3-4	1-4	3	12
Steve Bardo.	29	3-8	3-5	3-4	4	9
Glynn Blackwell.	27	4-6	5-7	1-1	0	13
Larry Smith	16	4-8	1-1	1-1	2	9
Ervin Small.	1	0-0	0-0	0-0	1	0
Lowell Hamilton	9	2-3	3-6	0-2	1	7
Totals		31-61	18-30	14-30	17	81

Three-point goals: 1-4 (Gill 1-3, Blackwell 0-1). Assists: 13 (Gill 4, Blackwell 2, Anderson 2, Bardo 2, Kujawa 2, Smith). Turnovers: 17 (Gill 5, Smith 3, Blackwell 2, Battle 2, Kujawa 2, Anderson, Bardo, Hamilton). Blocked shots: 1 (Battle). Steals: 12 (Battle 4, Gill 3, Blackwell 3, Smith 2).

Kansas	33	42 — 75
Illinois	48	33 — 81

Technical foul: Kansas coach Brown. Officials: Jim McDaniels, Wayne Samford, Donovan Lewis. Attendance: 350.

" . . . it's probably the worst game this KU team played. A lot of nasty things were said. But everybody was upset, coach and all of us."

— CHRIS PIPER

There were plenty of times when Larry Brown didn't like what he saw.

Richard Gwin

Sophomore Mark Randall would be held out so he could undergo surgery to correct an elongated jaw, and senior Sean Alvarado, in a move that would spawn some second thoughts later on, would be given an extra year to improve his strength and conditioning.

There were other disappointments. Piper wasn't able to suit up for the games after injuring his right knee in practice on Nov. 17. He underwent arthroscopic surgery in what turned out to be a minor operation five days later. Sophomore forward Keith Harris was left behind in Lawrence for undisclosed reasons. After the Italian exhibition game, Brown had said Harris wouldn't play until he "shows the team and everybody he'll be responsible about the right things."

In addition, Milt Newton had to sit out the Chaminade game because of an NCAA ruling based on the handling of billing for his personal travel. On three occasions the KU athletic department had collected payment from Newton for personal travel, then forwarded the money to a travel agent. The NCAA judged those transactions inappropriate. Newton was ordered to miss two games — the exhibition with Italy and the season opener against Chaminade. The junior from Washington, D.C., did play against Iowa and Illinois, but for only nine minutes against the Hawkeyes and seven against the Illinois. His combined totals were eight points and six rebounds.

With Newton hardly a factor, KU used the same starting lineup in all three Maui Classic contests — Manning and Marshall up front with Branch at center and Lincoln Minor and Pritchard in the backcourt. It was a lineup that wouldn't last much longer.

"The effort in Hawaii, in those two games, was the poorest of any team I've coached. It's scary. Everybody must care like Kevin and Archie."

— LARRY BROWN

Brown's analysis of the Iowa and Illinois games was as rough as the play on Maui. "The effort in Hawaii, in those two games," he said, "was the poorest of any team I've coached. It's scary. Everybody must care like Kevin and Archie. We've got to have everybody with that attitude. I want to have fun, to be a cheerleader on the bench. That's what I hope will happen."

To get the point across, Brown had made his team watch film of the 100-81 loss to Iowa. "To be brutally honest, we got our butts kicked against Iowa," he concluded. "That game embarrassed everybody."

With its record standing at 1-2, Kansas had dropped from seventh to 16th in the AP weekly poll. A crowded early December schedule and more road games loomed. First, though, came a kind of reunion, and the season's most lopsided victory.

Only two days after the blues of Hawaii, Kansas made its regular-season debut in Allen Fieldhouse before a crowd of 15,100 and blasted Pomona-Pitzer, 94-38, to extend the homecourt win streak to a Big Eight-record 49 games. In the California school, Kansas didn't face the collegiate equivalent of the Los Angeles Lakers. An NCAA Division III team with its tallest player standing 6-4, the Sagehens were on the schedule only because their coach, Greg Popovich, had spent a sabbatical on Brown's staff the previous season. Brown had agreed to the game so Pomona-Pitzer's players could experience play at the Division I level.

The view was sobering. The Jayhawks shot a school record 75.9 percent. Pomona-Pitzer scored a grand total of 13 points in the second half, while Kansas had 49. Manning, playing only 19 minutes,

DEC. 1 AT LAWRENCE

Pomona-Pitzer (38)

	MIN	FG	FT	REB	PF	TP
		m-a	m-a	o-t		
David Todd	27	3-10	0-0	0-2	2	7
Rick Duque	27	8-17	2-4	2-3	0	18
James Johnson	30	2-6	1-2	2-5	4	5
Ethan Caldwell	18	1-4	0-0	1-1	0	2
Matt Weyer	25	0-1	0-0	2-2	4	0
G. Hendricksen	24	0-3	0-0	0-0	4	0
Keith Davis	12	0-2	0-0	0-0	1	0
Ashanti Payne	21	2-6	0-1	1-3	3	4
C. Buckholtz	10	1-1	0-1	0-0	0	2
John Peterson	1	0-0	0-0	0-0	0	0
Evan Lee	3	0-0	0-0	0-0	1	0
Raymond Struck	1	0-0	0-0	0-0	0	0
Bernie Wharton	1	0-0	0-0	0-0	0	0
Totals		17-50	3-8	8-16	19	38

Three-point goals: 1-8 (Todd 1-4, Caldwell 0-2, Weyer 0-1, Payne 0-1). **Assists:** 10 (Payne 4, Caldwell 2, Weyer 2, Hendricksen, Davis). **Turnovers:** 27 (Caldwell 5, Duque 4, Payne 4, Johnson 3, Todd 3, Hendricksen 2, Davis 2, Struck 2, Weyer, Bucholtz). **Blocked shots:** 2 (Hendricksen 2). **Steals:** 4 (Hendricksen 2, Payne 2).

Kansas (94)

	MIN	FG	FT	REB	PF	TP
		m-a	m-a	o-t		
Danny Manning	19	6-7	0-0	0-2	1	12
Archie Marshall	23	3-6	0-0	1-4	0	6
Marvin Branch	29	7-8	3-7	2-12	2	17
Lincoln Minor	12	2-2	0-0	0-0	2	4
Kevin Pritchard	20	7-9	3-4	0-2	2	17
Otis Livingston	14	3-3	1-2	0-0	1	7
Mike Masucci	16	2-5	0-0	0-2	2	4
Jeff Gueldner	18	3-4	2-2	2-2	0	8
Milt Newton	17	3-3	0-0	2-3	2	6
Scooter Barry	16	3-3	0-0	0-0	0	6
Mike Maddox	16	2-4	3-5	2-5	2	7
Totals		41-54	12-20	9-32	14	94

Three-point goals: 0-0. **Assists:** 24 (Pritchard 6, Newton 5, Marshall 3, Minor 3, Livingston 2, Barry 2, Branch, Masucci, Gueldner). **Turnovers:** 18 (Livingston 5, Barry 5, Branch 2, Manning, Marshall, Pritchard, Masucci, Newton, Maddox). **Blocked shots:** 5 (Manning 3, Marshall, Branch). **Steals:** 17 (Pritchard 7, Manning 2, Minor 2, Livingston 2, Barry 2, Branch, Newton).

Pomona-Pitzer	25	13 — 38
Kansas	45	49 — 94

Officials: Mike Kouri, Charles Greene, Roger Baldwin. **Attendance:** 15,100.

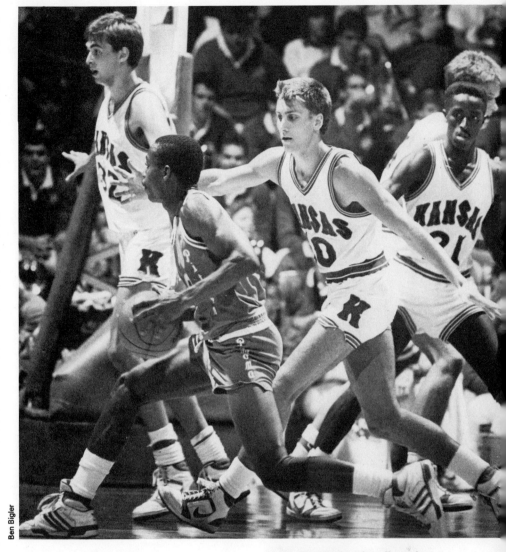

Ben Bigler

The taller Jayhawks allowed Pomona-Pitzer only 13 points in the second half. But when it came to effort, Larry Brown said KU came up short.

scored just 12 points, tying his season low. With Manning's output down, Branch and Pritchard led the Jayhawks with 17 points apiece. It was to be one of only three times all season that someone other than Manning would be the team scoring leader. Pritchard also had seven steals and six assists and, said Brown, was "an unbelievable example" of how the team should be playing.

Though Kansas won by 56 points, the coach saw little overall improvement over the Iowa and Illinois

defeats on Maui. "He's upset . . . he's very upset," senior Archie Marshall told sportswriters after the game. "He's mad." Why? "We've got such a long way to go," Brown said. "It's gut-wrenching. It's scary. It's just not there. Some kids are trying. We didn't have enough. I think they're a little tired, but hell, this is a game. Hell, all our kids were lying on the beach. We didn't get tired the way we played in Hawaii."

Some fatigue was inevitable, though, because of the crowded schedule ahead. It was evenly spaced with odd numbers — games on the 1st, 3rd, 5th and 7th of December. First it was off to

Marvin Branch put the arm on Pomona-Pitzer's Sagehens for 17 points and 12 rebounds.

13 of 16 attempts and finishing with 30 points. But his six rebounds didn't impress the KU coach, and Brown also felt a crucial intangible was missing. "Danny is not comfortable with his leadership role, something all great players learn to accept," he said.

Prodded by Brown and by the loss of key teammates to injury and academics, Manning would eventually accept that role. However, Kansas' fans absolutely could not accept the yellow uniforms the Jayhawks had worn for the first time at Western Carolina. A gift from the team's uniform outfitter, the amber togs brought Brown a load of negative mail, mainly from critics

Cullowhee, N.C. — you can barely get there from here, or anywhere else — for a Dec. 3 meeting with Western Carolina.

On the road, a win is a win is a win, but when the Jayhawks led 66-44 in the late going and then surrendered 17 unanswered points, Brown sensed deep problems. "Our team is tremendously overrated," he said. But he felt the Jayhawks could learn from their 68-63 victory regardless. "We have no direction right now. We have a lot of kids trying to find themselves. It'll take time," he said. But "to play with adversity in games like this will help prepare you. There were a lot of good lessons out there tonight."

Manning shot brilliantly, making

DEC. 3 AT CULLOWHEE, N.C.

Kansas (68)

	MIN	FG m-a	FT m-a	REB o-t	PF	TP
Danny Manning	37	13-16	4-7	3-6	1	30
Archie Marshall	17	3-6	1-1	2-6	3	7
Marvin Branch	33	4-11	0-0	3-11	0	8
Lincoln Minor	25	3-6	0-1	0-1	2	6
Kevin Pritchard	37	6-9	1-3	0-0	2	13
Otis Livingston	14	0-0	0-1	0-0	2	0
Jeff Gueldner	16	2-3	0-0	0-1	3	4
Mike Masucci	5	0-0	0-0	0-0	1	0
Milt Newton	7	0-1	0-0	0-0	0	0
Scooter Barry	4	0-2	0-0	0-0	0	0
Chris Piper	5	0-1	0-0	0-0	0	0
Totals		31-55	6-13	8-25	14	68

Three-point goals: 0-0. **Assists:** 10 (Minor 3, Gueldner 2, Manning, Marshall, Branch, Livingston, Masucci). **Turnovers:** 19 (Manning 4, Branch 3, Minor 3, Livingston 3, Gueldner 3, Marshall, Pritchard, Piper). **Blocked shots:** 4 (Manning 3, Branch). **Steals:** 6 (Manning 2, Marshall, Minor, Pritchard, Gueldner).

Western Carolina (63)

	MIN	FG m-a	FT m-a	REB o-t	PF	TP
Robert Hill	38	3-11	0-0	3-4	3	6
Bennie Goettie	37	4-13	7-8	2-10	4	15
Andre Gault	39	8-14	1-1	5-9	4	17
Robert Hutchison	36	7-10	1-3	1-2	0	17
Kenny Brown	31	4-12	0-2	1-4	4	8
Maurice Johnson	9	0-0	0-0	0-0	1	0
Mitch Madden	9	0-0	0-0	0-1	1	0
Jim Yates	1	0-0	0-0	0-1	0	0
Totals		26-60	9-13	12-31	17	63

Three-point goals: 2-9 (Hutchison 2-4, Hill 0-2, Brown 0-3). **Assists:** 16 (Hutchison 7, Brown 5, Hill 2, Goettie, Gault). **Turnovers:** 21 (Brown 6, Goettie 5, Johnson 3, Madden 2, Hill 2, Gault 2, Hutchison). **Blocked shots:** 3 (Goettie, Gault, Madden). **Steals:** 8 (Gault 3, Goettie 2, Hill, Hutchison, Brown).

Kansas	35 33	68
Western Carolina	22 41	63

Officials: Rich Eichhorst, Bill Summers, Verl Sell. **Attendance:** 4,603.

who said they made the Jayhawks look more like Missouri than Kansas. "I like them, but they're history," the coach announced later. True to his word, Brown never had the Jayhawks wear yellow again.

KU's next opponent loomed as the toughest test since Iowa and Illinois. St. John's, unbeaten in four games, came to Allen Fieldhouse for a nationally televised Saturday afternoon game, and the Redmen ran into a buzzsaw — a Kansas team that seemed to have learned its lessons. The Jayhawks were ready to play defense.

St. John's arrived with a much-ballyhooed backcourt tandem of Greg "Boo" Harvey and Michael Porter, who had starred for San Jacinto (Texas) Junior College a year earlier. Thanks to defensive pressure from guards Minor, Livingston and Pritchard, the two St. John's newcomers combined for just 14 points on seven of 22 shooting, Harvey going three of 14 for six points.

"We played better on defense," said Minor, who like Livingston, had two steals. "If we played like this in Hawaii, I think we'd have won more than one game." The Jayhawks' pressure paid off early. Kansas forced 10 first-half turnovers and stormed to a 33-24 halftime lead. Manning scored 12 of his game-high 21 points in the half, putting KU in front to stay. Kansas won, 64-53, as Manning, Pritchard (17) and Marshall (12) combined for 50 points. The defense — missing in action in Hawaii — was devastating. "If you take away their offensive boards (14), we had a great defensive night," Brown said.

St. John's coach Lou Carnesecca agreed, saying Kansas had ". . . an excellent defense. It's the best we've

DEC. 5 AT LAWRENCE

St. John's (54)

	MIN	FG m-a	FT m-a	REB o-t	PF	TP
Shelton Jones	39	7-14	3-5	4-10	0	17
Matt Brust	17	0-3	2-2	1-1	5	2
Marco Baldi	37	3-4	0-0	0-3	2	6
Greg Harvey	36	3-14	0-0	2-4	3	6
Michael Porter	34	4-8	0-0	1-3	2	8
J. Williams	24	5-9	1-2	5-6	2	11
Elander Lewis	11	1-3	0-0	0-0	0	2
Sean Muto	2	1-1	0-0	0-0	0	2
Totals		24-56	6-9	13-27	14	54

Three-point goals: 0-4 (Jones 0-1, Brust 0-1, Harvey 0-1, Lewis 0-1), Assists: 8 (Jones 3, Harvey 3, Baldi, Porter). Turnovers: 14 (Harvey 6, Jones 4, Brust 2, Porter, Lewis). Blocked shots: 1 (Williams). Steals: 5 (Jones, Baldi, Harvey, Porter, Lewis).

Kansas (63)

	MIN	FG m-a	FT m-a	REB o-t	PF	TP
Danny Manning	38	9-15	3-3	2-5	3	21
Archie Marshall	37	6-11	0-0	1-5	3	12
Marvin Branch	29	1-3	0-0	0-4	1	2
Lincoln Minor	20	2-6	0-0	1-2	0	4
Kevin Pritchard	31	8-11	1-2	0-3	2	17
Otis Livingston	20	0-0	3-4	0-1	2	3
Chris Piper	14	1-1	0-0	0-0	0	2
Keith Harris	2	0-0	0-0	0-0	1	0
Scooter Barry	9	1-1	0-0	0-0	0	2
Totals		28-48	7-9	4-20	12	63

Three-point goals: 0-1 (Marshall 0-1). Assists: 15 (Livingston 5, Manning 2, Branch 2, Minor 2, Pritchard 2, Barry 2). Turnovers: 13 (Manning 4, Branch 3, Livingston 3, Minor 2, Pritchard). Blocked shots: 1 (Manning). Steals: 11 (Minor 2, Livingston 2, Piper 2, Manning, Marshall, Branch, Pritchard, Barry).

St. John's	24	30	— 54
Kansas	33	30	— 63

Technical fouls: Pritchard. Officials: Verl Sell, Mike Tanco, Woody Mayfield. Attendance: 15,800.

seen this year. They had so many fast breaks. It was like we were wearing galoshes." Less than a month later the overshoes would be on the other feet, however, when KU met St. John's in the championship game of the ECAC Holiday Festival.

Everybody wanted to talk about KU's rugged man-to-man pressure after this Allen Fieldhouse meeting. "I wouldn't say we played great defense. I want it to be great at the end of the year," said Pritchard. "I'd call it good defense." Manning, who had held 6-9 senior Shelton Jones to 17 points, said, "Coach has been on us at practice, trying to make us become a better defensive team. We're always out there trying, but

It wasn't the best of times for St. John's Lou Carnesecca.

Richard Gwin

22

KU's quickness produced so many fast breaks that Carnesecca said it was as if St. John's was wearing galoshes.

Richard Gwin

"I started very slowly, took some shots out of my range. Coach Brown told me to slow it down and gradually get into the game."

— DANNY MANNING

tonight we were really intense."

Brown had actually benched Manning for a spell in the first half, and it served as a wakeup call. "I thought he took some quick shots," the coach said. "We've been having trouble with kids not making extra passes and I told him he needs to set an example. He came back and was phenomenal the rest of the way."

"I started very slowly, took some shots out of my range," Manning confirmed. "Coach Brown told me

to slow it down and gradually get into the game. He told me to slow down." A sidelight was Harris making his first exit from Brown's doghouse. He played two minutes but didn't score. "He's back in good graces," Brown reported.

The Jayhawks were working on a three-game winning streak, but their performances hadn't won raves in the AP poll. KU had dropped two notches, to 18th, in that week's rankings. Then, on the night of the day of the poll's release, they dropped more than two notches — in Brown's estimation anyway — after a sluggish 73-62 win over Appalachian State in Allen Fieldhouse.

Manning scored 19 points, Marshall 14, Branch 11 and Scooter Barry a career-high 10. Kansas had an unsightly 23 turnovers, but Appalachian State had 28, and shot only 34.7 percent (17 of 49) to KU's 51 percent (27 of 53). "I'm shocked we won," Brown said. "We won by 11 points. That's the biggest joke ever. They were better coached and better prepared. I've done a terrible job with this team. We don't do things that require effort. The only thing this team understands is discipline and punishment. That's

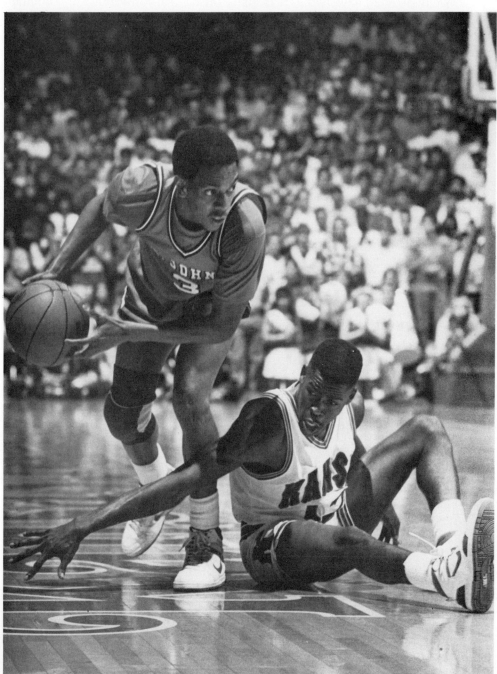

"The only thing this team understands is discipline and punishment. That's the only way they'll become a team. We'll be prepared from now on."

— LARRY BROWN

Otis Livingston played 20 minutes against the Redmen, picking up a pair of steals.

Mike Yoder

The Jayhawks needed effort and more effort, Brown told Scooter Barry and his teammates.

the only way they'll become a team. We'll be prepared from now on."

After four games in a week, the schedule showed only two games in the next 12 days, and Brown told his players, in effect, that they were about to enlist in basic training. "Coach Brown said these will be the hardest three weeks we'll ever experience," Barry reported. "He said we're going to have two-a-days, that we'll practice like hell. He said we'll play the way he wants us to play. And the only way to do it is to make us fear him."

DEC. 7 AT LAWRENCE

Appalachian State (62)

	MIN	FG m-a	FT m-a	REB o-t	PF	TP
R. Christian	39	1-5	6-8	1-5	3	8
Ben Miller	26	4-8	2-2	1-2	5	10
Sam Gibson	18	1-6	4-4	3-6	4	6
Kemp Phillips	36	6-14	4-5	1-5	3	20
Rodney Peel	37	3-11	4-5	0-4	1	13
Jerry Holmes	21	1-1	1-2	1-2	5	3
Jimmy Stewart	12	1-4	0-1	1-2	5	2
Ed Ward	8	0-0	0-1	0-1	1	0
S. Killian	2	0-0	0-0	1-1	1	0
Bruce Falkner	1	0-0	0-0	0-1	0	0
Totals		17-49	21-28	9-29	28	62

Three-point goals: 7-14 (Phillips 4-6, Peel 3-7, Christian 0-1). Assists: 9 (Christian 3, Miller 2, Phillips 2, Peel, Ward). Turnovers: 28 (Phillips 7, Stewart 5, Christian 4, Gibson 4, Miller 3, Holmes 2, Ward 2, Peel). Blocked shots: 3 (Gibson 2, Stewart). Steals: 5 (Gibson 2, Christian, Peel, Holmes).

Kansas (73)

	MIN	FG m-a	FT m-a	REB o-t	PF	TP
Danny Manning	37	8-16	3-6	2-5	3	19
Archie Marshall	24	6-7	2-2	0-4	2	14
Marvin Branch	15	3-3	5-7	2-7	3	11
Kevin Pritchard	20	0-5	2-2	0-0	5	2
Lincoln Minor	14	2-7	0-0	0-1	5	4
Otis Livingston	6	0-1	0-0	0-0	1	0
Chris Piper	27	4-4	1-2	3-6	0	9
Scooter Barry	30	2-4	6-7	1-5	4	10
Milt Newton	10	0-1	0-1	1-6	0	0
Jeff Gueldner	17	2-5	0-0	1-2	3	4
Totals		27-53	19-27	10-36	26	73

Three-point goals: 0-4 (Pritchard 0-2, Minor 0-1, Gueldner 0-1). Assists: 19 (Barry 5, Piper 5, Manning 3, Minor 3, Marshall, Livingston, Newton). Turnovers: 23 (Manning 4, Minor 4, Pritchard 3, Barry 3, Marshall 2, Branch 2, Livingston 2, Newton 2, Piper). Blocked shots: 3 (Manning 2, Newton). Steals: 11 (Branch 3, Marshall 2, Manning 2, Pritchard, Minor, Livingston, Gueldner).

Appalachian State	32 30	— 62
Kansas	37 36	— 73

Officials: Woody Mayfield, David Hall, Dennis Schmidt. Attendance: 15,300.

The Appalachian State game also featured a public confrontation between Brown and point guard Otis Livingston, just before halftime in front of the KU bench. "We were in a press and I had to play a specific position," Livingston recalled after the season. "He (Brown) started yelling and I said, 'I got this guy.' I yelled it back. I didn't feel like I was being disrespectful or anything because I wouldn't do that. He just yelled at me and I just reacted fast. I didn't mean to embarrass him or anything. First he took me out of the game, then he talked to me about some stuff and then he sent me out."

Livingston was told to go to the locker room, but he changed clothes and left the fieldhouse. The next day, the two met and Brown announced the matter had been resolved. Livingston returned to practice. "I told him that what happened was over, and I wouldn't hold it against him. I don't anticipate any problem," Brown said. He was overly optimistic. Almost exactly three months later, a similar problem would result in Livingston's suspension from the team.

Brown also announced after the game that all practices would be closed to the public and, in an unusual move, to the media as well. "It's been a circus," he said. "People have been walking in and out. There's commotion . . . it's not a good environment for learning. This team doesn't need any distractions."

A few weeks later, Brown would relax that ban, but for the time being what the Jayhawks needed, he had determined, was practice, practice, practice. And more practice. Or as Piper said: "We made our own bed. I don't want to sleep in it, but we'll all have to."

Archie's out

And so, as Larry Brown decreed, the Jayhawks ran and they listened and they drilled and they ran some more. Then they ran and listened and drilled again — for four hours the day after the Appalachian State game, for three hours on each of the three days after that.

"I wouldn't say they were extremely hard physically," senior Chris Piper recalled. "He (Brown) works on you mentally. That's why his teams succeed. We worked mostly on defense. The thing he stressed at practice all year was defense."

Like a ringmaster, Brown ran the show during KU practice sessions. Assistant coaches Ed Manning, Alvin Gentry and R.C. Buford played lesser roles. The assistants, Piper said, ". . . do individual stuff. They are there to remind you to rebound and play defense. Coach (Brown) is the overall picture." Aiding the KU coaches were student assistant Mark Turgeon and graduate assistant John Robic.

One thing the rugged workouts accomplished was to make the Jayhawks eager for a game, and they rode herd on Rider, 110-72,

the next time out. It was the only time all season KU would surpass the century mark and, unlike after the blowout against Pomona-Pitzer, Brown was pleased. "I was glad to have a laugher," he said. "It was a good situation to look down the bench and see everybody played (at least) 10 minutes. When you do that, you become a team."

Rider, a Division I school from Lawrenceville, N.J., played into the Jayhawks' hands by launching 29 three-point goal attempts — the most against KU all season — and connecting on only five. Two dozen three-point misses led to a bundle of fast-break opportunities. Danny Manning made 14 of 16 shots, scored 30 points and collected 14 rebounds. Lincoln Minor added a dozen points, Kevin Pritchard 11 and freshman Mike Masucci a career high 10.

"It's nice to see coach like this," Archie Marshall remarked afterward. "Speaking for myself, I don't feel comfortable going out and having a good time after we have a bad game. I'd like to take advantage of that, go out and have a good time."

In his first lineup change of the season, Brown inserted Scooter

"We worked mostly on defense. The thing he stressed at practice all year was defense."

— CHRIS PIPER

Barry at point guard in place of Minor, and he announced Minor would be switched to off-guard. Permanently. Brown said Minor, who had more turnovers than assists at the time, "was more comfortable" at the off-guard slot. Thus the point guard position now belonged to Barry and Otis Livingston, who came off the bench for nine points and four assists.

Another encouraging sign was a team-high six assists from Piper, the fifth-year senior who had been nursing a tender knee and a nagging groin pull. Brown had been trying to give Piper as much playing time as

possible by using him as a substitute for Manning and Marvin Branch. "We rated our players — the coaches did and the players did — and Piper came out second, on both lists," Brown said. Also noteworthy was Manning's 116th career start, the most ever by a Kansas basketball player. Manning, who often played with at least one knee in a thin rubber support and with a tape-wrapped finger, had proven remarkably durable in his four seasons at KU. Partly that was sheer

KU's point production soared against Rider. The Jayhawks' 110 points were a season high and the only time KU scored more than 100.

Mike Yoder

DEC. 12 AT LAWRENCE

Rider (72)

	MIN	FG m-a	FT m-a	REB o-t	PF	TP
Ed Titus	20	2-10	3-3	2-4	4	7
Ron Simpson	25	7-14	2-2	3-3	3	17
Jim Cleveland	30	7-16	7-10	4-5	4	22
Lee Nesmith	24	1-6	2-2	2-3	3	4
Ramon Rosado	19	5-10	0-0	0-1	1	12
Bill Vogt	9	0-1	0-0	0-2	5	0
Matt Zaleski	18	1-10	0-0	2-6	4	3
C. Carothers	25	1-5	0-0	1-1	3	2
Bob Urbanik	13	0-4	2-2	1-1	2	2
John Jordan	17	0-5	3-4	0-1	2	3
Totals		24-81	19-23	15-27	31	72

Three-point goals: 5-29 (Zaleski 1-9, Rosado 2-5, Titus 0-5, Simpson 1-4, Cleveland 1-4, Jordan 0-1, Urbanik 0-1). **Assists:** 15 (Simpson 4, Carothers 3, Titus 3, Nesmith 2, Jordan, Zaleski, Rosado). **Turnovers:** 16 (Rosado 6, Zaleski 4, Carothers 3, Titus 2, Jordan). **Blocked shots:** 0. **Steals:** 10 (Zaleski 3, Carothers 2, Cleveland 2, Nesmith 2, Simpson).

Kansas (110)

	MIN	FG m-a	FT m-a	REB o-t	PF	TP
Archie Marshall	15	3-6	1-2	3-4	2	7
Danny Manning	26	14-16	2-4	2-14	2	30
Marvin Branch	13	2-2	2-2	2-4	2	6
Scooter Barry	22	1-2	2-2	1-3	0	4
Kevin Pritchard	18	4-5	3-6	0-1	3	11
Chris Piper	17	1-1	2-2	1-2	1	4
Otis Livingston	17	4-5	1-3	1-4	2	9
Lincoln Minor	12	3-4	6-8	0-1	3	12
Mike Maddox	13	4-4	0-2	1-4	3	8
Jeff Gueldner	14	0-1	1-2	1-1	1	1
Milt Newton	14	3-8	0-0	2-7	0	6
Mike Masucci	10	4-5	2-3	1-6	1	10
Keith Harris	9	0-2	2-4	1-3	1	2
Totals		43-61	24-40	16-54	21	110

Three-point goals: 0-0. **Assists:** 28 (Piper 6, Barry 5, Marshall 4, Livingston 4, Manning 2, Pritchard 2, Minor 2, Gueldner 2, Branch). **Turnovers:** 25 (Barry 4, Branch 3, Minor 3, Piper 2, Pritchard 2, Livingston 2, Newton 2, Masucci 2, Maddox 2, Manning, Gueldner, Harris). **Blocked shots:** 5 (Manning 3, Minor 2). **Steals:** 8 (Pritchard 2, Livingston 2, Minor 2, Barry, Newton).

Rider	36 36	— 72
Kansas	52 58	— 110

Officials: J.C. Leimbach, Charles Greene, Duane Smith. **Attendance:** 15,800.

drive. Manning, trainer Mark Cairns noted, never complained about injuries that would have distracted many other collegians. The senior forward, in fact, would finish his college career by setting an NCAA record for games played (147).

Despite their slide in the polls, these were good times for the Jayhawks. Final exams were almost over, the winning streak had reached five and Christmas was two weeks away. Now the team faced another full week of practice before the next game — a nationally televised clash with North Carolina State in Raleigh.

Meanwhile, the roster had expanded by one. Clint Normore, the starting free safety on KU's football team, showed up for Monday's practice, and Brown put him to work. A two-year letterman in basketball at Wichita State, Normore had switched to football at WSU, then transferred to KU the previous spring when the Shockers dropped football. WSU's loss was Brown's gain: He picked up an experienced point guard, even if Normore was rusty and coming off a broken wrist suffered during the football season. Normore had planned to go out for basketball all along, but had to wait until the cast was removed from his shooting hand.

Normore had few illusions about big-time basketball, or football — "There are more six-foot safeties in the NFL than there are six-foot guards in the NBA," he said — but he knew the Jayhawks were unstable at point guard. "My goal is to contribute where I can, to give as much help as needed," he said. "I am and always will be a role player."

With the semester winding down as the Jayhawks prepared for the trip to Raleigh, the question of

Brenda Steele

grades invariably came up. Brown painted a dark picture. "A lot of guys are up in the air right now, a lot," he said. Who were they? "You can take your pick. But hopefully nobody will be ineligible." In a season in which little went smoothly for the Jayhawks, academic troubles would strike soon enough, but this wasn't the time to worry about that. The focus was on the Wolfpack.

"We're better than we were two weeks ago, but I don't know if we'll see that progress when we play North Carolina State," Brown said. ABC Television had concocted this match. The national network wanted to bring Manning back to

"I am and always will be a role player."

— CLINT NORMORE

Football player Clint Normore found his role with the Jayhawks, and a way to be late for spring practice.

North Carolina, where he had lived for seven years before moving to Lawrence. Manning, on the other hand, didn't necessarily relish the return. Many in the Tar Heel State thought that by hiring his father, Ed Manning, as an assistant coach, Brown had stolen Danny Manning away from his natural destiny — which was, in their view, to lead North Carolina State, Duke or

Danny Manning took his ball-handling ability on the road.

Mike Yoder

North Carolina to a national championship or two. As a KU sophomore, he'd been booed when he played in Greensboro against the Wolfpack two years earlier.

Sure enough, a record crowd of 12,715 in Reynolds Coliseum booed Manning early and often this time. But his 32 points and dominating play in the last four minutes silenced the crowd. "He was awesome," said Marshall. "A great player takes over, and that's what Danny did," said Pritchard. "When we needed him most, he rose to the occasion."

Here's what he did:

— With 4:06 left, Manning hit two free throws to give KU 66-65 lead, its first since the first half.

— 3:40: Manning hit a short jumper for a 68-65 lead.

— 2:30: Manning deflected a pass out of Wolfpack center Charles Shackleford's hands and KU regained possession.

— 1:45: Manning's basket gave KU a 72-67 lead, and KU went on to win 74-67.

Manning had 16 points in each half, but five of his six rebounds and all three of his blocked shots came after intermission. "I think the second half was one of the best second halves of basketball I've ever seen him play," said a smiling Brown. "He did everything. The whole team was good. We competed. I thought we competed in the second half."

Still, the search for a point guard continued. Against North Carolina State, Livingston had become the third player to start at the position. He failed to score, and fouled out with 4:21 remaining. Brown wasted no time using his new acquisition, Normore, inserting him for the last three minutes of the first half. Still, Brown said he had faith in Livingston. "I truly believe Otis is going

DEC. 19 AT RALEIGH, N.C.

Kansas (74)

	MIN	FG m-a	FT m-a	REB o-t	PF	TP
Archie Marshall	29	5-12	2-3	2-7	1	12
Danny Manning.	39	13-25	5-9	0-6	2	32
Marvin Branch.	14	0-2	2-3	0-4	2	2
Otis Livingston	17	0-0	0-0	0-1	5	0
Kevin Pritchard	33	5-8	4-5	0-2	0	14
Scooter Barry	20	1-3	2-3	0-1	3	4
Chris Piper	27	2-2	0-0	2-7	2	4
Lincoln Minor	7	1-2	0-0	1-2	0	2
Milt Newton.	3	0-1	0-0	0-0	0	0
Clint Normore	3	1-1	0-0	0-0	0	2
Jeff Gueldner.	8	1-1	0-0	2-2	0	2
Totals		29-57	15-23	7-32	15	74

Three-point goals: 1-2 (Manning 1-2). Assists: 21 (Barry 7, Pritchard 4, Piper 2, Branch 2, Manning 2, Livingston, Minor, Newton, Gueldner). Turnovers: 16 (Pritchard 7, Manning 3, Gueldner 2, Branch, Livingston, Piper, Minor). Blocked shots: 3 (Manning 3). Steals: 3 (Livingston 2, Manning).

North Carolina State (67)

	MIN	FG m-a	FT m-a	REB o-t	PF	TP
Brian Howard	11	1-3	0-0	0-2	1	2
Chucky Brown.	33	8-10	0-1	2-6	0	16
Charles Shackleford .	32	5-15	0-1	5-9	1	10
Chris Corchiani	27	2-3	4-4	0-1	4	9
Vinny DelNegro.	33	8-18	1-3	1-3	0	17
Rodney Monroe	25	4-14	1-2	2-4	3	11
Avie Lester.	14	0-2	0-0	1-4	4	0
Kelsey Weems.	6	1-1	0-0	0-0	1	2
Sean Green	11	0-5	0-0	1-1	1	0
Quentin Jackson. . . .	8	0-0	0-0	0-0	3	0
Totals		29-71	6-11	12-30	18	67

Three-point goals: 3-10 (Monroe 2-7, Corchiani 1-1, Green 0-2). Assists: 16 (Corchiani 7, Jackson 2, Howard 2, DelNegro 2, Monroe 2, Weems). Turnovers: 11 (Corchiani 4, Monroe 3, Weems 2, Howard, Shackleford). Blocked shots: 4 (Shackleford 2, DelNegro, Monroe). Steals: 8 (Corchiani 3, Monroe 2, Shackleford, DelNegro, Jackson).

Kansas	36	38 — 74
N.C. State	41	26 — 67

Officials: Ed Hightower, Ron Zetcher, Rich Eichhorst. Attendance: 12,715.

to have to step forward and we'll bring Scooter off the bench," he said. "Otis has always played that position and he feels more relaxed."

Brown certainly felt more relaxed. His team was rolling with a six-game win streak. Kansas was leading the nation in field goal percentage (shooting 58.9 percent), was ranked No. 18 in the AP poll and was picking up momentum. Brown wasn't even noticeably perturbed when a reporter asked about reports linking him with the Carolina Hornets, the NBA expansion team. "There's no

truth to the rumor," he answered. "I'm not going anywhere."

His players were, though. Brown turned them loose for four days with orders not to report for practice again until Christmas Eve. KU wasn't scheduled to play again until the post-Christmas ECAC Holiday Festival in New York City. It was a team with its mind on basketball — not the Big Apple — that showed up in New York a few days later. "To come and play in Madison Square Garden is a challenge," Brown said. "Playing in the Holiday Festival, it's a big deal. It's what we want. It prepares you for later." As for the city's celebrated nightlife, "We did a lot of walking around the hotel," Pritchard said. "We're here to play basketball." Nonetheless, he found time to see a Broadway show, along with his mother and freshman Mike Maddox.

The tourney's first round went well for the Jayhawks, but not for their shooting percentage. They faced Memphis State, a team riddled by NCAA probation and player losses, and won, 64-62, despite shooting only 37.9, some 21 points below their nation-leading percentage.

Fortunately, the Tigers shot worse — terribly in fact, making only 18 of 63 shots for 28.6 percent. Kansas also made only 10 of 22 free throws. Had the eight-day layoff — four without practice — played hob with the Jayhawks' shooting? Probably.

Even Manning missed more shots (nine) than he made (eight) and settled for 19 points. And with all those missed shots flying around Madison Square Garden, Manning snared 16 rebounds. It was to be his second highest rebounding total of the season; he was to save the best for last.

"It was one of those nights," said

"There's no truth to the rumor. I'm not going anywhere."

— LARRY BROWN

"They had good defense. You'd think you were open and a guy would jump up at you."

— KEVIN PRITCHARD

"You've heard coaches say, 'This kid is the greatest.' With Archie you mean it."

— LARRY BROWN

Pritchard, who had 11 points on three of 12 shooting and four of five free throws. "They had good defense. You'd think you were open and a guy would jump up at you. They were really working hard on defense."

"They played good, hard defense," added Livingston, who was two for two, including a driving layup off a steal with 2:04 left that increased a three-point KU lead to five at 62-57. "We were getting the shots we wanted. We just weren't hitting them."

DEC. 28 AT NEW YORK CITY

Memphis State (62)

	MIN	FG m-a	FT m-a	REB o-t	PF	TP
Steve Ballard	32	1-6	4-6	4-7	4	6
Rodney Douglas	28	2-5	4-5	2-4	1	8
Dewayne Bailey	18	3-7	1-2	3-5	4	7
Dwight Boyd	24	0-8	1-2	1-2	5	1
Elliot Perry	28	7-18	6-6	2-5	1	23
Cheyenne Gibson	23	2-8	2-3	0-5	2	6
Ronald McClain	17	0-4	0-0	0-2	1	0
Russell Young	23	3-6	3-4	2-10	1	9
John McLaughlin	5	0-1	2-2	0-0	2	2
Bret Mundt	2	0-0	0-0	0-0	0	0
Totals		18-63	23-30	14-40	21	62

Three-point goals: 3-9 (Perry 3-8, McLaughlin 0-1). Assists: 10 (Gibson 4, Perry 2, McClain 2, Bailey, Boyd). Turnovers: 16 (Perry 4, Boyd 3, Gibson 3, Ballard 2, Bailey 2, Douglas, McLaughlin). Blocked shots: 3 (Ballard, Douglas, Perry). Steals: 9 (Perry 4, McClain 3, Douglas, McLaughlin).

Kansas (64)

	MIN	FG m-a	FT m-a	REB o-t	PF	TP
Danny Manning	36	8-17	2-5	4-16	4	19
Archie Marshall	26	6-14	2-6	3-8	3	16
Marvin Branch	16	2-6	0-2	2-4	2	4
Otis Livingston	22	2-2	0-0	1-2	4	4
Kevin Pritchard	29	3-12	4-5	1-4	2	11
Lincoln Minor	14	2-6	0-0	1-1	2	4
Scooter Barry	4	0-1	2-2	0-1	1	2
Chris Piper	25	0-1	0-0	1-4	4	0
Jeff Gueldner	13	1-6	0-2	2-2	2	2
Clint Normore	12	1-1	0-0	0-0	2	2
Mike Maddox	3	0-0	0-0	0-1	0	0
Totals		25-66	10-22	15-43	26	64

Three-point goals: 4-8 (Marshall 2-3, Pritchard 1-2, Manning 1-1, Gueldner 0-2). Assists: 18 (Livingston 4, Normore 4, Pritchard 3, Marshall 2, Minor 2, Manning, Branch, Gueldner). Turnovers: 19 (Manning 6, Livingston 3, Pritchard 3, Minor 2, Piper 2, Marshall 2, Branch). Blocked shots: 2 (Marshall, Livingston). Steals: 8 (Livingston 3, Manning, Pritchard, Minor, Gueldner, Maddox).

Memphis State	27 35	— 62
Kansas	32 32	— 64

Technical fouls: Piper. Officials: Mickey Crowley, Joel Mingle, David Day. Attendance: 12,900.

The sloppy game — Memphis State had 16 turnovers to KU'S 19 — went down to the wire, despite the fact the Tigers were playing without Sylvester Gray and Marvin Alexander, declared ineligible two weeks earlier for accepting money from an agent. Freshman guard Elliott Perry, who had been recruited by Kansas and Oklahoma, led the Tigers with 23 points on seven of 18 shooting. He hit seven of seven free throws.

"They were shorthanded without Gray and Alexander," said Brown. "The kids they had played hard and our kids respected them." MSU coach Larry Finch saw some hope for his depleted squad: "If you'd told me we'd play a team like Kansas that close without those two, I'd say, 'Whoa, back up.'"

St. John's, the same team Kansas had beaten 63-54 three weeks earlier in Lawrence, also advanced in the four-team tourney, setting up a rematch. The Redmen made the most of their opportunity in a game that came to matter much less for the final score than for the injury that ended Marshall's season. While working under the basket in the first half, the 6-6 forward bumped his left knee against another player's knee and went down in a heap. "I passed it to Archie." Piper said. "He was sandwiched between Danny, Jayson Williams and Matt Brust. Somebody hit him and he went down." Film later showed that Marshall had made contact with Manning underneath the goal. But who and how didn't matter much. The diagnosis — two torn ligaments — did. So did the prognosis: the end, almost, of a college career.

On the bench, Brown wept. Many of Marshall's teammates also had tears in their eyes.

One of the most popular players on the team, Marshall had spent the entire 1986-87 season rehabilitating his right knee, which he'd injured in the 1986 Final Four game against Duke. "I've never seen a kid work harder to get himself back, ready to play," a distraught Brown said. "Now he's back where he was. I don't care about how this affects the team right now. You've heard coaches say, 'This kid is the greatest.' With Archie you mean it."

"You can't lose Archie," said Piper. "Losing Archie is like losing two starters. He's such a hard worker. He's quiet, never says much, but he leads by example. He's shown courage before and will again. He's always optimistic and we'll be optimistic for him."

When Marshall went down, Kansas was leading St. John's, 21-20. The Jayhawks clung to a 31-29 advantage at intermission, but in the second half, fully aware of the seriousness of Marshall's injury, their competitive edge vanished. They were outscored 41-25. "I don't want to take anything away from St. John's," Brown said. "We tried, but it was hard without Archie." The Redmen won, 70-56.

The Jayhawks had shot even worse than they had against Memphis State, making only 18 of 55, or 32.7 percent. "We came in as the nation's best shooting team and didn't shoot well," Brown said. "We didn't play for nine days (before the tourney), and they played good defense." He added: "Hey, there's pressure on the kids. Playing in the Holiday Festival is a big deal."

So as the Jayhawks headed back to Lawrence on New Year's Eve, they tried to extract something positive from their New York experience. But what? It didn't seem

much like a happy New Year.

To Brown fell the problem of finding a replacement for the injured Marshall, who had been averaging 8.8 points and four rebounds a game. "Somebody will have to step forward," the coach said simply as KU began packing for another cross-country trip, this one westward to play the University of Washington in Seattle. Brown seemed to lean toward Piper for the job. The Lawrence High graduate, despite his injuries, was already logging

DEC. 30 AT NEW YORK CITY

Kansas (56)

	MIN	FG m-a	FT m-a	REB o-t	PF	TP
Danny Manning.....	32	8-17	8-13	2-5	4	24
Archie Marshall.....	8	0-1	0-0	0-3	1	0
Marvin Branch......	26	3-6	2-4	3-12	3	8
Otis Livingston	27	2-4	2-2	1-3	2	6
Kevin Pritchard	23	1-6	2-2	0-0	5	4
Scooter Barry	12	0-0	0-0	0-0	4	0
Chris Piper	20	0-1	0-0	0-2	3	0
Milt Newton........	11	1-2	1-2	1-1	2	4
Lincoln Minor	15	0-3	0-2	1-4	0	0
Clint Normore	2	0-2	0-0	0-0	2	0
Mike Masucci	4	1-3	0-1	3-4	0	2
Jeff Gueldner.......	14	1-6	4-5	2-3	2	6
Keith Harris	3	0-1	0-0	0-0	0	0
Mike Maddox.......	3	1-3	0-0	1-2	3	2
Totals		18-55	19-31	14-39	31	56

Three-point goals: 1-5 (Newton 1-1, Manning 0-1, Normore 0-1, Gueldner 0-2). Assists: 13 (Minor 3, Livingston 3, Branch 2, Barry 2, Manning, Marshall, Piper). Turnovers: 21 (Livingston 5, Minor 4, Normore 3, Manning 3, Branch 2, Piper 2, Maddox, Harris). Blocked shots: 4 (Manning 2, Branch, Normore). Steals: 5 (Livingston, Minor, Gueldner, Harris, Maddox).

St. John's (70)

	MIN	FG m-a	FT m-a	REB o-t	PF	TP
Matt Brust	40	5-10	4-7	5-9	3	14
Shelton Jones	30	5-13	7-11	2-8	4	17
Marco Baldi	25	3-4	2-4	1-6	4	8
Greg Harvey........	38	1-7	11-12	0-0	3	13
Michael Porter......	28	1-10	3-4	1-6	2	5
Jayson Williams	17	0-3	1-6	1-2	4	1
Terry Bross	7	1-2	0-0	1-2	2	2
Elander Lewis	14	3-6	2-3	1-4	0	8
Sean Muto	1	0-0	2-2	0-0	1	2
Totals		19-55	32-49	12-37	23	70

Three-point goals: 0-0. Assists: 8 (Jones 2, Porter 2, Brust, Baldi, Harvey, Lewis). Turnovers: 14 (Baldi 4, Brust 3, Jones 2, Harvey 2, Porter, Williams, Lewis). Blocked shots: 2 (Brust, Porter). Steals: 13 (Porter 3, Lewis 3, Brust 2, Harvey 2, Jones, Baldi, Williams).

Kansas.............................	31	25 — 56
St. John's	29	41 — 70

Technical fouls: Piper, Baldi, St. John's coach Carnesecca, Kansas coach Brown. Officials: Larry Lembo, Jim Burr, Jack Hannon. Attendance: 10,077.

Archie Marshall's passing, rebounding and scoring would be missed.

Richard Gwin

considerable time in relief of Branch and, to a lesser extent, Manning. Now, Brown indicated, Piper was the logical choice to replace Marshall.

Pregame newspaper stories in Seattle made it seem as if it didn't matter. Manning, after all, was the entire team. One sportswriter called him ". . .a majestic team player on a sub-majestic team." Sub-majestic? The Jayhawks were 8-3 and ranked No. 18 in the AP poll and they were about to prove they could mount a majestic comeback against the Huskies. They would need to.

In a surprise move, Brown picked Milt Newton, not Piper, to start in Marshall's spot against Washington. Newton, a fourth-year junior, had started only three of the 71 Kansas games he'd played in. "Coach told me two hours before the game," Newton said. "I wasn't nervous. I knew what I had to do, rebound and play defense."

Newton grabbed six rebounds, worked hard defensively and, even better, scored 12 points — his most ever for KU — as the Jayhawks staged a ferocious, defense-keyed rally from a 19-point deficit in Edmondson Pavilion, site of the only NCAA championship Kansas had ever won. Why start Newton? "Milt deserves to play," Brown said. "He tries hard every day in practice." Later, after Newton came to play a major role in the Jayhawks' season, Brown would frequently look back and wonder why he hadn't used him earlier and more often. "I was too dumb to play him," the coach would tell anyone who would listen.

Newton was hardly sensational that night in Seattle, but he was solid — just what Kansas needed after falling behind 29-10 after the first 10 minutes against a Washington team playing without its leading scorer,

> "It was scary, but I told the kids I didn't think they'd make every outside shot the whole game. And if they did, I told them not to worry because we wouldn't win anyway."
>
> — LARRY BROWN

JAN. 4 AT SEATTLE, WASH.

Kansas (67)

	MIN	FG m-a	FT m-a	REB o-t	PF	TP
Danny Manning.....	39	7-11	3-6	2-5	1	17
Milt Newton........	29	5-12	0-2	2-6	2	12
Marvin Branch......	14	1-3	2-2	1-2	0	4
Lincoln Minor	34	7-15	1-1	5-7	2	15
Kevin Pritchard	26	3-8	2-2	2-2	3	8
Chris Piper	23	2-2	3-3	1-2	1	7
Mike Maddox.......	5	1-3	0-0	0-0	0	2
Otis Livingston	16	1-1	0-0	0-2	1	2
Jeff Gueldner.......	5	0-0	0-0	1-1	0	0
Mike Masucci	4	0-1	0-0	0-0	2	0
Scooter Barry	5	0-0	0-0	0-0	0	0
Totals		27-56	11-16	14-27	12	67

Three-point goals: 2-8 (Newton 2-4, Minor 0-2, Manning 0-1, Pritchard 0-1). Assists: 17 (Livingston 4, Minor 3, Manning 2, Newton 2, Pritchard 2, Gueldner 2, Barry, Piper). Turnovers: 14 (Newton 3, Branch 3, Minor 3, Manning 2, Pritchard, Livingston, Barry). Blocked shots: 1 (Maddox). Steals: 16 (Livingston 4, Manning 2, Minor 2, Barry 2, Newton, Branch, Pritchard, Maddox, Gueldner, Masucci).

Washington (57)

	MIN	FG m-a	FT m-a	REB o-t	PF	TP
Mike Hayward	33	6-8	0-0	0-4	5	14
Jeff Sanor	40	5-10	0-1	0-2	3	14
Mark West	40	5-11	0-0	6-13	2	10
Anthony Jenkins....	35	2-7	1-1	1-2	1	5
Troy Morrell	40	6-11	0-1	1-2	4	14
David Wilson	5	0-0	0-0	0-1	0	0
Tom Robinson......	1	0-0	0-0	0-0	0	0
Todd Lautenbach ...	6	0-0	0-0	0-0	0	0
Totals		24-47	1-3	8-24	15	57

Three-point goals: 8-13 (Sanor 4-7, Hayward 2-3, Morrell 2-3). Assists: 16 (Morrell 6, Sanor 4, Jenkins 4, Hayward, West). Turnovers: 24 (West 7, Hayward 6, Morrell 5, Jenkins 3, Lautenbach 2, Sanor). Blocked shots: 1 (West). Steals: 10 (Morrell 5, Jenkins 3, Hayward, Sanor).

Kansas............................	28 39	— 67
Washington........................	35 22	— 57

Officials: Booker Turner, Jimmy Clark, John Dabrow. Attendance: 6,079.

guard Eldridge Recasner, who was home in New Orleans with his ill mother. Even without Recasner, the Huskies made 10 of their first 12 shots, including four of five from three-point range.

"It was scary, but I told the kids I didn't think they'd make every outside shot the whole game," Brown said. "And if they did, I told them not to worry because we wouldn't win anyway." Added Newton: "Like coach said, even the Celtics wouldn't beat them if they kept doing that."

Eventually, a full court press by KU produced 16 steals, and the

Jayhawks caught up at 44-44 with 11:21 remaining. Key baskets included a couple of breakaways by Minor, who put together his best game of the season with 15 points and seven rebounds. Minor was another surprise starter, Brown giving him the nod, he said, because several relatives were there.

"It was a struggle," Brown said after KU beat the Huskies, 67-57. "You've got to be so thankful you could win. After losing to St. John's last week and losing Archie, we could have packed it in when we were down early." Not that the come-from-behind road win soothed all wounds. "It's hard . . . it's really hard," admitted Manning, who scored 17 points despite yet another sagging zone defense aimed at preventing him from touching the ball. "We're a group and we all love Archie, and we know he cares about us." Manning showed he cared by writing No. 23 — Marshall's number — on his wristband for the next game. It would stay there for the rest of the season.

Two days later, back in Allen Fieldhouse for the first time in more than three weeks, the Jayhawks faced American University. Marshall was still on their minds. He'd undergone a 4½-hour operation earlier that day. His surgery had taken a long time, and so did the game, because the visiting Eagles committed 37 fouls, sending KU to the foul line a clock-stopping 54 times — they made 35 of them — in its 90-69 victory. Manning, who started a Big Eight-record 116th straight game, scored 18 points and had 14 rebounds. Branch made 12 of his 16 free throws and finished with a team-high 20 points, the highest total of his short-lived season.

Despite the KU victory, there

Richard Gwin

All-American Manning versus American University.

34

"The two kids who give our team character, Archie and Piper, have these things happen. It's indicative of our season — a struggle."

— LARRY BROWN

Kevin Pritchard eyed a transition from shooting guard to point guard.

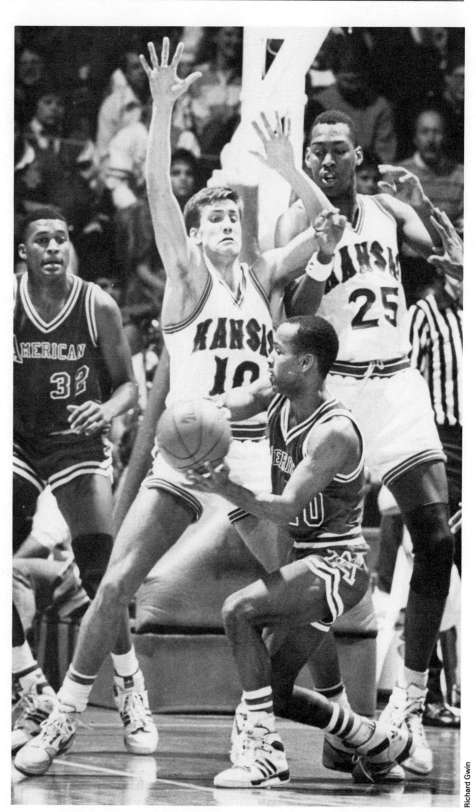

KU's eagle-eyed defense held the Eagles to 69 points. Danny Manning was outscored by Marvin Branch, who played two fewer minutes.

American (69)

	MIN	FG m-a	FT m-a	REB o-t	PF	TP
Mike Sumner	22	6-9	5-7	2-2	4	17
Daryl Holmes	20	2-9	2-4	2-3	5	6
Tom Scherer	22	2-2	3-4	1-3	5	7
Mike Sampson	30	1-6	1-2	1-1	3	3
Brock Wortman	19	5-8	0-0	1-2	3	11
Dale Spears	24	4-14	0-0	2-7	3	9
Andy BonSalle	20	1-4	2-2	1-4	4	4
Eric White	27	2-5	2-3	3-10	5	6
L. Harrison	9	1-3	0-0	1-1	1	2
Fred Tillman	1	0-1	0-0	0-0	1	0
C. Broderdorp	6	2-5	0-0	1-3	3	4
Totals		26-66	15-22	15-36	37	69

Three-point goals: 2-13 (Wortman 1-2, Spears 1-3, Sampson 0-3, White 0-2, Broderdorp 0-2, Tillman 0-1). Assists: 9 (Sampson 4, White 3, Holmes, Spears). Turnovers: 18 (BonSalle 4, Sumner 3, Sampson 3, Wortman 3, Spears 2, White 2, Scherer). Blocked shots: 0. Steals: 6 (Sampson 2, Sumner, Scherer, Wortman, Spears).

Kansas (90)

	MIN	FG m-a	FT m-a	REB o-t	PF	TP
Danny Manning	29	4-7	10-14	8-14	4	18
Milt Newton	18	5-8	1-3	1-3	1	11
Marvin Branch	27	4-8	12-16	4-10	2	20
Scooter Barry	15	1-5	2-2	2-2	2	4
Lincoln Minor	17	2-7	0-0	0-0	1	4
Otis Livingston	15	0-0	0-1	0-3	2	0
Chris Piper	4	2-2	0-0	0-1	0	4
Kevin Pritchard	20	6-9	3-3	2-3	2	15
Mike Maddox	12	0-1	0-2	0-3	0	0
Mike Masucci	14	2-3	0-0	1-1	2	4
Keith Harris	11	0-1	3-5	0-3	1	3
Clint Normore	10	1-1	0-0	0-3	0	3
Jeff Gueldner	8	0-1	4-8	1-1	0	4
Totals		27-53	35-54	19-47	17	90

Three-point goals: 1-3 (Normore 1-1, Newton 0-1, Pritchard 0-1). Assists: 15 (Manning 3, Pritchard 3, Livingston 2, Harris 2, Gueldner 2, Newton, Barry, Minor). Turnovers: 15 (Pritchard 4, Branch 3, Manning 2, Newton, Barry, Minor, Harris, Normore, Gueldner). Blocked shots: 3 (Branch 2, Manning). Steals: 6 (Manning, Branch, Livingston, Pritchard, Masucci, Normore).

American	22	47 — 69
Kansas	44	46 — 90

Officials: John Dabrow, Steve Nicollerat, Meryl Wilson. Attendance: 15,400.

were troublesome undercurrents. Piper's groin injury clearly wasn't improving; Brown used the senior co-captain for only four minutes against American. As for Branch, rumors surfaced that he might be declared academically ineligible when the second semester began, in exactly a week. So Marshall was gone, Piper was hurting, Branch was on egg shells and red-shirt Mark Randall had just undergone surgery in Denver to correct his elongated jaw and drain his sinus cavities.

"It's been a real unusual year,"

Brown remarked. "The two kids who give our team character, Archie and Piper, have these things happen. It's indicative of our season — a struggle. So many have high expectations, but it's not the team we expected to have." Manning also sensed the potential for trouble. "Losing Archie knocked me down a notch and knocked the team down a notch," he said. "I think we're starting to get our confidence level almost back where it was. This is when we'll find out what this team is made of — whether it'll play or give up."

"This is when we'll find out what this team is made of — whether it'll play or give up."

— DANNY MANNING

Richard Gwin

In conference

4

Lincoln Minor and Milt Newton, opposite page, battle Missouri's Mike Sandbothe on the boards. Although the Tigers were rated the preseason favorite in the Big Eight, Kansas, Oklahoma, Iowa State and Kansas State would fight to dethrone the defending champions.

Ricky Grace issued an early warning. Oklahoma's senior guard, speaking at the Big Eight Media Day on Nov. 1 in Kansas City, promised "We'll be better than last year. We lost 10 games. I guarantee you we won't lose 10 this year. I don't see why we can't win the Big Eight."

Many analysts dismissed Grace's remarks as preseason hype. The Sooners were returning only two of their top five scorers (Grace and center Harvey Grant) from the year before, when OU had tied Kansas for second place in the Big Eight. Both Oklahoma and KU had finished 9-5, two games behind the surprising conference champion, Missouri.

This time, Missouri seemed a clear-cut favorite. And why not? Norm Stewart, dean of the conference's coaches, had every starter back for his 21st year at MU, including second-team All-American Derrick Chievous, already the school's career scoring leader. Other starters were Nathan Buntin and Lee Coward, both standouts as freshmen, senior Lynn Hardy and junior Mike Sandbothe. Stewart had picked up Byron Irvin, a red-shirt who had transferred from Arkansas, and Doug Smith, a 6-10 freshman from Detroit who had been the outstanding performer in the National AAU Junior Tournament. The Tigers headed the annual Big Eight preseason media poll, followed by Kansas, Oklahoma, Kansas State, Iowa State, Oklahoma State, Nebraska and Colorado.

"I hope whoever picked us knows what they're talking about," Stewart said. "We have expectations every year. Hopefully, our players will expect and demand as much from themselves as others will." The Tigers rolled to a 9-2 record before conference play began. Their Big Eight expectations would get an early test on Jan. 9 in Allen Fieldhouse, where the Jayhawks' home winning streak stood at 53.

As Grace had indicated, the Sooners weren't a bit bashful about trumpeting their own high hopes. "Fans in the Big Eight feel Oklahoma players have big egos," said OU's Grant. "We do. If you don't have a big ego, there's nothing to shoot for. Right now we're unproven. By January we should be the team to beat." Added Grace, who would go on to compile a Big Eight-record 280 assists, "If you're quiet and not conceited, you will not make it on Oklahoma's team . . . I guess it's good we all have big egos.

It means we all have something to prove."

OU coach Billy Tubbs mentioned that Grace's backcourt partner, junior college transfer Mookie Blaylock, was "the quickest defensive player we've had at Oklahoma in a long time. He has great hands." By the season's end, those hands

At times, Danny Manning was a one-man band for KU.

would account for 150 steals, an NCAA season record. When Grace predicted that Oklahoma wouldn't lose 10 games, he also announced that by January the Sooners would be the team to beat in the conference race. He forecast as well as he dished out assists: Oklahoma roared out of the chute, not only going undefeated in its first 13 games but scoring more than 100 points in 10 of them. Punishments inflicted by the Sooners included wins of 152-84 over Centenary, 151-99 over Dayton and 144-93 over Oral Roberts University.

Why such strength? Grant and Grace had been joined by Stacey King and Dave Sieger, reserves the year before, and newcomer Blaylock to form a potent team. Grant and the fast-developing King gave the Sooners a strong inside game, while Sieger was known for his three-pointers. OU scored many of its points off fast-breaks keyed by an aggressive defense.

There was another factor in the high point totals. Besides Blaylock, Tubbs' roster included four other junior college transfers — among them forward Tyrone Jones, who had started his college career at Kansas — plus a couple of redshirts. But as the conference season approached, Tubbs revealed he didn't have much faith in his bench. Following a 109-69 trouncing of Austin Peay, he said, "I'm not going to worry about substitutions anymore. We might play five on five and try to score 200 points. If you want to see sorry teams play, go somewhere else. The day of mass substitutions is over. The subs that came in the last five minutes (of the game) made me sick." Much later, Tubbs would find time for only one substitute in the season's most important game.

Mike Yoder

Oklahoma's improvement was the biggest surprise in the Big Eight during the early season, but the Sooners didn't have the most surprising player. That was Iowa State's Lafester Rhodes, a 6-8 senior who had been a seldom-used reserve during his first three years with the Cyclones. Rhodes blossomed in coach Johnny Orr's up-tempo offense early in the 1987-88 season, scoring 54 points in a 102-100 overtime victory over cross-state rival Iowa, the team that had embarrassed Kansas in Hawaii. The Cyclones, off to an 11-2 start after going 13-15 the year before, also rode the 1-2 punch of Rhodes and 6-5 senior Jeff Grayer to an impressive 104-96 win at Purdue, later accorded the No. 1 seed in the NCAA Midwest Regional.

Kansas State, which would come within one victory of the Final Four, was a lukewarm commodity early in the season. In the Wildcats' only meeting with a noteworthy foe they had been beaten 101-72 at Purdue, a loss they would later avenge. Otherwise, K-State, featuring 6-5 senior Mitch Richmond, had dropped a pair of two-point decisions to Southern Mississippi — one in Manhattan, the other in Hattiesburg — and a marathon four-overtime home game to Southwest Missouri State. As Richmond continued to improve, the Wildcats would make their mark in the conference race.

Nothing much had been expected of Colorado, Oklahoma State and Nebraska, and in the early going none of the three had changed anyone's opinion. Nebraska's Danny Nee, however, found an appropriate label for what would turn out to be the best basketball season in conference history. "It's the Year of the Superstar in the Big Eight," Nee said. "You have five legitimate No. 1 (NBA) picks in Grayer, Richmond, Manning, Grant and Chievous."

An Associated Press poll released just before the January conference openers gave some indication of the Big Eight's strength. Oklahoma was ranked No. 8, Iowa State No. 17 and Kansas No. 18. Missouri just missed the Top Twenty, coming in with the 21st highest vote total.

Manning and Chievous, two of the five Big Eight "superstars," were scheduled to meet on the conference season's opening weekend. KU's Marvin Branch, however, received almost as much pregame publicity. Branch was, of course, rumored to be headed for academic ineligibility. And he would be playing against former high school teammates Buntin and Coward. All three had attended Murray-Wright High in Detroit. "On the court it's going to be all business," Branch stressed. "After that, we can all be friends again."

Milt Newton was all business as he scored the Jayhawks' first eight points, including a three-pointer, on the way to a 34-31 halftime lead in a jam-packed Allen Fieldhouse. Manning settled for nine points in the opening half. "I knew they'd sag on Danny and when they did I knew I'd have open shots, so I shot it," Newton said.

Missouri battled back to tie the game seven times in the second half, the last at 58-58 with six minutes remaining. Then KU ran off an 8-1 flurry, but Chievous' three-pointer at 1:29 cut the Jayhawk lead to 70-67. At :27, following a Coward three-pointer, Kansas led 74-72. Kevin Pritchard's layup at :19 boosted the margin to 76-72 before Greg Church, with a stickback at :08, brought the Tigers to within two again. Two seconds later, Scooter

Norm Stewart wanted the calls to go Missouri's way.

Richard Gwin

"It's the Year of the Superstar in the Big Eight. You have five legitimate No. 1 (NBA) picks in Grayer, Richmond, Manning, Grant and Chievous."

— DANNY NEE

Manning (28 points) was head and shoulders above Nathan Buntin and Missouri's defense.

Richard Gwin

JAN. 9 AT LAWRENCE

Missouri (74)

	MIN	FG m-a	FT m-a	REB o-t	PF	TP
Greg Church	33	2-8	4-4	7-13	3	8
Nathan Buntin	38	7-12	3-4	3-6	3	17
Doug Smith	21	1-5	2-2	1-5	4	4
Lee Coward	33	7-10	1-2	0-0	4	19
Byron Irvin	19	2-6	0-1	1-2	0	4
Gary Leonard	4	1-1	0-0	0-0	0	2
Derrick Chievous....	20	4-14	7-11	3-4	2	16
Mike Sandbothe	26	0-5	1-2	4-8	3	1
John McIntyre......	6	1-1	0-0	0-0	1	3
Totals		25-62	18-26	19-38	20	74

Three-point goals: 6-8 (Coward 4-6, Chievous 1-1, McIntyre 1-1). Assists: 13 (Church 4, Buntin 3, Smith 2, Coward 2, Chievous, Sandbothe). Turnovers: 17 (Church 4, Irvin 4, Chievous 4, Coward 2, McIntyre 2, Smith). Blocked shots: 1 (Smith). Steals: 4 (Coward, Irvin, Sandbothe, McIntyre).

Kansas (78)

	MIN	FG m-a	FT m-a	REB o-t	PF	TP
Danny Manning.....	35	12-21	4-5	3-7	2	28
Milt Newton	32	8-10	4-6	1-5	3	21
Marvin Branch......	33	2-9	4-6	3-7	3	8
Kevin Pritchard	27	3-6	2-3	1-3	4	8
Otis Livingston	23	1-2	2-2	1-3	3	4
Scooter Barry	17	0-0	3-4	0-1	1	3
Chris Piper	18	1-2	0-0	0-2	2	2
Lincoln Minor	13	2-4	0-0	0-0	3	4
Jeff Gueldner.......	2	0-0	0-0	0-0	1	0
Totals		29-54	19-26	9-28	22	78

Three-point goals: 1-1 (Newton 1-1). Assists: 17 (Livingston 6, Barry 3, Manning 2, Pritchard 2, Piper 2, Newton, Branch). Turnovers: 14 (Pritchard 4, Branch 3, Manning 2, Newton 2, Livingston 2, Minor). Blocked shots: 8 (Manning 4, Branch 2, Livingston, Minor). Steals: 7 (Livingston 2, Barry 2, Minor 2, Manning).

Missouri............................	31	43 —	74
Kansas.............................	34	44 —	78

Officials: Stan Reynolds, Rich Eichhorst, Ed Hightower. Attendance: 15,800.

Richard Gwin

Kevin Pritchard had two assists against the Tigers, and four turnovers.

Barry stepped to the foul line, knowing that if he made both free throws KU couldn't lose. Barry, who had converted 14 of 17 foul shots going into the game, hit both. Kansas won, 78-74, and Barry revealed afterward he'd never been in a similar situation before.

"I never even did that in high school." he said. "A lot of their players were saying 'He's going to choke, he's going to choke.' They were trying to psych me out. It's part of the game." In all, the Jayhawks made 10 of 11 foul shots in the last 4½ minutes and 19 of 26 overall — an improvement for a team then shooting only 62.2 percent at the line. "We're spending 10 to 15 minutes a day, plus our own time, on free throws," Chris Piper said, "and that's a lot more than ever before. It's a good idea, too, because we've been awful." Barry's two charities had been a factor in the win, and the fourth-year junior was gradually gaining a reputation as the Jayhawks' best foul shooter. He would go on to lead the team in that category for the season, making 53 of 65 for 81.5 percent.

From the field the Jayhawks shot 53.7 percent (29 of 54) against Missouri. Manning made 12 of 21 shots and finished with 28 points, 19 in the second half. Newton was eight for 10 and had 21 points, a career high in only his third start since replacing Archie Marshall. "Milt's always been there," Piper remarked. "He just hasn't had the confidence. The whole key to his game is confidence, and it looks like he's got it."

Chievous, in contrast, hadn't shot well — four of 14 from the floor, seven of 11 from the line — but was still the Tigers' third-leading scorer (16 points) behind Coward (19) and Buntin (17). Then again, Chievous played only 20 minutes. He started

With his long first step, Manning was a handful when he headed to the hoop.

Richard Gwin

the game on the bench, perhaps because he'd been involved in a minor automobile mishap the night before in Columbia.

With the win — KU's 10th victory in its last 11 games — the Jayhawks proved that if adversity pushed them down, they could jump right back up. But a knockout blow was coming. Branch, who scored eight points and had seven rebounds against Missouri, wouldn't play again. By the time the Jayhawks recovered from the loss of the 6-10 junior college transfer they had been all but written off.

Wednesday, Jan. 13, was the first day of KU's spring semester. It may have felt more like a Friday the 13th to Brown, a man who seemingly never met a superstition he didn't embrace. That morning, the Kansas sports information office issued a press release confirming that Branch was academically ineligible because he had "failed to satisfy NCAA certification standards." That night, Iowa State defeated the Jayhawks, 88-78; Hilton Coliseum in Ames remained the only Big Eight arena in which Brown's KU teams had never won. It wasn't a day to remember.

Branch's situation came as little surprise. Although he hadn't named names, Brown had all but conceded that the transfer was through for the season at a press conference the day before the Jayhawks flew to Iowa. But he did more than come close to confirming the rumors.

"If I commented about the way I really feel about the faculty," the coach said, "there'd be a lot more microphones in front of me." Moments later, Brown questioned the university's commitment to student-athletes from all walks of life. "I think we've made a real effort in tutoring and monitoring," he said. "What I'm saying is I don't think we've hit the problem. We don't have a curriculum set up for our students who don't have a normal background, a curriculum that gives them a chance to be successful. We don't have that."

Those remarks opened a can of worms that would wiggle for days. As Brown's position drew support and criticism it sparked a campus debate that wasn't settled by the end of the academic year. But on the basketball court, the Jayhawks quickly felt the loss of their starting center. They started to let big leads get away, a habit that would send them tumbling in the league's standings and nearly ruin their postseason chances.

Branch, after all, had averaged 8.4 points and 6.1 rebounds while starting all 14 of KU's games. He had either led or tied for the team lead in rebounds five times. Twice he was the Jayhawks' leading scorer, with 17 against Pomona-Pitzer and 20 against American University.

"I feel sorry for the kid . . . it's his life," Brown said. "It's just a sad situation. Those things happen and you've got to live with it." Branch would later say he found it ". . . hard accepting I was not eligible. As soon as I found out I was ineligible I wished it hadn't happened. I felt like I had let the team, my family and the fans down." Against Iowa State in Ames, the Jayhawks never enjoyed a lead big enough to fiddle away. Starting a lineup of Piper, Manning and Newton up front, with Pritchard and Otis Livingston in the backcourt, the Jayhawks fell behind by 17 points in the first half and couldn't recoup, finally falling to the Cyclones 88-78. The key stretch occurred late in the first half, when ISU ran off a 19-4 spurt to grab a 38-21 lead. Kansas battled back and clos-

ed to within six points with 1:14 remaining, but that was it.

Mainly because KU owned a 43-24 rebounding edge, Brown was quick to point out that even if Branch had played " . . . the outcome of the game wouldn't have been any different, I know that." Turnovers (25) and an inconsistent defense (ISU made 30 of 57 shots) were more costly. The Jayhawks were also zero for seven from three-point range while Iowa State made seven of 16 three-point attempts.

Piper, replacing Branch, logged a

JAN. 13 AT AMES, IOWA

Kansas (78)

	MIN	FG m-a	FT m-a	REB o-t	PF	TP
Danny Manning.....	38	12-25	8-8	4-14	5	32
Milt Newton........	25	7-13	1-3	4-12	1	15
Keith Harris	19	3-4	0-0	0-2	2	6
Kevin Pritchard	30	3-9	0-0	0-2	1	6
Otis Livingston	20	0-1	2-2	2-5	4	2
Clint Normore	5	0-0	0-0	1-1	1	0
Scooter Barry	4	0-0	0-0	0-1	2	0
Lincoln Minor	22	6-10	0-0	0-0	4	12
Chris Piper	28	2-7	1-2	4-6	2	5
Mike Maddox.......	7	0-1	0-0	0-0	1	0
Mike Masucci	2	0-0	0-0	0-0	0	0
Totals		33-70	12-15	15-43	23	78

Three-point goals: 0-7 (Newton 0-3, Manning 0-1, Minor 0-1, Maddox 0-1, Pritchard 0-1). Assists: 19 (Livingston 6, Newton 3, Pritchard 3, Manning 2, Harris 2, Piper 2, Minor). Turnovers: 25 (Livingston 6, Manning 5, Piper 4, Minor 3, Pritchard 2, Normore 2, Barry 2, Newton). Blocked shots: 1 (Maddox). Steals: 10 (Manning 3, Piper 3, Newton 2, Pritchard, Minor).

Iowa State (88)

	MIN	FG m-a	FT m-a	REB o-t	PF	TP
Jeff Grayer.........	30	7-15	1-4	1-4	4	15
Elmer Robinson.....	35	4-9	10-14	0-6	3	20
Lafester Rhodes	39	7-16	4-4	1-5	3	19
Gary Thompkins	30	4-5	4-4	0-4	2	13
Terry Woods	10	2-2	0-0	0-1	1	5
Mike Born	30	3-6	2-2	1-2	2	10
Marc Urquhart......	9	2-2	0-0	1-1	0	4
Mark Baugh........	6	0-0	0-0	0-0	0	0
Paul Doerrfeld	11	1-2	0-0	0-1	3	2
Totals		30-57	21-28	4-24	18	88

Three-point goals: 7-16 (Robinson 2-4, Born 2-5, Rhodes 1-4, Thompkins 1-1, Woods 1-1, Grayer 0-1). Assists: 22 (Rhodes 6, Thompkins 6, Born 5, Woods 2, Robinson, Urquhart, Baugh). Turnovers: 15 (Thompkins 5, Robinson 3, Grayer 2, Rhodes 2, Woods 2, Urquhart). Blocked shots: 6 (Rhodes 4, Grayer, Thompkins). Steals: 14 (Robinson 5, Doerrfeld 3, Grayer 2, Rhodes 2, Thompkins, Born).

Kansas.............................		31 47	— 78
Iowa State.........................		42 46	— 88

Technical fouls: Rhodes, Manning. Officials: Ron Zetcher, Ron Spitler, J.C. Leimbach. Attendance: 14,526.

"We don't have a curriculum set up for our students who don't have a normal background, a curriculum that gives them a chance to be successful. We don't have that."

— LARRY BROWN

Academic issues

On Jan. 26, despite fresh losses to Iowa State and Notre Dame, Larry Brown was focusing on more than basketball. In the wake of controversy stirred by his remarks on Marvin Branch's disqualification, the coach met with a faculty committee to express his concerns about academics. The implication in his initial remarks that athletes might need special courses in order to succeed at KU had drawn critical comment on a campus that took academic standards seriously.

"They were great," Brown said of the professors he spoke with. "Now I've got a forum and I feel a lot better." At the same time, he tossed a barb at the news media for the way remarks he had made on Jan. 12 had been reported.

"What I said, everybody wrote half of it," Brown charged. "The last thing I wanted anybody to feel was that I wanted to change the system here. I don't want it to be easy for kids. I'm not asking for a change, for an easy way out. The bottom line is we want a great academic program here and a great athletic program.

"But if you do that, you're going to take some kids that aren't up to normal standards. If we're going to bring them here, we've got to give them a chance for a legitimate degree. It's not about Marvin Branch. I'm sensitive and selfish about Marvin, but I'd hope I'd be sensitive and selfish about all kids involved."

One of those the coach met with, Mel Dubnick, associate professor of public administration, expressed sympathy. "We finally see it's not a narrow issue of Larry Brown mouthing off about the faculty," he said. The issue, he said, is concern that "the average student is being squeezed out of this place."

Some of Brown's points were echoed later in an April report by two faculty members, Ron Francisco, associate professor of political science, and Sharon Bass, associate professor of journalism. They had begun examining the issue of the "C" student at KU a year earlier, long before the Branch episode. Their report said that in response to rapidly rising enrollment at traditionally open-admissions KU, several schools within the university had imposed stiffer academic requirements. Such moves had the effect of eliminating options for the average student.

Stiffer grade-point requirements are in line with a trend at colleges across the country, the report noted. However, as KU's schools raised the grade point averages they require for admission, the choice of majors for average students has been narrowed. That, the professors said, forces some students into programs they are ill suited for, causes a "considerable imbalance in the distribution of minority students" and may result in some students leaving KU. By semester's end, no solutions — Brown's or anyone else's — were in hand.

season-high 28 minutes, scored five points and hauled down six rebounds. He then announced he wanted no more sympathy for his groin injury. "It's not fixable, as far as being able to play this season, so I'm just going to play through it," he said. "The most annoying thing is it limits my ability to practice, but I'm going to try and forget it from here on out. I figure if I'm going to sit out in practice, I may as well go all out in the games."

Against the Cyclones, Manning had faced a defense that wasn't stacked against him. He didn't shoot particularly well, though, missing 13 of his 25 shots. Still, he wound up with 32 points and 14 rebounds. "We love Marvin and we love Archie," Manning said afterward. "We'll miss them, but we've got to make do with what we can. As long as we have the effort, we'll be OK."

At Allen Fieldhouse on Jan. 16, three days after the ISU game, Kansas frolicked to a 95-69 victory over Hampton University. The Division II school from Hampton, Va., was inserted into the schedule when the athletic department had to make changes to accommodate three national TV games. Hampton became the 55th straight home victim as the Jayhawks continued to extend their Big Eight record. Manning, who played just 26 minutes, broke a record too: his three blocked shots made him KU's career leader in that category, with 157. Brown was smiling. "We were as unselfish as we've been," he said. "That was fun, because in a game like that, kids could be selfish."

Hampton provided a good, old-fashioned confidence boost — Piper called it "a good practice game" — and now the Jayhawks had a full week to prepare for a nationally televised game at Notre Dame. As

Brown saw it, the team needed the work. "The way the season has gone, with the injuries and Marvin, this has come at a great time," he said. "It gives us time to practice. I think we need it."

In South Bend, the Jayhawks would face a Notre Dame team anxious to prevent Manning from scoring 40 points — as he'd done the year before against the Irish in Lawrence, when KU won 70-60. Coach Digger Phelps' plan was to surround Manning and make the Jayhawks win with outside

Keith Harris rebounded from Larry Brown's doghouse to score 12 points against Hampton.

Brenda Steele

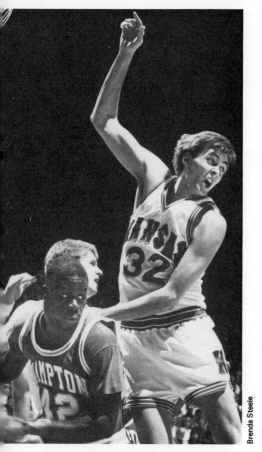

Freshman Mike Maddox won nine minutes of valuable playing time.

"We were as unselfish as we've been."

— LARRY BROWN

JAN. 16 AT LAWRENCE

Hampton (69)

	MIN	FG m-a	FT m-a	REB o-t	PF	TP
S. Hartfield	15	2-4	0-0	0-1	0	5
P. Williams	24	3-4	0-0	1-3	3	6
Derrick Dunson	29	0-2	2-4	3-7	3	2
Raymond Lee	32	5-10	7-9	1-2	3	17
Stacy Clark	32	10-20	4-5	4-8	1	25
Charles Battle	13	0-4	1-3	2-4	0	1
Jay Lane	11	1-2	0-2	1-1	4	2
Tony Woods	6	1-2	2-2	0-0	3	5
Deon Lewis	17	2-9	0-0	2-2	1	4
Ishmael Morley	3	0-2	0-0	2-2	2	0
Greg Ford	12	0-4	0-0	0-2	0	0
M. Draughon	2	1-1	0-0	0-0	0	2
Michael Smith	2	0-0	0-0	0-0	1	0
A. Blackmon	2	0-0	0-0	0-0	1	0
Totals		25-64	16-25	16-32	22	69

Three-point goals: 3-11 (Hartfield 1-3, Clark 1-3, Lee 0-3, Woods 1-1, Ford 0-1). Assists: 9 (Ford 2, Woods 2, Williams, Dunson, Lee, Clark, Smith). Turnovers: 24 (Clark 5, Lee 4, Battle 3, Williams 2, Dunson 2, Lane 2, Blackmon, Smith, Ford, Lewis, Woods, Hartfield). Blocked shots: 1 (Williams). Steals: 9 (Clark 3, Dunson 2, Woods 2, Lewis, Battle).

Kansas (95)

	MIN	FG m-a	FT m-a	REB o-t	PF	TP
Milt Newton	19	6-15	0-0	2-9	0	12
Chris Piper	18	4-4	1-1	1-3	4	9
Danny Manning	26	6-9	10-11	2-7	1	22
Kevin Pritchard	11	4-9	0-0	0-0	5	8
Otis Livingston	19	2-2	0-0	1-3	2	4
Scooter Barry	16	1-1	0-0	0-3	1	2
Keith Harris	23	4-7	4-7	2-4	2	12
Lincoln Minor	19	4-5	2-2	0-0	2	10
Mike Masucci	16	3-5	0-0	1-1	2	6
Mike Maddox	9	1-3	0-0	0-0	2	2
Clint Normore	8	1-2	2-2	0-1	2	4
Jeff Gueldner	16	2-4	0-0	0-0	0	4
Totals		38-66	19-23	9-31	23	95

Three-point goals: 0-6 (Newton 0-3, Pritchard 0-2, Manning 0-1). Assists: 23 (Livingston 7, Minor 4, Manning 4, Harris 3, Barry 2, Maddox 2, Newton). Turnovers: 15 (Minor 3, Normore 2, Newton 2, Pritchard 2, Livingston 2, Manning, Harris, Maddox, Gueldner). Blocked shots: 5 (Manning 3, Masucci, Normore). Steals: 14 (Minor 6, Livingston 2, Harris 2, Newton, Piper, Manning, Barry).

Hampton	30	39	— 69
Kansas	43	52	— 95

Officials: Dennis Schmidt, Samuel Banks, Duane Smith. Attendance: 15,450.

shooting. It was becoming a standard defense against KU, especially after rival coaches started to notice the Jayhawks' dismal 24.2 percent shooting from three-point range.

But Kansas, 0-13 from beyond the three-point line in its last two games, could hardly miss from the outside against the Irish. Newton hit three three-pointers and Pritchard a pair as the Jayhawks forged a 41-36 halftime lead. After intermission, KU drew out to an 11-point ad-

vantage, 57-46, with 13:39 showing. Then the edge started to wear away. As they had against so many visiting teams, the Irish fought back. With 15 seconds left, Notre Dame led 76-74. Manning, however, went to the foul line with a chance to tie the score. Instead, he missed the front end of the bonus opportunity — "Point blank I just missed it. That's the bottom line" — and the Irish went on to win, 80-76.

Notre Dame guard David Rivers had scored 29 points — he was 14 of 15 at the free throw line — and Phelps announced that the national player-of-the-year race was between Rivers and Manning. Brown, naturally, took a different view.

JAN. 23 AT SOUTH BEND, IND.

Kansas (76)

	MIN	FG m-a	FT m-a	REB o-t	PF	TP
Chris Piper	30	2-8	0-0	1-1	3	4
Milt Newton	30	6-9	0-1	1-7	3	15
Danny Manning	40	8-19	4-6	2-9	4	22
Otis Livingston	26	2-3	0-0	0-1	4	4
Kevin Pritchard	29	6-13	0-0	0-1	4	14
Scooter Barry	6	0-0	1-2	0-0	1	1
Lincoln Minor	20	2-6	2-2	0-1	2	6
Mike Masucci	4	1-1	1-1	1-1	3	3
Keith Harris	15	3-4	1-2	1-1	0	7
Totals		31-57	9-14	6-22	24	76

Three-point goals: 5-9 (Newton 3-4, Pritchard 2-4, Minor 0-1). Assists: 19 (Livingston 6, Minor 4, Newton 3, Pritchard 2, Barry 2, Piper, Manning). Turnovers: 10 (Minor 3, Piper 2, Newton 2, Manning, Livingston, Pritchard). Blocked shots: 4 (Manning 3, Pritchard). Steals: 7 (Minor 2, Manning, Livingston, Pritchard, Barry, Masucci).

Notre Dame (80)

	MIN	FG m-a	FT m-a	REB o-t	PF	TP
Mark Stevenson	36	7-9	1-2	0-1	3	15
Gary Voce	39	5-9	3-5	0-3	1	13
Scott Paddock	8	0-0	3-4	1-2	3	3
David Rivers	38	7-16	14-15	1-5	3	29
Jamere Jackson	31	3-8	2-3	0-2	1	8
Joe Fredrick	2	0-0	0-0	0-0	0	0
Tim Singleton	2	0-0	0-0	0-0	0	0
Sean Connor	11	1-1	0-0	0-3	0	2
Keith Robinson	33	4-6	2-3	3-10	3	10
Totals		27-49	25-32	5-26	14	80

Three-point goals: 1-6 (Rivers 1-4, Jackson 0-2). Assists: 12 (Rivers 7, Stevenson 2, Jackson 2, Paddock) Turnovers: 13 (Stevenson 6, Robinson 3, Rivers 2, Voce, Jackson). Blocked shots: 0. Steals: 6 (Robinson 3, Rivers 2, Jackson).

Kansas	41	35	— 76
Notre Dame	36	44	— 80

Officials: J.C. Leimbach, Stan Reynolds, Rich Eichhorst. Attendance: 11,418.

"You ask any kid in America who is the best player on any team and who would be the first person they'd take and they'll say Danny," he said, " . . . not to take anything away from David, though. He's phenomenal." Manning — who would have his own say later, on the court, about who would rank as player-of-the-year — finished with 22 points. But he took only 13 shots against a collapsing zone defense clearly designed to prevent the 6-10 All-American from beating the Irish, even if it left other Jayhawks open. "They weren't guarding me," said a disgusted Piper, who missed six of eight shots. "I was wide open. It was a good strategy by them. I couldn't stick it in."

The game had two postscripts: It was at Notre Dame that the KU players donned black ribbons to honor Roy Edwards, a longtime supporter of KU athletics who had died in December. They would remain on the uniforms throughout the season. And it was after the Notre Dame game that Kansas dropped out of the AP rankings, never to return to the AP's top 20 list.

Now, though, it was off to Lincoln, Neb., and the Cornhuskers. What were the odds of KU surrendering big leads in back-to-back games? A good bet, it turned out. This time Kansas wasted a 16-point advantage in the final 12 minutes and suffered a heartbreaking 70-68 loss to Nebraska. "We played like we were scared to death," Brown said after the Jayhawks missed the front end of three bonus free-throw opportunities in the last 2:43. None were by Manning, however. He was 11 of 11 at the foul line but didn't score in the last 6:39, partly because the Huskers fouled KU's guards before they could feed him the ball.

JAN. 27 AT LINCOLN, NEB.

Kansas (68)

	MIN	FG m-a	FT m-a	REB o-t	PF	TP
Milt Newton	21	4-8	3-5	2-4	4	11
Chris Piper	29	3-3	4-5	1-4	2	10
Danny Manning	39	5-13	11-11	0-5	4	21
Otis Livingston	29	1-2	1-3	1-1	1	3
Kevin Pritchard	25	4-6	1-3	0-2	3	9
Clint Normore	4	0-1	0-0	0-1	1	0
Scooter Barry	7	1-1	2-2	0-0	1	4
Lincoln Minor	15	2-2	0-0	0-2	2	4
Jeff Gueldner	16	1-2	2-2	1-2	2	4
Mike Masucci	12	1-2	0-0	0-2	3	2
Keith Harris	3	0-0	0-0	0-0	0	0
Totals		22-42	24-31	5-23	23	68

Three-point goals: 0-3 (Pritchard 0-2, Normore 0-1). Assists: 13 (Barry 3, Livingston 2, Pritchard 2, Gueldner 2, Masucci 2, Manning, Minor). Turnovers: 16 (Livingston 5, Pritchard 3, Minor 3, Newton, Manning, Barry, Harris, Gueldner). Blocked shots: 5 (Manning 3, Piper, Masucci). Steals: 5 (Piper 2, Manning 2, Masucci).

Nebraska (70)

	MIN	FG m-a	FT m-a	REB o-t	PF	TP
Jeff Rekeweg	28	6-9	3-5	0-4	5	15
Derrick Vick	33	5-7	6-9	1-6	3	16
Pete Manning	25	4-6	2-2	0-4	4	10
Henry Buchanan	33	7-11	4-4	0-1	3	21
Eric Johnson	32	1-6	3-4	0-3	4	5
Rich King	15	0-1	1-4	0-0	2	1
Clifford Scales	15	0-1	0-0	1-2	2	0
R. vanPoelgeest	3	0-0	0-0	0-0	0	0
Beau Reid	16	1-2	0-0	0-1	2	2
Totals		24-43	19-28	2-21	25	70

Three-point goals: 3-4 (Buchanan 3-4). Assists: 13 (Johnson 6, Reid 2, Rekeweg, Manning, Buchanan, King, Scales). Turnovers: 17 (Rekeweg 5, Reid 4, Vick 3, Buchanan 2, Johnson 2, Manning). Blocked shots: 2 (Vick 2). Steals: 8 (Buchanan 3, Johnson 2, Reid, Vick, Rekeweg).

Kansas	40 28	— 68
Nebraska	28 42	— 70

Officials: Rick Wulkow, Paul Sternberger, John Dabrow. Attendance: 14,015.

"I figure if I'm going to sit out in practice, I may as well go all out in the games."

— CHRIS PIPER

Finally, with the score knotted at 68, Manning brought the ball upcourt. Though a skilled ball-handler, this time he lost the handle. Nebraska took over on the turnover and won on Beau Reid's last-ditch 16-foot jumper at :01.

For the Jayhawks, it was the sixth straight Big Eight road defeat over the last two seasons. Their conference record dropped to 1-2. KU stood at 12-6 overall after losing three of its last four games.

"We're not that good," Brown said after the defeat in Lincoln. "Good basketball teams don't let that happen."

It's over

5

If there's anything Kansas State basketball fans can't stomach, it's losing to KU. To drop 10 straight games to the Jayhawks — as the frustrated Wildcats had during Larry Brown's tenure at Kansas — well, that was more than a bellyful for KSU backers.

Brown tried to downplay that dominance with observations that may not have entirely soothed Wildcat stomachs. "I've had better teams than they've had . . . we've been better," he explained. "It's as simple as that." Kansas had also won 55 straight games in Allen Fieldhouse, a Big Eight record, and, as KSU coach Lon Kruger conceded, "Anytime you go into Lawrence, winning is almost impossible."

So on the afternoon of Jan. 30 — Archie Marshall's knee had been injured exactly a month earlier — Kansas State came to town on the wrong side of 10-0 and 55-0 streaks. When the 'Cats bused back to Manhattan later that evening, those numbers would read 10-1 and 55-1.

K-State had come to town on a streak. Led by senior Mitch Richmond, who was rapidly gaining a reputation as a strong pro prospect, the Wildcats had knocked off Oklahoma at home, then posted wins at Colorado and Oklahoma State, snatching the conference lead.

Kansas, meanwhile, was in the doldrums, coming off the back-to-back losses in which the Jayhawks had blown big leads at Notre Dame and Nebraska. "We've got to find somebody to pull our kids together, to step forward as a leader," Brown said. "We've had it in Mark

KU couldn't get past Charles Bledsoe and his Kansas State teammates.

Mike Yoder

Ben Bigler

"We beat some great teams in this building and a great team beat us tonight."

— LARRY BROWN

KSU's Bledsoe scored only eight points but pulled down a dozen rebounds, seven of them on the offensive boards.

(Turgeon) and Cedric (Hunter) before."

Against Kansas State, the Jayhawks experienced some now familiar problems in a setting that, so far, had helped them avoid the defeats they'd suffered on the road. Yet for the third straight game they lost a double-digit lead. Playing the intense defense that was to become their trademark, KU had built a 22-12 lead with eight minutes left in the first half. The advantage disappeared in a hurry. The Wildcats tied the score at 29-29 just before inter-

The Jayhawks put up defensive barriers, but Bledsoe and the Wildcats found ways around.

Mike Yoder

mission, although a Danny Manning jumper put the Jayhawks up 31-29 at the break.

The second half was another story. K-State grabbed its first lead at 36-35, on a three-pointer by Will Scott with 16:23 left. Then Richmond, who had 23 of his game-high 35 points after intermission, followed with another three-pointer at 14:48, for a four-point lead.

Seven minutes later, however, Kansas had battled back to lead 48-47, and the game looked as if it might stay close all the way. It didn't. With six minutes left, KSU went on an 11-1 run built around two three-pointers by Richmond. The Wildcats forged a 58-49 lead. Jayhawk fans in the stands and around the state sensed that a pleasant piece of basketball history — the 55-game winning streak — was about to end. KU managed to close to 60-54 with 1:59 left, but then Lincoln Minor missed four shots in the last 1:43, and KSU, in contrast, made 10 of 10 free throws in last :54. The Wildcats won, 72-61.

Like the speed limit on two-lane roads, the nation's longest current winning streak would be stuck on 55. The streak, which began after Oklahoma posted an overtime win at the fieldhouse on Feb. 22, 1984, was over. KU's players were shattered. Manning, experiencing his first home loss while wearing a Kansas uniform, was so distraught he declined to talk to sportswriters. "It hurts so much," said Milt Newton. "I feel like the world is over."

Brown, in contrast, was unexpectedly upbeat. He accepted the defeat for what it was — a tremendous performance by a hungry KSU team. "We beat some great teams in this building and a great team beat us tonight," Brown stated. "It's tough to hold a streak. The bottom

line is we've got to get better and appreciate what we've accomplished. They made their shots and we didn't." In all, the Wildcats had made nine of 12 three-pointers and 21 of 26 foul shots.

Actually, Richmond and his cohorts didn't shoot that well overall — 45.7 percent — but Kansas shot only 44.1 percent against KSU's 3-2 zone. Manning scored 21, but took only a dozen shots, hitting eight. In putting the squeeze on Manning, the Wildcats dared Kansas to beat them from the outside. The Jayhawks couldn't do it. Starting guards Kevin Pritchard and Minor were a combined eight of 29 — and zero for nine from three-point range.

"I take responsibility for this loss," Pritchard said afterward. "I was three of 12 taking 15-footers. I should have hit them. To me, that's the game right there. If I hit those shots, we win." His shots, however, had come from unfamiliar territory: This was his first game at point guard. Against KSU, Brown had benched the turnover-prone Otis Livingston, shifted Pritchard to the point and inserted Minor as the off-guard. Livingston never took off his warm-ups against the 'Cats. "We played guys I thought we'd win with," Brown said. One was reserve guard Jeff Gueldner, a sophomore who came off the bench to score a career-high 10 points by hitting all four shots he attempted, half from beyond the three-point line.

Still, Richmond was too much. Despite missing 13 of 24 shots, he was three for four from three-point territory and finished with 35 points and 12 rebounds. He was also 10 of 10 at the line, with eight coming in the last minute and a half. "We had the ball in Mitch's hands and that's a good place to have it," said a smiling

Steve Henson, K-State's point guard. Henson also thought Allen Fieldhouse was the right place at the right time. "They were probably thinking about it (the winning streak) more than we were," he reflected. "We had nothing to lose. Then we started hitting some of those threes and I think that might have got on their minds."

When the other team hits nine of 12 from beyond the three-point line, it can be demoralizing, all right. "We hit some shots that if they don't go in we lose," said Kruger about his team's long-range shooting. "We're going to live and die by that." Weeks later, when Kansas and Kansas State met in the Pontiac Silverdome for the right to go to the

Keith Harris hounded, but Mitch Richmond burned KU for 35 points and 12 rebounds.

Mike Yoder

Breaking a 55-game homecourt winning streak was reason enough for the Wildcats to celebrate.

"We're not a great basketball team. We're a little short-handed now. But we've got to keep working and it'll come."

— LARRY BROWN

JAN. 30 AT LAWRENCE

Kansas State (72)

	MIN	FG m-a	FT m-a	REB o-t	PF	TP
Mitch Richmond	37	11-24	10-10	6-12	1	35
Charles Bledsoe.....	36	3-8	2-3	7-12	2	8
Fred McCoy	17	1-3	3-4	1-4	4	5
Steve Henson	40	2-4	2-2	0-2	2	8
Will Scott	34	4-7	4-5	0-4	2	16
Buster Glover.......	5	0-0	0-0	0-0	1	0
Ron Meyer	19	0-0	0-2	0-2	2	0
Mark Dobbins	8	0-0	0-0	0-0	1	0
Carlos Diggins	3	0-0	0-0	0-0	0	0
Mark Nelson	1	0-0	0-0	0-0	0	0
Totals		21-46	21-26	14-36	15	72

Three-point goals: 9-12 (Henson 2-2, Richmond 3-4, Scott 4-6). Assists: 12 (Henson 6, Scott 2, Richmond, Bledsoe, McCoy, Dobbins). Turnovers: 17 (Henson 5, Richmond 4, McCoy 3, Scott 3. Bledsoe 2). Blocked shots: 0. Steals: 3 (Richmond, Bledsoe, Meyer).

Kansas (61)

	MIN	FG m-a	FT m-a	REB o-t	PF	TP
Milt Newton........	28	4-7	0-0	1-3	5	8
Chris Piper	23	0-1	0-0	0-1	5	0
Danny Manning.....	39	8-12	3-4	3-8	2	21
Lincoln Minor	35	5-15	0-0	2-3	0	10
Kevin Pritchard	31	3-12	1-2	0-2	2	7
Mike Masucci	11	0-3	1-1	0-1	2	1
Keith Harris	11	1-2	0-0	2-3	2	2
Scooter Barry	14	1-2	0-0	0-1	3	2
Clint Normore	2	0-1	0-0	0-0	2	0
Jeff Gueldner.......	6	4-4	0-0	0-0	1	10
Totals		26-59	5-7	8-22	24	61

Three-point goals: 4-16 (Manning 2-2, Gueldner 2-2, Newton 0-2, Minor 0-5, Pritchard 0-4, Barry 0-1). Assists: 17 (Pritchard 8, Newton 3, Piper 2, Minor 2, Barry, Gueldner). Turnovers: 9 (Newton 5, Minor, Pritchard, Harris, Barry). Blocked shots: 5 (Newton 2, Manning 2, Piper). Steals: 8 (Pritchard 4, Minor 2, Barry, Gueldner).

Kansas State.........................	29	43 — 72
Kansas	31	30 — 61

Officials: Ron Spitler, Rick Wulkow, Stan Reynolds. Attendance: 15,800.

NCAA Final Four, the Wildcats died. They would make just seven of 22 three-pointers that afternoon.

At the time of the streak-breaking win, though, the second-year KSU coach was a gracious winner and a happy man. "It's a special feeling. It's an honor to beat them here. There've been a lot of good teams come through here and leave with a loss. The fact we were down by 10 makes it a little bit sweeter. Kansas was controlling things with its defense, but we hung together and kept scratching and gave ourselves a chance at halftime."

The win moved KSU to 4-0 in the Big Eight, while the Jayhawks, expected before the season to challenge for the lead, skidded to 1-3. Kansas was an enigma. The Jayhawks ranked No. 7 nationally in field goal percentage but, at 26.7 percent, were one of the worst three-point shooting teams in the country. And KU hadn't found a replacement for Branch. Piper, unable to practice, was playing poorly. He had no points and one rebound in 23 minutes against the Wildcats.

Still, the man in charge maintained he saw something to build on. "I'm encouraged with the way we played," Brown said at time. "We're not a great basketball team. We're a little short-handed now. But we've got to keep working and it'll come."

Looking back later, Brown saw the loss to KSU as a turning point in his relations with his players, and vice versa. "I had fun on the bench that game," he recalled. "Prior to that, I had to yell at kids to play unselfish. I didn't like yelling that all the time and didn't like the way the kids reacted. That game, everything I said, they listened.

"This was a most difficult year,"

Long faces were the order of the day for Milt Newton, Chris Piper and Clint Normore.

Brown added. "I didn't like the way I acted early in the season. From January on, I grew up in a lot of ways. I'm hopeful that in the future I'll be a better coach, more responsible to the kids. Sometimes I'm a little too vocal."

For the Jayhawks, however, the turnaround didn't happen right away. In fact, shortly after the groundhog emerged on a cloudy day to promise an early spring, many Kansas basketball fans figured the rodent was actually forecasting a short season for KU. After Feb. 3 it was difficult — almost impossible, really — for anyone to imagine six more weeks of good basketball in Lawrence. Or, as Oklahoma guard Ricky Grace said sarcastically: "Maybe they can start a 55-game losing streak at home."

Four days after Kansas State had ended the Jayhawks' invincibility at home, Oklahoma came to Lawrence in a peevish mood. The high-flying Sooners, averaging over 100 points a game and often accused of showing their opponents little mercy, clearly had wanted to end KU's home streak themselves.

"I was disappointed because they broke our home winning streak a couple of years ago," said Grace, who had made his feelings about the Jayhawks clear before the season when he remarked: "I won't say I hate Kansas but I'd rather lose to anybody else but Kansas. It's kind of like the Oklahoma-Nebraska rivalry in football. Of any place I play, I like to silence the people in Kansas."

The Jayhawks, meanwhile, went into the game wondering if recent nightmares would ever end, and Manning's bad dreams were no doubt dominated by zone defenses. "It's frustrating, but I can't show my frustration on the court," he said. "Once I get frustrated at people sagging, packing it in, I can't concentrate on the game. I can't get caught up in talking to the refs, begging for calls. I've got to go out and do what I can."

When Brown had switched Pritchard to point guard against K-State, he also advised Manning to abandon, from time to time, his accustomed spot under the basket. "I've been given permission to go out on the perimeter," Manning said. "Coach Brown wants me to step out on the floor to get people off my back. If I can dart out, then in, it's easier. Maybe if Oklahoma sags we'll hit the 15-footer."

During their skid, though, the Jayhawks hadn't been able to drop a 15-foot shot with a 15-foot spoon. "The bottom line is we have to step forward and hit a jump shot,"

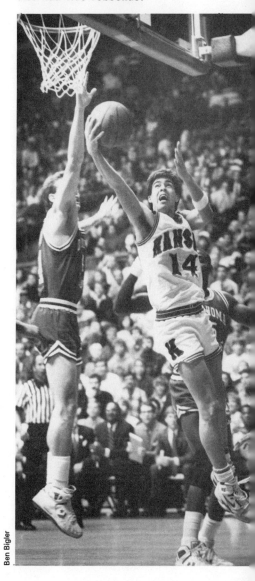

Kevin Pritchard drove through the Sooner defense for a dozen points. The KU guard also had five rebounds.

Billy Tubbs exhorted Harvey Grant, who was held to 12 points.

Brown noted. Something else the coach wanted was for Manning to play with more fire: "If we're to be competitive, he'll have to play his best basketball. He'll do it. I told Danny they won't pay him money (in the NBA) to look good in a program."

Mike Yoder

OU's Terrence Mullins reached for another Sooner steal against Pritchard. OU collected nine in all.

Ben Bigler

Playing at a packed Allen Fieldhouse, KU forged a 31-29 halftime lead — the same as against K-State. Early in the second half, Kansas stayed on top, 35-33. Then Grace and Dave Sieger unloaded three-pointers to begin an 11-2 spurt. Outside shooting like that — along with pressure defense, relentless running and tough inside play — was why Oklahoma was considered one of the most explosive college teams in years. With 14:17 remaining, OU was up 44-37, and six minutes later, the Sooners put together a 22-8 run. Kansas was down by a dozen, 55-43. KU came right back, however, and cut that bulge to 55-51 at 5:52. The Sooners wouldn't fold. OU made six of six free throws in the last minute to wrap up a 73-65 victory.

The loss looked like the crusher of KU's hopes — for the Big Eight race, for an outstanding season, and even for making the NCAA Tournament field. The Jayhawks had now lost four in a row and five of their last six. Their record stood at 12-8, with three of the victories coming

FEB. 3 AT LAWRENCE

Oklahoma (73)

	MIN	FG m-a	FT m-a	REB o-t	PF	TP
Harvey Grant	33	6-15	0-2	4-10	4	12
Dave Sieger	32	3-7	3-4	2-8	2	11
Stacey King	31	9-18	1-2	4-8	3	19
Mookie Blaylock	34	3-13	1-2	2-3	4	9
Ricky Grace	40	6-14	4-4	2-3	3	19
Tyrone Jones	8	0-1	0-0	0-0	1	0
Anthony Martin	16	1-4	1-2	2-5	1	3
Terrence Mullins	6	0-1	0-0	1-2	2	0
Totals		28-73	10-16	17-39	20	73

Three-point goals: 7-16 (Sieger 2-3, Grace 3-6, Blaylock 2-6, Jones 0-1). Assists: 20 (Blaylock 7, Grace 3, Sieger 3, Grant 2, Martin 2, King, Jones, Mullins). Turnovers: 11 (Grant 4, Sieger 2, Blaylock 2, Grace, Jones, Mullins). Blocked shots: 3 (King 3). Steals: 9 (Grace 3, Grant 2, King 2, Martin, Blaylock).

Kansas (65)

	MIN	FG m-a	FT m-a	REB o-t	PF	TP
Milt Newton	28	3-8	2-3	0-4	2	8
Mike Masucci	14	0-2	0-0	1-2	3	0
Danny Manning	33	12-20	4-5	7-16	4	28
Lincoln Minor	29	4-12	1-3	2-4	3	9
Kevin Pritchard	33	4-7	4-5	0-5	1	12
Chris Piper	23	0-3	0-0	0-1	1	0
Scooter Barry	5	1-3	0-0	0-1	0	2
Keith Harris	12	1-2	0-0	0-3	0	2
Otis Livingston	4	0-0	0-0	1-1	1	0
Mike Maddox	10	2-3	0-0	1-3	1	4
Jeff Gueldner	9	0-0	0-0	0-0	1	0
Totals		27-60	11-16	12-40	17	65

Three-point goals: 0-6 (Minor 0-3, Barry 0-1, Manning 0-1, Pritchard 0-1). Assists: 14 (Minor 7, Manning 2, Pritchard 2, Piper 2, Masucci). Turnovers: 16 (Pritchard 6, Minor 4, Manning 2, Piper 2, Barry, Newton). Blocked shots: 3 (Manning, Minor, Piper). Steals: 6 (Manning 2, Minor 2, Pritchard, Livingston).

Oklahoma .... 29 44 – 73
Kansas .... 31 34 — 65

Officials: Ed Hightower, Jim Harvey, Ron Zetcher. Attendance: 15,800.

against non-Division I schools — that is, non-games in the NCAA computer. The schedule ahead, marked by a murderous stretch in February and March against Kansas State, Duke, Oklahoma and Missouri — all but the Duke game on the road — seemed to make the Jayhawks' chances prohibitive. Danny Manning's senior season — the one he'd given up certain riches in the pro ranks to play — wasn't shaping up as one to savor. There was talk that Manning, once considered a near-certain bet for national player-of-the-year awards, might lose out, perhaps to Hersey Hawkins of Bradley who would lead

the nation in scoring with a 36.3 average.

Later on, Brown admitted he thought it was possible that the Jayhawks wouldn't make the tournament field. "We were wondering if we'd make the NIT," he confided later. But at the time he was doing his second straight Pollyanna impression.

Slowed by injuries, Chris Piper couldn't get a handle on his game against Oklahoma. He played 23 minutes but didn't score.

Ben Bigler

"We've got to keep
growing, building,
get a couple of wins
and who knows,
something funny
might happen."

— LARRY BROWN

Richard Gwin

Both the Jayhawks and the Sooners took their games to new heights but OU came out on top, 73-65. It was KU's second straight loss in Allen Fieldhouse and, some said, the low point of the season.

"If we give this kind of effort, play as well defensively as we did tonight, we'll be fine," he emphasized. "We've got to keep growing, building, get a couple of wins and who knows, something funny might happen."

It did, of course. But the something funny happened to Oklahoma almost two months later, in Kansas City's Kemper Arena. Looking back in the hectic days of the Final Four, on the eve of the rematch with the Sooners, a sportswriter asked Chris Piper what would have happened if someone had walked into the KU locker room after that first OU game, seen all those long faces and told the Jayhawks to cheer up — that in 61 days they'd be playing Oklahoma for the NCAA title. "What," Piper replied, smiling, "are your chances of winning the Pulitzer?"

Piper himself didn't even start that OU game in Allen Fieldhouse. Freshman Mike Masucci earned the call instead. But Masucci took a Stacey King elbow to the head early in the second half, suffered a mild concussion and was out for 10 days.

"We couldn't get it done," Brown said afterward. "We battled. I thought we got tired when Masucci got hurt. We didn't have a lot of depth." Despite not starting, Piper had to play more than Brown

wanted, 23 minutes, because of Masucci's injury. Piper had also logged 23 minutes in the K-State game. He didn't score a point in either one. There was one difference this time, however. He was booed.

"It's sad," Brown said of the booing. "He didn't practice all week. He can't turn. He has no legs on his shot. If we do something about it (an operation) he's finished for the season, and he's a senior. It's a Catch 22."

As the Oklahoma game wore down, the Kansas crowd polarized. While some booed, others tried to drown the boos with cheers. Finally, with the game in the closing moments and obviously lost, hundreds of fans stood up and began leaving. That unusual early exodus prompted, mostly from the student section, chants of "Don't come back, don't come back, don't come back . . . ." Early February was a dark time for the KU faithful, and the not-quite-so-faithful.

"Right now they're struggling," observed the Sooners' King, who had scored 19 points, "but when they get their confidence back, they'll do all right in the Big Eight Tournament and in the NCAAs."

Manning, for one, agreed with King's assessment. Although Brown had wanted two things against Oklahoma — a more aggressive Manning and improved outside shooting — he'd had to settle for one out of two. Manning, freed up by the Sooners' man-to-man defense and fast-paced style, had 28 points and 16 rebounds. "Nobody here has quit," he emphasized. "Nobody's packing their bags. If we do the things we're supposed to do, we're capable of beating a lot of teams. We've got to go out and get a victory. We're going to go out and practice hard for Colorado."

Turnaround

6

Larry Brown didn't snap his fingers and turn the Kansas basketball season around. He didn't push a button or feed his players a magic potion or sell his soul. Instead he made a series of subtle moves.

First he decided he wanted Kevin Pritchard to take over most of the ball-handling duties. That was in the K-State game on Jan. 30. At the same time, he encouraged Danny Manning to roam away from the basket on offense, and Manning began to do just that. Then, before the Colorado game on Feb. 6, Brown granted a request that Chris Piper had made the day after the loss to Oklahoma. The senior forward asked that despite his injuries he be allowed to practice, as well as play in games. The fans' booing had convinced Piper to make the change. "I'm playing bad when I don't practice," he said. "I don't have any timing on the floor. I guess maybe 99 percent of it is mental, but there's no way I can be halfway effective without practicing." For the first time in weeks, Piper practiced with the team. Time would prove his self-analysis correct. For a while, though, he would continue to struggle, as would the team. At least one more move remained for Brown to

make, but it wouldn't come until after the Colorado game in Allen Fieldhouse.

Although the season still had weeks to run, opposing teams had already learned to spell confidence C-O-L-O-R-A-D-O. The Buffaloes, with a record of 4-14 and with five losses so far in the Big Eight race, were coming off a 99-69 pasting at Missouri. Kansas needed to follow suit: "Right now it's probably the most important game we've played all year," Piper said.

A crowd of only 14,100 — 1,700 under capacity — was on hand in the fieldhouse. KU bolted to a 16-10 lead and then, astonishingly, the Buffs made seven of eight shots and scored 15 unanswered points, taking a 25-16 lead. The boo-birds returned for what was to be their last appearance of the season. KU scrambled back to take a 34-32 halftime lead and eventually won, 73-62, despite missing seven of 16 free throws in the last four minutes.

It was a spotty performance, but no one wanted to give it back. "I hate to say it, but if we lost this one, it was all over," Piper said. Manning had 23 points and nine big rebounds despite being whistled for his fourth foul with 12:17 remaining. "When

> *"I guess maybe 99 percent of it is mental, but there's no way I can be halfway effective without practicing."*
>
> — CHRIS PIPER

Danny picked up his fourth foul so early, it was scary," Brown said. "But Danny was great. He made some big hoops."

So did Kevin Pritchard, who was five of eight from the floor. Pritchard went into the game shooting 48.2 percent, and mentioned that he'd received letters on how to improve the figure. "I appreciate it," the sophomore guard said. "It's constructive criticism. There's a guy in Topeka who's sent me three or four letters. I look at the films and he's been right every time. He said I've been using my left hand too much and I haven't had enough rotation. Your left hand has nothing to do with your shot."

With Piper ailing, Masucci out and Keith Harris temporarily suspended — "Keith has personal problems; he missed two practices," Brown said — two members of the

Colorado gave KU a spell of relief in Allen Fieldhouse. Kevin Pritchard, on five of eight shooting, scored 17 points.

Richard Gwin

FEB. 6 AT LAWRENCE

Colorado (62)

	MIN	FG m-a	FT m-a	REB o-t	PF	TP
Dan Becker	34	5-11	1-4	6-13	5	11
Brian Robinson	33	3-9	0-2	2-5	1	6
Scott Wilke	39	7-14	2-5	3-7	2	16
Steve Wise	19	3-6	0-0	0-0	4	9
Brian Molis	23	2-4	0-0	0-0	2	6
Michael Lee	34	3-9	0-0	0-1	3	7
Brent Vaughan	14	0-3	4-4	1-3	1	4
David Kuosman	2	1-4	0-0	0-0	4	3
T. Chapmon	1	0-0	0-0	0-0	0	0
Rodell Guest	1	0-0	0-0	0-0	0	0
Totals		24-60	7-15	12-29	22	62

Three-point goals: 7-18 (Wise 3-4, Molis 2-3, Lee 1-3, Kuosman 1-4, Vaughan 0-3, Wilke 0-1). **Assists:** 12 (Molis 4, Lee 3, Becker 2, Robinson, Wilke, Wise). **Turnovers:** 16 (Wilke 5, Molis 3, Becker 2, Robinson 2, Wise 2, Lee 2). **Blocked shots:** 1 (Vaughan). **Steals:** 5 (Lee 2, Wilke 2, Becker).

Kansas (73)

	MIN	FG m-a	FT m-a	REB o-t	PF	TP
Lincoln Minor	21	1-6	0-0	0-1	2	2
Kevin Pritchard	33	5-8	7-10	0-3	2	17
Milt Newton	23	6-7	3-4	1-3	1	15
Danny Manning	34	10-13	3-4	2-9	4	23
Chris Piper	32	1-4	0-2	2-6	3	2
Jeff Gueldner	16	1-4	2-2	1-2	2	4
Scooter Barry	8	0-0	2-2	0-0	0	2
Mike Maddox	19	2-3	0-1	0-1	2	4
Otis Livingston	14	1-1	2-3	0-0	1	4
Totals		27-46	19-28	6-25	17	73

Three-point goals: 0-1 (Pritchard 0-1). **Assists:** 16 (Manning 4, Maddox 3, Pritchard 3, Minor 2, Newton 2, Piper 2). **Turnovers:** 15 (Manning 5, Newton 4, Minor 2, Gueldner 2, Pritchard, Piper). **Blocked shots:** 4 (Minor, Newton, Manning, Piper). **Steals:** 10 (Manning 4, Pritchard 3, Newton 2, Piper).

Colorado . . . . 32 30 — 62
Kansas . . . . 34 39 — 73

Technical fouls: Colorado bench. **Officials:** J.C. Leimbach, Paul Kaster, Ed Schumer. **Attendance:** 14,100.

Danny Manning carried Kansas to the top, but it took some prodding from coach Larry Brown. "I want him to be assertive," Brown said. "It's not an equal opportunity sport when you're that talented."

Pressure defense was KU's game. Scooter Barry showed how against Iowa State.

Mike Yoder

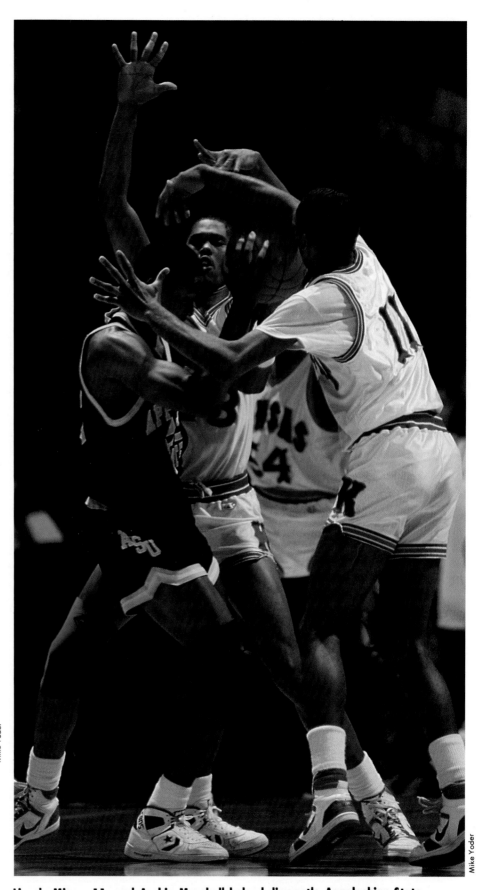

Mike Yoder

Lincoln Minor, 11, and Archie Marshall helped dismantle Appalachian State.

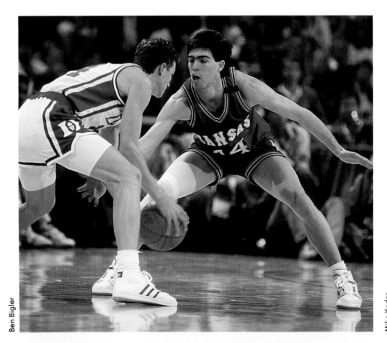

Ben Bigler

Head to head: Kevin Pritchard vs. Duke's Quin Snyder. Below, Brown vs. the ref.

Mike Yoder

Ben Bigler

Giving chase: Danny Manning hounded a Nebraska player at the edge of the court.

The season had highs — and lows — for Brown, but the ending was perfect.

Switching from football to basketball, Clint Normore knew when a block was needed.

Counted on for his rugged inside play, Marvin Branch was lost midway through the season, an academic casualty.

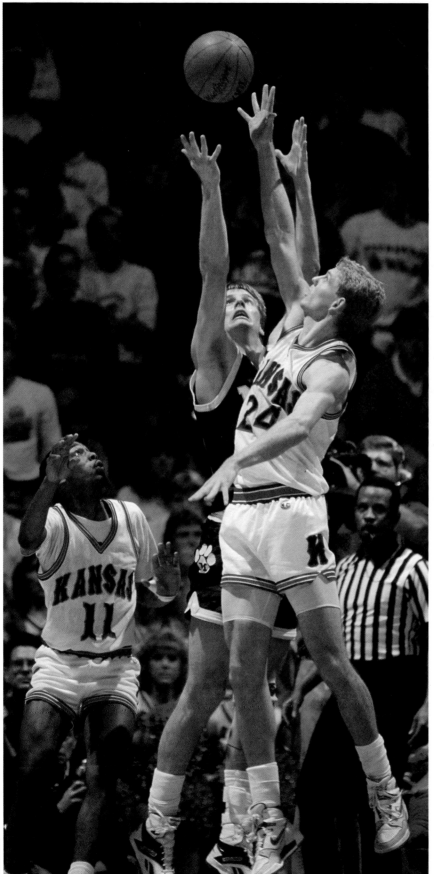

Richard Gwin

In Big Eight play against Nebraska, Keith Harris and Lincoln Minor made a play for a loose ball.

Ben Bigler

Richard Gwin

Manning took stock of the situation.

Chris Piper, playing injured much of the season, was described by Danny Manning as the heart and soul of the KU team.

Adoring fans loved Super-Manning and the Jayhawks. One of the most loyal of fans was Ryan Gray of Lawrence, an inspiration to the team.

Milt Newton took on Kansas State star Mitch Richmond.

Against Iowa State, Danny Manning rose above the crowd.

Kevin Pritchard was a force from the perimeter.

Next page: Surrounded by Oklahoma Sooners, Kansas All-American Danny Manning still found a path to the basket. Photo by Mike Yoder.

Jeff Gueldner, above, went over Duke's Billy King. At right, Kevin Pritchard ignored the pressure from Duke's Quin Snyder.

Larry Brown directed his team from the sidelines.

Chris Piper escorted his mother during a ceremony honoring KU's seniors before their final home game.

Clint Normore battled for the ball in NCAA tournament action against Xavier.

Scooter Barry, with a career-high 15 points, shocked Kansas State during the NCAA Midwest Regionals in Pontiac, Mich.

After the Jayhawks won a Final Four spot, KU fans in Lawrence went to the streets to celebrate. At right, a superfan left no doubt about his Kansas loyalty.

Chris Piper helped KU surge past Duke to gain
a berth against Oklahoma in the title game.

Mike Yoder

Ben Bigler

Ben Bigler

In a Final Four battle, Kevin Pritchard won the race to the ball against Duke's Danny Ferry.

Ben Bigler

Mike Yoder

Kansas celebrated victory in Kansas City. At right, Stacey King sat alone and dejected after Oklahoma fell to KU in the championship game.

Mike Yoder

Watching from the sidelines, Jayhawk players Marvin Mattox, left, and Archie Marshall lifted their arms in a victory salute as KU knocked off Big Eight rival Oklahoma and won the 1988 NCAA basketball championship.

Ben Bigler

Mike Yoder

KU assistant coach Ed Manning and his son Danny both went to the net after the Jayhawks' victory over Oklahoma.

The No. 1 Jayhawks met President Reagan at the White House and gave him a KU letter jacket.

Manning lifted the NCAA trophy.

Mike Yoder

Richard Gwin

60,000 fans turned out for a parade in downtown Lawrence to honor KU's champions. Here Scooter Barry greeted the KU faithful. And it was only fitting that Cinderella would lead the parade for the Cinderella team.

Richard Gwin

junior varsity squad, football player Marvin Mattox and walk-on Brad Wahl, suited up. Mattox would remain with the team for the rest of the season, but Wahl went back to JV status once Harris returned.

So worried was Brown about having enough healthy bodies that he seriously considered pulling 6-10 Sean Alvarado from red-shirt status. "We're running out of people," he said. "You look down the bench and our kids in street clothes could probably beat the ones who are playing. It'd be a helluva game." Alvarado, though, remained a red-shirt. He recalled later, "I suited up

when Masucci got hurt. I was leaning toward playing. These guys have done so much for me, I was ready to do something for them." Brown confirmed it was a close call. "It wouldn't have been fair to him, but we said if anybody else went down we'd probably have to play him. We were able to win without Sean, and he'll be back."

Now, as the Jayhawks headed for Stillwater and Oklahoma State, a final change remained as Brown fine-tuned the Jayhawks. He started Jeff Gueldner in the backcourt in place of Lincoln Minor, who had been plagued by poor outside shooting and turnovers. Gueldner, a 6-5 sophomore, had no outstanding strengths but no real weaknesses either. And he played hard. All the time.

"I don't think it's an accident we started winning after (Gueldner) started playing," Brown remarked later. "He helped us win." Gueldner, from Illinois, had been an unheralded recruit. He had averaged 17 points and nine rebounds for

"There's a guy in Topeka who's sent me three or four letters. I look at the films and he's been right every time. He said I've been using my left hand too much . . . ."

— KEVIN PRITCHARD

FEB. 10 AT STILLWATER, OKLA.

Kansas (78)

	MIN	FG m-a	FT m-a	REB o-t	PF	TP
Chris Piper	35	1-1	6-6	2-4	3	8
Milt Newton	26	6-10	2-3	1-6	3	17
Danny Manning	40	8-16	7-9	2-9	3	23
Kevin Pritchard	39	6-8	6-6	0-2	3	20
Clint Normore	6	1-1	0-1	0-1	1	2
Scooter Barry	3	0-0	0-0	0-0	0	0
Otis Livingston	22	0-0	1-2	0-2	4	1
Mike Maddox	8	1-1	0-0	0-0	3	2
Jeff Gueldner	18	1-2	2-4	0-2	3	5
Keith Harris	3	0-0	0-0	0-0	1	0
Totals		24-39	24-31	5-26	24	78

Three-point goals: 6-6 (Newton 3-3, Pritchard 2-2, Gueldner 1-1). **Assists:** 17 (Pritchard 6, Livingston 5, Gueldner 3, Newton, Manning, Maddox). **Turnovers:** 17 (Livingston 7, Pritchard 4, Newton 2, Manning 2, Normore, Barry). **Blocked shots:** 3 (Manning 2, Gueldner). **Steals:** 8 (Pritchard 4, Livingston 2, Manning, Gueldner).

Oklahoma State (68)

	MIN	FG m-a	FT m-a	REB o-t	PF	TP
Richard Dumas	36	1-12	9-11	1-6	3	11
William Woods	22	1-5	0-0	3-3	2	2
S. Kincheon	16	1-4	0-0	1-2	2	2
Derrick Davis	19	0-0	5-6	0-0	2	5
John Starks	38	7-11	4-4	0-4	4	21
Chuck Davis	8	1-1	0-0	0-0	0	2
Todd Christian	21	4-8	0-0	1-2	4	8
Royce Jeffries	26	7-9	3-5	4-6	5	17
Robert Smith	13	0-2	0-0	0-1	1	0
Bryan Fowler	1	0-0	0-0	0-0	1	0
Totals		22-52	21-26	10-24	24	68

Three-point goals: 3-9 (Starks 3-5, Christian 0-4). **Assists:** 14 (Woods 5, Starks 3, Davis 3, Christian 2, Smith). **Turnovers:** 14 (Kincheon 3, Jeffries 3, Dumas 2, Davis 2, Starks 2, Christian, Smith). **Blocked shots:** 1 (Smith). **Steals:** 6 (Starks 2, Dumas, Woods, Davis, Christian).

Oklahoma State	28 40 —	68
Kansas	33 45 —	78

Officials: Rick Wulkow, Paul Kaster, Woody Mayfield. **Attendance:** 6,381.

Mike Yoder

Jeff Gueldner was a winner for KU after Larry Brown made him a starter against Oklahoma State.

Charleston High, but wasn't a prep All-American or even an all-state selection. However, he compiled nearly a perfect grade point average, something Brown didn't take lightly. Steve Simons, Charleston High's coach, had worked in Brown's camp one summer, and he asked if KU would take a look at Gueldner. Brown did, and saw a player comparable, he thought, to Jeff Hornacek, the former Iowa State walk-on currently on the roster of the NBA Phoenix Suns. "It's an eight-hour drive to Charleston," said Gueldner, whose only other firm offer was from Eastern Illinois, his hometown university. "So I was lucky coach Brown got to see me play. He recruited me honestly. He was sincere."

"I remember going to see Gueldner play at the Five Star camp in Pennsylvania," said Brown. "They put the best prospects on what they call the NBA team. The other kids are on the NCAA team. He was on the NCAA team. I went up to a guy and said, 'We've offered him a scholarship.' So he put him on the NBA team as a favor to me. This kid helped the NBA win the championship. Gueldner finds a way to win, and that's the bottom line."

In his first start, on Feb. 10 in Stillwater, Gueldner had only one basket, but it was important. It was a three-pointer in the opening minutes, and it set the tone for an unprecedented exhibition by the Jayhawks. Kansas took six long-range shots — and made all six.

Prior to the game in refurbished Gallagher Hall, OSU coach Leonard Hamilton said he was worried about facing KU, although some thought needlessly. The Cowboys, after all, were coming off

their best Big Eight road trip in years — back-to-back wins at Nebraska and Iowa State. "Kansas is fighting to come back from adversity, and sometimes the struggle will make you stronger," Hamilton pointed out. "I feel we're catching them at the most dangerous time possible because their pride is hurt a little bit."

Hamilton was right about that, but he couldn't know the Jayhawks were going to step out of character with long-range gunnery. "I was looking for it and it was dropping," explained Milt Newton, who made half the six three-pointers on the way to a 17-point effort. "They were playing zone against us like everybody else, so coach said look for it and I did."

KU never trailed after bolting to a 19-8 lead after 8½ minutes. The Jayhawks led 33-28 at the half, but it took solid free-throwing down the stretch to halt their six-game Big Eight road losing streak. Kansas made 10 of 12 charities in the last 2:12 to seal the 78-68 win. The last time they'd played a league road game — at Nebraska — poor foul shooting down the stretch cost them dearly. This time the shots dropped. "We didn't play scared, and that was the key," said Manning, who had 23 points and nine rebounds.

Pritchard was six for six at the foul line and wound up with a season-high 20 points. Also noteworthy was the defensive job Piper did on OSU standout Richard Dumas. The 6-7 forward, later named Big Eight freshman-of-the-year, missed 11 of 12 shots, mostly with Piper on him.

Effective, too, were those unexpected three-point goals. KU was shooting 24.7 percent in that category — worst in the Big Eight and one of the worst percentages in the country. Why the turnaround at

---

"Gueldner finds a way to win, and that's the bottom line."

—LARRY BROWN

OSU? "If I knew the answer, we'd shoot well every game," Pritchard said. Going into the game, KU's new point guard had made only three of 23 three-point tries. He would wind up the season 17 for 54, including seven of 13 in the six NCAA Tournament games. All 17 were away from home. For the season, Pritchard was zero for 15 from three-point range in Allen Fieldhouse.

"I've been begging our kids to shoot three-pointers against zones all year," Brown said. "We hadn't been successful. But hopefully we'll be a better three-point team." Not since the rule had gone into effect before the 1986-87 season had Kansas made as many as six three-pointers in one game. The new record would last only a little longer than a week.

Still, the Oklahoma State game was a watershed. It proved the Jayhawks could win on the road, and it showed that they could convert three-pointers. And it marked Gueldner's debut as a starter. "Deep down I was nervous, I guess," he recalled. "Once I got over that, I just wanted to go out and do what I can do." In all, he played 18 minutes, with five points and two rebounds.

The Jayhawks also tried six three-point goals next time out — in a home game against Iowa State that opened the second half of the Big Eight round-robin schedule. They made only two of the six, not that it mattered much. Against the Cowboys, the three-pointers were crucial; against the Cyclones they were next to meaningless, thanks to Manning. The All-American downplayed his performance. "I think I had a good game, but not an excellent one," he said. Manning scored 39 points — on 13-of-18 shooting from the field and 12 of 13

at the line — and added seven rebounds, seven assists and six steals. It was the best all-around statistical game of his career. "Manning was just too much for us," sighed ISU coach Johnny Orr. "He's just a fantastic player."

In the first half, Manning had 19 points on the way to a 44-34 halftime Kansas lead. With 11:08 left, KU led by 19. With Manning picking up an extra 20 points in the second half, the Jayhawks coasted

Danny Manning and Pritchard helped KU fast-break the game open against Iowa State.

Mike Yoder

to an 82-72 victory. "Just another day at the office for him," teammate Clint Normore said of Manning. "I was just watching him," echoed Pritchard. "Finally I said, 'I'm out here, too. I can't just watch. I've got do something.'"

In his best all-around game, however, Manning suffered his most serious injury of the season. He sprained the index finger on his left hand. He didn't complain, but for the rest of the campaign he would have the digit taped.

Kansas, now 4-4 in the league and 15-8 overall, had such a big lead

The KU defensive cyclone: ISU's Lafester Rhodes tried the middle but was met by Keith Harris and Manning, who blocked his shot.

Coach Johnny Orr of Iowa State watched the Jayhawks avenge their loss in Ames. "Manning was just too much for us," Orr said.

at the end against the Cyclones that Wahl and Mattox, the two JV players added to the roster the previous week, made their debuts. It was also Wahl's finale. And Masucci, coming off his concussion, saw three minutes of duty.

In the meantime, the backlash of the back-to-back home losses to Kansas State and Oklahoma continued to cut into the crowd. This one was 300 under capacity. "It's remarkable to me to see some empty seats now," Brown said. He would see twice as many empty

seats at the next home game, against Nebraska. But with the season drawing to a close and the Jayhawks improving, the rest of the home games would be standing-room-only.

In the fieldhouse on Feb. 16, Nebraska faced big odds. The Cornhuskers hadn't won in Lawrence since 1983, and the Jayhawks hadn't forgotten that 76-68 loss in Lincoln back on Jan. 27 — a defeat Brown termed ". . . as disappointing a loss as I've been associated with. We had that game won and we

Mike Maddox and Lincoln Minor, going up against Nebraska's Rich King, helped KU continue its rebound against Big Eight foes.

FEB. 13 AT LAWRENCE

Iowa State (72)

	MIN	FG m-a	FT m-a	REB o-t	PF	TP
Jeff Grayer	40	11-17	8-12	3-7	4	30
Lafester Rhodes	25	6-17	2-2	6-8	4	14
Paul Doerrfeld	11	0-3	0-0	0-1	3	0
Marc Urquhart	29	2-3	4-4	1-1	1	8
Terry Woods	23	0-5	2-2	0-0	3	2
Mike Born	28	1-3	2-2	2-3	2	5
Elmer Robinson	18	1-3	0-0	0-3	5	2
V. Alexander	10	4-7	0-0	3-4	0	8
Mark Baugh	14	0-4	3-4	1-2	2	3
R. Johnson	2	0-0	0-0	0-0	0	0
Totals		25-62	21-26	16-29	24	72

Three-point goals: 1-6 (Born 1-2, Baugh 0-2, Rhodes 0-1, Robinson 0-1). Assists: 13 (Born 5, Woods 3, Grayer 2, Urquhart 2, Baugh). Turnovers: 19 (Rhodes 7, Grayer 3, Urquhart 2, Woods 2, Born 2, Robinson 2, Doerrfeld). Blocked shots: 4 (Robinson 2, Grayer, Rhodes). Steals: 8 (Doerrfeld 2, Woods 2, Grayer, Rhodes, Urquhart, Baugh).

Kansas (82)

	MIN	FG m-a	FT m-a	REB o-t	PF	TP
Milt Newton	18	1-7	0-3	1-4	4	2
Chris Piper	34	3-7	2-2	4-7	3	8
Danny Manning	33	13-18	12-13	1-7	3	39
Kevin Pritchard	37	5-10	0-0	0-2	4	10
Jeff Gueldner	22	4-6	2-4	1-2	1	10
Keith Harris	16	1-1	0-0	1-1	1	2
Clint Normore	23	2-3	2-3	0-1	1	7
Scooter Barry	4	0-1	2-2	0-2	0	2
Mike Maddox	7	1-2	0-0	1-2	1	2
Mike Masucci	3	0-0	0-0	0-0	0	0
Otis Livingston	2	0-0	0-0	0-0	1	0
Marvin Mattox	1	0-0	0-0	0-0	0	0
Totals		30-55	20-27	9-28	19	82

Three-point goals: 2-6 (Normore 1-1, Manning 1-1, Newton 0-3, Gueldner 0-1). Assists: 18 (Manning 7, Pritchard 4, Newton 2, Normore 2, Piper, Gueldner, Barry). Turnovers: 19 (Manning 4, Gueldner 3, Harris 3, Normore 3, Barry 2, Piper 2, Maddox, Livingston). Blocked shots: 2 (Piper, Harris). Steals: 11 (Manning 6, Piper 4, Pritchard).

Iowa State	34	38 — 72
Kansas	44	38 — 82

Officials: Ed Hightower, Terry Turlington, Rich Eichhorst. Attendance: 15,500.

Ben Bigler

"I doubt any team in the country will face four Top 20 teams, three on the road. But that's what makes basketball fun."

— LARRY BROWN

Beau Reid, who ruined the Jayhawks in Lincoln, managed only two points against Milt Newton and the KU defense in Allen Fieldhouse.

basically gave it away."

"Before the game, we were really pumped up," said Newton. "The last time, in Lincoln, we came close to blowing them out but ended up losing. We had to prove something tonight." The proof came early. KU hammered Nebraska with a 20-4 spurt at the outset, then raced to 46-23 halftime lead. The dominance disappeared in the second half, and Nebraska outscored KU 25-24. But

FEB. 16 AT LAWRENCE

Nebraska (48)

	MIN	FG m-a	FT m-a	REB o-t	PF	TP
Derrick Vick	26	2-5	0-1	1-7	3	4
Pete Manning	38	8-9	5-8	0-4	4	21
Richard King	26	1-5	2-3	0-6	4	4
Jeff Rekeweg	21	3-6	0-0	2-2	2	6
Eric Johnson	28	0-4	2-2	1-3	4	2
Henry Buchanan	15	1-4	0-1	0-0	1	3
R. van Poelgeest	15	0-0	2-2	0-2	3	2
Beau Reid	15	0-4	2-2	0-0	4	2
Cliff Scales	12	2-2	0-0	0-1	2	4
Rodney Curtis	4	0-0	0-0	0-0	0	0
Totals		17-39	13-19	6-31	27	48

Three-point goals: 1-4 (Buchanan 1-2, Johnson 0-1, Reid 0-1). **Assists:** 9 (King 4, Scales 2, Vick, Johnson, van Poelgeest). **Turnovers:** 19 (King 5, Johnson 5, Rekeweg 2, van Poelgeest 2, Reid 2, Vick, Manning, Scales). **Blocked shots:** 2 (King 2). **Steals:** 5 (Vick, Manning, Rekeweg, Reid, Scales).

Kansas (70)

	MIN	FG m-a	FT m-a	REB o-t	PF	TP
Milt Newton	22	5-9	0-0	3-6	2	12
Chris Piper	27	3-7	4-6	3-3	2	10
Danny Manning	35	9-20	3-4	3-8	3	21
Kevin Pritchard	23	0-5	4-5	0-2	2	4
Jeff Gueldner	17	0-2	0-0	0-0	2	0
Clint Normore	17	2-4	2-2	0-3	1	6
Lincoln Minor	14	1-3	3-4	2-4	1	5
Keith Harris	18	2-5	0-0	2-4	1	4
Otis Livingston	4	0-1	0-0	0-0	1	0
Mike Masucci	12	0-0	0-0	1-2	2	0
Scooter Barry	5	1-2	4-4	0-2	1	7
Mike Maddox	5	0-1	1-2	0-0	3	1
Marvin Mattox	1	0-0	0-0	0-0	0	0
Totals		23-59	21-27	14-34	21	70

Three-point goals: 3-10 (Newton 2-2, Barry 1-2, Pritchard 0-2, Manning 0-1, Gueldner 0-1, Livingston 0-1). **Assists:** 10 (Manning 2, Newton, Piper, Pritchard, Gueldner, Normore, Minor, Livingston, Masucci). **Turnovers:** 7 (Gueldner 2, Newton, Manning, Pritchard, Harris, Maddox). **Blocked shots:** 2 (Newton 2). **Steals:** 10 (Manning 3, Newton 2, Piper, Gueldner, Minor, Harris, Barry).

Nebraska	23	25 — 48
Kansas	46	24 — 70

Technical fouls: Nebraska bench. **Officials:** Woody Mayfield, John Dabrow, Charles Greene. **Attendance:** 15,200.

Kansas won, 70-48, despite shooting only 39 percent, the team's lowest percentage at home all season.

Manning, coming off his Iowa State performance, returned to reality with 21 points. He missed 11 of 20 shots, but he looked like a ballet star to the beleaguered Huskers. "I guess you can say they danced with who brought them to the dance . . . Danny Manning," said Beau Reid, whose last-second shot had ruined the Jayhawks in Lincoln. "He's the best player in the nation."

With the victory, Kansas had won four straight, and, said Brown, "Right now we're playing as well as we can play. I'm going to enjoy this a bit. Then it's the death march." Death march, murderer's row, call it what you wanted. The Jayhawks faced a 10-day stretch that included games at Kansas State, Oklahoma and Missouri, and a home date with Duke. Three of the schools were ranked in the Top 20, while K-State had dropped out only the week before. "I doubt any team in the country will face four Top 20 teams, three on the road," Brown said. "But that's what makes basketball fun."

Less than thrilling for the coach was another rumor, this one centering on Brown taking over the Charlotte, N.C., NBA expansion franchise. He denied even talking to Hornets' officials and wondered aloud when the rumors would ever end. "I honestly think it'll never change until Danny leaves," he said. "Once Danny leaves and people see me here, then they won't have as much ammunition." With Manning around, Brown had lots of firepower for Jayhawk opponents, and he and his team would need it during the games ahead.

7

Rough road

S ome things in sports are hard to explain, even in hindsight. How could Kansas play consecutive regular-season games against Kansas State, Duke and Oklahoma, then meet the same teams in the same order in the NCAA Tournament? In postseason play KU would find ways to win against all three schools, but now, in the toughest part of a tough regular season, Larry Brown and the Jayhawks knew they'd be hard-pressed to win at all. They also knew that many of their earlier high hopes would rest on the KSU, Duke, Oklahoma sequence, and that two of the three games would be away from home. The road didn't get any smoother after that: Two other traditionally tough games followed, at Missouri and Colorado. Somehow, the Jayhawks had to find new ways to win.

The first chance came against Kansas State. Back on Jan. 30 the Wildcats had ended KU's 55-game homecourt winning streak. Now they thirsted to end another KU streak. Brown was unbeaten in Ahearn Fieldhouse, where his teams had won four straight. The 'Cats hardly needed an extra incentive, but there was one: The 1987-88

season marked the finale for KSU's 38-year-old fieldhouse. For the K-State faithful, Ahearn was filled to the rafters with as many memories as Allen held for Kansas fans. Next year, the Wildcats would play in the new Bramlage Coliseum. Now, a win over the Jayhawks would sweeten Ahearn's final season.

"I don't know if I'm sorry to see it closed down," Brown said. "It's a tough place to play." Traditional Ahearn distractions included flying chickens during pregame KU player introductions. Then, Brown knew, Kansas would again run into a stifling 3-2 zone defense designed to frustrate Danny Manning and force KU to score from the outside. In the first meeting in Lawrence, KU had been unable to do so, and that, as much as the Wildcats' inspired play, had decided the game.

This time was different. The Jayhawks threw up three-point attempts every chance they got; Ahearn was raining three-pointers. Even Manning launched four, making two. Overall, Kansas was eight of 18 — both season highs — from beyond the stripe. And it was a Kevin Pritchard three-point shot with :29 showing that broke a 61-61

Richard Gwin

Jeff Gueldner scrambled for 30 minutes against Steve Henson and the Wildcats.

Richard Gwin

FEB. 18 AT MANHATTAN

Kansas (64)

	MIN	FG	FT	REB	PF	TP
		m-a	m-a	o-t		
Milt Newton	27	6-13	1-2	3-6	2	14
Chris Piper	21	1-2	0-0	1-1	5	2
Danny Manning	40	8-15	0-0	4-8	2	18
Kevin Pritchard	34	4-10	1-1	1-3	1	12
Jeff Gueldner	30	4-5	1-1	4-5	3	10
Keith Harris	23	2-5	1-3	1-3	2	5
Mike Masucci	9	0-1	0-0	1-1	2	0
Lincoln Minor	8	0-2	0-0	0-0	0	0
Otis Livingston	1	0-0	0-0	0-0	0	0
Clint Normore	7	1-1	0-0	0-1	0	3
Totals		26-54	4-7	15-28	17	64

Three-point goals: 8-18 (Pritchard 3-8, Manning 2-4, Newton 1-3, Gueldner 1-1, Normore 1-1, Minor 0-1). **Assists:** 17 (Pritchard 6, Gueldner 5, Normore 2, Harris, Newton, Piper, Manning). **Turnovers:** 12 (Piper 3, Manning 3, Pritchard 3, Gueldner, Minor, Livingston). **Blocked shots:** 0. **Steals:** 5 (Newton 2, Manning, Pritchard, Harris).

Kansas State (63)

	MIN	FG	FT	REB	PF	TP
		m-a	m-a	o-t		
Mitch Richmond	39	4-17	2-2	0-1	1	11
Charles Bledsoe	38	3-10	0-1	5-8	2	6
Ron Meyer	18	4-6	3-3	4-4	4	11
William Scott	22	2-3	0-0	0-0	0	6
Steve Henson	40	4-6	2-2	0-3	3	13
Fred McCoy	20	5-10	2-4	4-7	2	12
Mark Dobbins	4	1-1	0-0	1-1	1	2
Buster Glover	18	1-2	0-0	1-3	0	2
Carlos Diggins	1	0-0	0-0	0-0	1	0
Totals		24-55	9-12	15-27	14	63

Three-point goals: 6-9 (Henson 3-3, Scott 2-2, Richmond 1-4). **Assists:** 14 (Richmond 7, Henson 5, Glover 2). **Turnovers:** 9 (Meyer 2, Henson 2, McCoy 2, Richmond, Bledsoe, Scott). **Blocked shots:** 0. **Steals:** 2 (Dobbins, Scott).

Kansas	38	26 — 64
Kansas State	34	29 — 63

Officials: Ron Spitler, Rick Wulkow, Mike Tanco. **Attendance:** 11,220.

deadlock late in the game.

Pritchard wasn't the star of this one, though. The role went to Jeff Gueldner. Making only his fourth start, the 6-5 sophomore had 10 points, five rebounds and five assists, and he was involved in crucial plays during the final two minutes. At 1:59, Gueldner made a left-handed stickback to give KU a 61-59 lead. Then he lunged, tipping Milt Newton's errant shot out to Pritchard with about a minute left, setting the stage for the game-winner. Gueldner also ruined the Wildcats' last chance by stealing the ball from Fred McCoy at midcourt with about one second remaining. "Luckily he (McCoy) lost control of the ball," Gueldner said, realizing he could have been called for a foul. He wasn't, and KU won a 64-63 nail-biter that had Jayhawk fans in Lawrence and across the state cheering around their television sets.

It was Kansas' 11th win in its last 12 meetings against KSU. "I don't know why we've been so successful against them," said Chris Piper, "except for Danny Manning." Actually, KU had featured as balanced an attack as it was to show all season. Manning had 18 points, Newton 14, Pritchard 12 and Gueldner 10. At the heart of the win was KU's ability to do what it had to, scoring from long range while the K-State zone crimped Manning. "If they're going to play Danny the way they're playing him, that's the way we're going to have to play," Brown said. "I don't like it, but that's the way we have to do it."

KSU standout Mitch Richmond,

who had buried the Jayhawks with 35 points and 11 rebounds in Lawrence, had one of his least effective games, scoring 11 points and getting one rebound. Hounded by Newton and Keith Harris, Richmond missed 13 of 17 shots. "They did a good job on me," he said of the KU defenders. "I was pretty frustrated, but I tried to stay in the game and not let it bother me. I just missed my shots. I'll have nights like this." Later, Richmond would have

another game like that against Kansas, in the NCAA Tournament. For now, KU was surging. Once 1-4 in the Big Eight, the Jayhawks stood at 6-4 and 17-8 overall after their fifth win in a row. Just two days later, it appeared that streak might reach an unlikely six. In a packed Allen Fieldhouse the Jayhawks were pummeling the No. 6-ranked team in the nation.

A national television audience joined the fieldhouse crowd to

"I just missed my shots. I'll have nights like this."

— MITCH RICHMOND

Richard Gwin

Mitch Richmond had run wild in Lawrence, but in Manhattan he faced well-armed KU defenders like Chris Piper and Milt Newton. Richmond was only 4 of 17 from the field.

Richard Gwin

Gueldner and Danny Manning celebrated the win over arch-rival KSU.

"The crowd took us out of the game . . . that's the loudest crowd we've ever heard."

— QUIN SNYDER

watch as Duke and Kansas, two teams that had met in the 1986 Final Four in Dallas, went at it again. The Jayhawks hit their first nine shots and stormed to a 23-8 lead in the first 12½ minutes. The fieldhouse rocked as fans yelled, whistled, clapped and stomped their feet on the steel flooring. "The crowd took us out of the game . . . that's the loudest crowd we've ever heard," Duke guard Quin Snyder said. Added forward Kevin Strickland, "We read in the papers that Kansas wanted revenge on us for what happened at the Final Four, but I didn't anticipate them coming out like that." Duke's coach, Mike Krzyzewski, concurred. "That's as hard as a team has come out against us, emotionally and physically," he said. "I don't know if anybody would have been ready for Kansas today."

But Duke hadn't earned its ranking by bowing to crowd noise and inspired defense. Although the Blue Devils missed 16 of their first 18 shots, the Jayhawks let Duke regroup by missing 13 of 14 attempts after their early run. At halftime, KU's lead had withered to one point, 28-27. And led by Strickland, who scored five points, and Robert Brickey and Danny Ferry, with four apiece, Duke outscored KU, 14-7, to start the second half. The Blue Devils took a 41-35 lead with 14:27 left. A three-pointer and layup by Snyder boosted the lead to 50-43 three minutes later. Then the Jayhawks, led by eight points from Manning, went on a 13-2 run to take a 56-52 lead at 6:06. The game was tied at 58-58 and 60-60. That was the score with 20 seconds left in regulation.

"I wanted us to run the clock down and get it inside," Brown said. "We've run that play before, but we

didn't run it that time. We took a horrible shot." Manning threw up an off-balance 18-footer that hit nothing but glass and rim with :05 showing. Overtime.

If the miss could be traced to fatigue, Manning didn't show it in the extra period. After just 45 seconds the senior had scored five points and KU led, 65-60. But Manning didn't take another shot and eventually fouled out just before the game ended. With 3:15 still to go, KU led 67-61. But moments later Snyder, who scored a career-high 21 points, hit a three-point basket,

FEB. 20 AT LAWRENCE

Duke (74)

	MIN	FG	FT	REB	PF	TP
		m-a	m-a	o-t		
Robert Brickey......	34	4-7	2-6	5-9	4	10
Billy King	34	0-4	2-4	1-4	4	2
Danny Ferry........	39	6-16	7-7	4-8	5	20
Kevin Strickland	36	2-11	0-0	5-8	3	5
Quin Snyder........	39	6-11	7-9	1-4	2	21
John Smith	15	4-6	2-2	0-1	1	10
Phil Henderson	19	3-6	0-0	0-5	1	6
Greg Koubek	8	0-2	0-0	0-0	1	0
Alaa Abdelnaby.....	1	0-2	0-0	0-0	0	0
Totals		25-65	20-28	16-39	21	74

Three-point goals: 4-11 (Snyder 2-2, Ferry 1-3, Strickland 1-5, Koubek 0-1). **Assists:** 10 (Snyder 5, Strickland 2, King 2, Brickey). **Turnovers:** 22 (Ferry 6, Snyder 4, Brickey 4, Henderson 3, King 2, Strickland 2, Smith). **Blocked shots:** 3 (Brickey, Ferry, Strickland, Team). **Steals:** 9 (Strickland 3, Snyder 3, King, Ferry, Henderson).

Kansas (70)

	MIN	FG	FT	REB	PF	TP
		m-a	m-a	o-t		
Milt Newton........	28	7-12	0-0	3-5	5	15
Chris Piper	32	2-4	2-3	2-4	3	6
Danny Manning.....	43	11-21	9-11	6-12	5	31
Kevin Pritchard	42	4-11	1-2	0-4	2	9
Jeff Gueldner.......	27	1-3	0-0	0-4	5	2
Keith Harris	12	0-2	0-0	1-2	1	0
Clint Normore	18	0-1	1-2	0-1	3	1
Mike Masucci	7	0-3	0-0	1-1	0	0
Scooter Barry	11	0-1	0-0	0-2	0	0
Lincoln Minor	5	3-5	0-0	0-0	0	6
Totals		28-63	13-18	13-35	24	70

Three-point goals: 1-6 (Newton 1-2, Pritchard 0-2, Normore 0-1, Minor 0-1). **Assists:** 17 (Newton 5, Pritchard 5, Gueldner 3, Piper 2, Manning, Harris). **Turnovers:** 21 (Manning 5, Pritchard 5, Newton 3, Normore 2, Barry 2, Piper, Gueldner, Harris, team). **Blocked shots:** 6 (Manning 3, Newton, Harris, Minor). **Steals:** 13 (Normore 4, Manning 4, Pritchard 2, Newton, Gueldner, Barry).

Duke...........................	27	33	14 — 74
Kansas.........................	28	32	10 — 70

Officials: Tom Fraim, David Dodge, Lenny Wirtz. **Attendance:** 15,800.

Ben Bigler

Clint Normore scrambled for a Duke fumble. So did the Blue Devils' Kevin Strickland and KU's Scooter Barry. The game was an intense struggle for 45 minutes.

Richard Gwin

KU ganged up on Danny Ferry and held the Duke star to 20 points on six-for-16 shooting, but a career-high 21 points from Quin Snyder helped the Blue Devils pull away in over-time.

Larry Brown and KU's bench found little to cheer in a great effort that came to nothing. Next stop after the frustrating home loss to Duke: Fourth-ranked Oklahoma, in Norman.

Richard Gwin

and at :52, Strickland's stickback gave the Devils a 69-68 lead. They went on to a 74-70 win.

Kansas, which hadn't lost at home in three years, had now dropped three games at home within the span of a month. "The effort was great, but we don't have a lot to be thankful for," Brown reflected. "I think this team is doing the best it can. We just don't have a lot of strength in terms of rebounding." On the other hand, Kansas still played defense: KU ranked No. 4 in the nation in field goal percentage defense. Jayhawk opponents were shooting only 41.3 percent, and Duke had managed only 38.5 percent. "They did a great job defensively," said Snyder. "They were really tough denying the passing lanes."

The Jayhawks had to forget the

frustrating loss. Ahead, in Norman, Okla., lay a Feb. 24 rematch with the Sooners, 24-2 and ranked No. 4 nationally. This year, Oklahoma was attracting attention with its defense as well as relentless scoring.

At least one KU veteran, though, thought the Jayhawks had a chance to win in Noble Arena, even if the Sooners' home record stood at 12-0. Mark Turgeon, the former guard working as a student assistant under Brown, called the current OU team even better than the one he faced during his senior season. He pointed to the play of 6-10 Stacey King and 6-8 Harvey Grant, averaging 20.3 and 21.6 points a game respectively. The two, he said, complemented each other well — "Grant is so unselfish. He doesn't force shots. He lets King do his thing." But Turgeon saw hope for KU in the Jayhawks' defense and in improved rebounding. "We can beat teams if we don't give up second shots . . . . Teams are shooting 41 percent against us. If we weren't giving up second shots, it would be something like 33 percent." Handling Oklahoma's prime defensive weapon, the press, would be a key. "They've always been a pressing team," Turgeon noted. "We've been able to beat it in the past."

On the road and up against another national power, the Jayhawks played a strong first half. Clint Normore made his only start of the season, replacing Gueldner, who had sprained an ankle in practice. Manning scored 20 first-half points on eight of 13 shooting. OU held only a 35-32 lead at intermission, but blasted to a 59-44 lead in the first 4½ minutes of the second half, largely on the strength of outside shooting by Mookie Blaylock and Ricky Grace. "It seemed like we'd get in striking distance and then they'd hit a three-pointer," said Newton.

Kansas wasn't through, however. The Jayhawks got to 64-56 on a tip by Lincoln Minor and to 68-62 on a shot by Manning at 9:07. After a driving layup by King, Pritchard hit a pair of free throws and Piper a 17-foot jumper; KU had crept to within four at 70-66. With 1:59 left, Oklahoma's advantage had been trimmed to 83-80. Then, just 11 seconds later, Manning fouled out. Despite Newton's 19 points in the second half, the Sooners, with King leading the way with 22 points, went

FEB. 24 AT NORMAN, OKLA.

Kansas (87)

	MIN	FG m-a	FT m-a	REB o-t	PF	TP
Milt Newton	27	8-14	3-5	2-6	4	21
Chris Piper	35	3-7	0-0	2-7	4	6
Danny Manning	37	13-24	4-4	4-11	5	30
Kevin Pritchard	36	6-9	4-4	0-6	4	16
Clint Normore	15	1-1	0-0	0-1	2	3
Scooter Barry	18	3-5	1-1	0-1	3	7
Lincoln Minor	10	1-3	0-0	1-1	1	2
Otis Livingston	2	0-0	0-0	0-0	0	0
Mike Masucci	3	0-0	0-0	0-2	1	0
Keith Harris	17	1-2	0-0	1-4	2	2
Totals		36-65	12-14	10-39	26	87

Three-point goals: 3-5 (Newton 2-3, Normore 1-1, Barry 0-1). **Assists:** 14 (Normore 5, Barry 4, Harris, Newton, Piper, Pritchard, Minor). **Turnovers:** 24 (Newton 5, Manning 5, Harris 4, Pritchard 3, Piper 2, Minor 2, Masucci, Normore, Barry). **Blocked shots:** 4 (Manning 4). **Steals:** 9 (Harris 3, Pritchard 2, Newton, Piper, Manning, Minor).

Oklahoma (95)

	MIN	FG m-a	FT m-a	REB o-t	PF	TP
Harvey Grant	38	7-13	3-7	1-3	2	17
Dave Sieger	38	3-9	4-4	2-8	4	12
Stacey King	33	9-19	4-7	7-10	4	22
Mookie Blaylock	40	6-15	4-8	2-3	0	19
Ricky Grace	29	5-12	2-2	1-1	5	16
Tyrone Jones	3	0-2	0-0	0-0	0	0
Terrence Mullins	11	0-2	2-2	0-2	1	2
Tony Martin	8	2-2	3-3	5-6	0	7
Totals		32-74	22-33	18-33	16	95

Three-point goals: 9-26 (Grace 4-10, Blaylock 3-7, Sieger 2-6, Jones 0-2, Mullins 0-1). **Assists:** 18 (Blaylock 6, Grace 5, Sieger 3, King 2, Grant, Mullins). **Turnovers:** 13 (Blaylock 4, King 3, Martin 2, Sieger 2, Grace 2). **Blocked shots:** 3 (Grant, Sieger, King). **Steals:** 14 (Grant 5, Blaylock 4, Sieger 2, Grace 2, King).

Kansas		32 55	— 87
Oklahoma		35 60	— 95

Officials: Ron Zetcher, Jim Harvey, Rich Eichhorst. **Attendance:** 9,785.

on to a 95-87 victory. It was only the second time in 13 games in Noble Arena that the Sooners had been held under 100 points.

The free-throw count — Oklahoma hit 22 of 33 to KU's 12 of 14 — wasn't the only statistic worth noting. A Manning 12-footer that hit the front of the rim and rolled in with 4:42 remaining put him atop the Big Eight record books. Before a Sooner crowd, Manning had broken Oklahoma standout Wayman Tisdale's career-scoring record of 2,661 points. In all, the KU senior scored 30 points — he had needed 27 to surpass Tisdale — but he showed little if any elation in the locker room. "It's no consolation to lose the game," said Manning, who would go on to score 2,951 career points. "A victory is more important. It just doesn't mean much now."

Brown, though, praised nearly everyone — his own team and the opponents. He termed the Sooners "just great. I don't know what you can do to beat Oklahoma. Heck, I was proud of our kids. This team is as good a one as I've ever coached against."

Actually, Brown didn't praise everyone. He wasn't including the referees in his litany. He accused them of blindness toward the conference's new career-scoring leader. "The poor kid can't get to the line," Brown said of Manning. "He shoots 24 times (hitting 13) with people all around him and he can't get to the line." Noting that Manning attempted only four free throws, Brown added, "Something is wrong. He gets inside, you'd expect some foul shots. He's not invisible. As great as he is, he's not invisible."

King begged to differ. "I don't want to be a crybaby," said the

"I don't know what you can do to beat Oklahoma. Heck, I was proud of our kids. This team is as good a one as I've ever coached against."

— LARRY BROWN

With 13 straight wins at home, Derrick Chievous and the Tigers were flying high in Columbia. Their woes came on the road.

junior center. "He's a great player, but he comes over the back on tips. He does it thoughout the game and no fouls are called until the end. I'm really surprised he fouled out."

Kansas was 17-10 now and on the NCAA bubble, but Brown was optimistic. "I've never seen a team play up to its potential like this one has the last six games," he stressed. "I have to believe there's justice, that we're going to get a break and win one of these."

The next stop on the rugged road was Columbia, Mo. Missouri was on a homecourt roll — 13 straight wins, the longest home streak in the Big Eight — and the Antlers were loving it. The Tigers' infamous jeering section had already caused a stir earlier in the season, and now they were honing their barbs for Kansas.

The Antlers, however, had been thrown off their game a bit lately, and by Missouri's own athletic director at that. As the Antlers saw it, their antics hadn't gone all that far out of bounds — even though they'd riled Iowa State standout Jeff Grayer with uncomplimentary references to his ailing mother, awakened ISU players at their motel late at night and accompanied the Cyclones' bus to the game — but Missouri athletic director Jack Lengyel stepped in nonetheless. He made the Antlers promise to cut out the vocal rough stuff, the late phone calls and the bus escorts.

So they were forced to devise other schemes. For Kansas, they unveiled an Antler wearing a Larry Brown mask and carrying a cardboard replica of a U-Haul trailer. They chanted and hurled insults at the Jayhawks. Then, not far into the first half, KU quieted them down.

Kansas and Missouri had gone into the game with identical 6-5 league records. The Tigers, defending con-

MU's infamous Antlers had a lot to say, and so did coach Norm Stewart.

ference champions and the preseason favorite, had struggled on the road, never more so than in an 87-78 loss to Colorado in Boulder a few days earlier. "I'm shocked Missouri would have five losses in the conference," Brown said. "I think they have the potential to be a Final Four team. Just because Colorado beat them I'm not going to change my mind."

The record crowd of 13,160 at Columbia's Hearnes Center did in fact get a preview of a Final Four team and the dominating style it was beginning to display. With 16:49 showing in the first half, Kansas held an 8-6 lead. Exactly eight minutes later, the Jayhawks were up by 28-6. KU had outscored the Tigers 20-0.

"That's the best we've played," Brown said. "We played great defense. We had them way out on the floor." The Jayhawks had followed virtually the same script at home against Duke — leading 23-8 but then losing. Would they surrender a big lead again? Missouri began its comeback in the last 3½ minutes of the first half, after Manning went to the bench with his second foul. KU's 22-point bulge shrank to 38-29 at halftime.

Manning returned to start the second half, but Missouri maintained the momentum. With 12:19 left, Lee Coward's basket brought the Tigers within two at 52-50. Those 20 straight first-half points were almost gone. Not quite, though: Missouri never crept any closer than two. At the end, Scooter Barry was a hero, and nearly a goat. The junior guard made four free throws in the last minute and a half, including two at :22 that put the icing on the victory cake, but that was after he nearly needed a jaw X-ray. The clock showed :32 and Kansas ahead 80-74 when Barry broke away for what looked like an easy layup against Missouri's press. Instead of laying the ball in, Barry tried for a stuff, and, to his horror — and Brown's — he blew it. "I was going to knock him out," Brown exaggerated later. "He was as mad as I was," Barry said, "but coach stayed positive with me and that really helped me. I shrunk. I was about an inch tall after I missed it." Brown stuck with Barry because of his foul shooting. By the Missouri game, Barry had made 33 of 38 free throws, nine in a row and 10 of his last 11.

So the Jayhawks had nearly wasted a 20-point first-half binge but had won, 82-77, hiking their record to 18-10. It would be harder for the NCAA to ignore them now, and the players knew it. "A lot of people have written us off this year," Manning said. "We feel different." He had played one of his best games: 37

Mike Yoder

points — 15 of 21 from the field; seven of eight at the line — eight rebounds and three blocked shots. "That's an average game for him," Piper said matter-of-factly. "Manning's performances are always incredible. That's something we expect."

Helping out were Newton with 16 points and Pritchard with 10. Gueldner, back after missing the OU

Danny Manning wasn't able to get a hand on all of Gary Leonard's shots. Leonard powered for 17 points, but Manning scored 20 more as KU ended the Tigers' home streak.

The Antlers' angle: Brown, you see, had moved around a lot....

Chris Piper put in 38 minutes of defense against the likes of Doug Smith. KU's man-to-man pressure held the Tigers to 43.5 percent shooting for the game. Kansas shot 55.7 percent and outscored Missouri 82-77.

Mike Yoder

FEB. 27 AT COLUMBIA, MO.

Kansas (82)

	MIN	FG m-a	FT m-a	REB o-t	PF	TP
Milt Newton	29	6-10	2-4	0-3	4	16
Chris Piper	38	1-3	3-4	1-3	4	5
Danny Manning	36	15-21	7-8	1-8	3	37
Kevin Pritchard	36	4-8	1-1	0-4	4	10
Jeff Gueldner	32	0-2	0-0	3-5	3	0
Clint Normore	4	0-1	0-0	0-0	1	0
Scooter Barry	7	1-2	4-4	1-2	0	6
Mike Masucci	5	0-1	0-0	0-0	2	0
Keith Harris	13	2-4	4-4	1-2	3	8
Totals		29-52	21-25	7-27	24	82

Three-point goals: 3-8 (Newton 2-5, Pritchard 1-1, Gueldner 0-1, Manning 0-1). **Assists:** 12 (Gueldner 5, Piper 2, Pritchard 2, Newton, Manning, Normore). **Turnovers:** 13 (Piper 3, Pritchard 3, Gueldner 2, Harris 2, Newton, Masucci, Manning). **Blocked shots:** 3 (Manning 3). **Steals:** 9 (Pritchard 3, Manning 2, Newton, Piper, Normore, Masucci).

Missouri (77)

	MIN	FG m-a	FT m-a	REB o-t	PF	TP
Derrick Chievous	23	4-10	11-13	6-11	3	20
Mike Sandbothe	9	1-3	0-0	1-1	2	2
Nathan Buntin	23	3-6	1-2	3-6	1	7
Lee Coward	29	4-8	0-2	0-0	1	11
Byron Irvin	30	1-6	1-2	0-0	2	4
John McIntyre	17	1-4	2-2	1-2	2	4
Lynn Hardy	4	0-0	0-0	0-0	1	0
Greg Church	10	1-2	0-1	0-1	4	2
Doug Smith	31	5-12	0-0	4-9	2	10
Gary Leonard	25	7-11	3-5	3-5	4	17
Totals		27-62	18-27	18-35	22	77

Three-point goals: 5-14 (Coward 3-5, Chievous 1-2, Irvin 1-5, McIntyre 0-2). **Assists:** 16 (Coward 3, McIntyre 3, Smith 3, Chievous 2, Irvin 2, Leonard 2, Buntin). **Turnovers:** 11 (Chievous 2, Church 2, Leonard 2, Sandbothe, Coward, McIntyre, Hardy, Smith). **Blocked shots:** 0. **Steals:** 9 (Coward 3, Irvin 2, Chievous, McIntyre, Hardy, Leonard).

Kansas	38	44	— 82
Missouri	29	48	— 77

Officials: Bill Summers, Ed Hightower, Ron Spitler. **Attendance:** 13,610.

Mike Yoder

game with a sprained ankle, didn't score but contributed five rebounds and five assists and helped hold Missouri to 43.5 percent shooting. Tiger standout Derrick Chievous, who didn't show up for pre-game drills because of an upset stomach, played 23 minutes and scored 20 points, but was just four of 10 from the field.

"I think we're realizing we're becoming a good team," Piper said. With the win, many fans believed KU had concluded the "death march" with a 2-2 record. Brown decreed that there would be a rubber game. "It's not over," he said. "We're still traveling." The road portion of the Jayhawks' Big Eight schedule was about to end with a trip to Boulder, Colo., where good KU teams often had run into bad trouble. Last year in Boulder, for instance, Colorado had won, 66-56. And Kansas would fly west without reserve center Mike Masucci, left behind because, Brown said, he was "struggling in school."

Manning, however, was surging. For three years he'd endured criticism that he wasn't eager enough to step forward, to carry the load that his talents could obviously bear. Now he was carrying the Jayhawks. The All-American had scored 30 or more points in the last three games. He was shooting 59.1 percent from the floor, 87 percent from the free throw line. He was making his case for the Jayhawks, and, incidentally, for national player-of-the-year honors.

By the standards of the three previous games, his 25-point, 11-rebound, three-block performance in Boulder was slightly under par and unremarkable. Yet an incident in the Colorado game was the most unusual of Manning's long college career. He was to play in 147 NCAA games during his four years at Kansas; the March 2 game in Boulder was the only one in which he was kicked out for fighting.

It happened with 3:54 left and Kansas ahead by 14 points. Milt Newton and Colorado's Brian Robinson started flailing in the lane. Official Ed Schumer intervened and pushed Robinson away and under the basket. Suddenly, Manning was all over Robinson, throwing soft punches before the officials broke it up. Nobody had been hurt, but Manning and Newton, the Jayhawks' top two scorers, were thrown out.

"Brian threw a punch and Milt retaliated and Danny retaliated," Brown said. "The official had to do that. The fortunate thing is no one left the benches. Nothing else happened." And fortunately Kansas was able to win with all that point production grounded. In fact the 14-point lead grew to 21 points in a 85-64 victory, the Jayhawks' biggest margin in Boulder in 27 years.

With Newton and Manning out, Pritchard took over, scoring seven of his 16 points after the ejections. "I just love what he's doing," Brown said about the sophomore guard. "He's becoming a great player." Pritchard was low-key. "As the point guard you have to be somewhat of a leader," he said. "We just wanted to take time off the clock."

Intense defense, by now a Jayhawk trademark, showed again in the final statistics. Kansas had led by just 37-34 at halftime, but the Buffs made only 25 percent of their second-half shots. Overall, CU hit only 38.3 percent, becoming the 11th straight opponent to shoot under 50 percent.

The victory, boosting KU to 8-5 in the league and 19-10 overall, clinched the No. 3 seed for the Big Eight

"We don't try to pick fights every game, but we're not going to back down."

— DANNY MANNING

"Brian Robinson had it coming the whole game, and we've always looked out for our own."

— CHRIS PIPER

Tournament. All that was left was for Manning to explain his pugilistic outburst. "Young children are out there watching and I really apologize for it," he said. At the same time, he offered a glimpse of the more asser-

Kansas (85)

	MIN	FG m-a	FT m-a	REB o-t	PF	TP
Milt Newton	28	7-8	2-2	1-5	2	18
Chris Piper	29	3-6	1-2	1-2	1	7
Danny Manning	33	11-20	3-3	2-11	1	25
Kevin Pritchard	36	5-10	6-8	0-3	1	16
Jeff Gueldner	18	1-3	5-6	3-4	2	7
Scooter Barry	19	2-3	2-2	1-2	2	6
Mike Maddox	6	2-3	0-0	2-2	1	4
Clint Normore	9	0-2	0-0	0-2	2	0
Keith Harris	11	0-1	0-0	0-4	1	0
Otis Livingston	7	0-0	2-3	0-0	0	2
Marvin Mattox	2	0-1	0-0	3-4	0	0
Lincoln Minor	2	0-3	0-0	1-2	0	0
Totals		31-60	21-26	14-41	13	85

Three-point goals: 2-5 (Newton 2-3, Pritchard 0-1, Normore 0-1). Assists: 17 (Gueldner 5, Pritchard 3, Barry 3, Newton 2, Piper, Manning, Harris, Livingston). Turnovers: 15 (Newton 4, Piper 4, Manning 4, Pritchard, Barry, Minor). Blocked shots: 5 (Manning 3, Newton, Normore). Steals: 3 (Manning, Pritchard, Barry).

Colorado (64)

	MIN	FG m-a	FT m-a	REB o-t	PF	TP
Brian Robinson	28	5-9	1-2	1-3	4	11
Brent Vaughan	27	1-2	0-0	0-4	2	2
Scott Wilke	30	7-17	3-4	5-9	3	17
Steve Wise	29	5-10	5-5	0-2	2	16
Michael Lee	27	1-7	4-4	1-2	2	6
Torrance Chapmon	9	0-0	0-0	0-1	1	0
Dan Becker	26	3-7	3-6	3-4	4	10
Brian Molis	6	0-2	0-0	0-0	2	0
Rodell Guest	12	0-0	0-0	0-0	0	0
David Kuosman	2	1-3	0-0	1-1	2	2
Jeff Penix	2	0-2	0-0	0-1	0	0
Kerry Nash	2	0-1	0-0	0-0	0	0
Totals		23-60	16-21	11-27	22	64

Three-point goals: 2-10 (Becker 1-1, Wise 1-3, Wilke 0-1, Lee 0-1, Kuosman 0-2, Penix 0-2). Assists: 14 (Lee 6, Robinson, Wilke, Wise, Chapmon, Becker, Molis, Guest, Kuosman). Turnovers: 11 (Lee 3, Wilke 2, Wise 2, Chapmon 2, Vaughan, Becker). Blocked shots: 2 (Lee, Becker). Steals: 6 (Wise 3, Vaughan, Wilke, Penix).

Kansas .... 37 48 — 85
Colorado .... 34 30 — 64
Technical fouls: Normore, Newton (ejected), Manning (ejected), Robinson (ejected). Officials: Ed Schumer, Veryl Sell, John Dabrow. Attendance: 6,886.

Ben Bigler

Manning had the right stuff to finish the season on a high note. Against Colorado, however, he suffered the only ejection of his college career for fighting.

tive player he had become. "I regret it, but I don't regret it," he added. "We don't try to pick fights every game, but we're not going to back down. I just saw people pushing and shoving and I just went over there." Manning's teammates weren't embarrassed by what he'd done. "They (Colorado) deserved it," Piper said. "Brian Robinson had it coming the whole game, and we've always looked out for our own." Echoed Pritchard: "That's part of being a team, protecting each other."

Now only one game remained in the regular season. It meant nothing, and everything. Win or lose, the home finale against Oklahoma State wouldn't improve the Jayhawks' seeding for the conference tourney, but it would be the last game in Allen Fieldhouse for seniors Manning, Piper and Archie Marshall.

"I'd like to see everybody get the opportunity to play," Manning said. "I'd like to sit on the bench the last few minutes of the game and reminisce about all the good times we've had here." He also wished there was some way Marshall, still hobbling as he recovered from knee surgery, could suit up and step on the floor.

Brown shared the feeling. "I'd love that he be introduced as a starter, but his knee is pretty darned bad," the KU coach said. "Danny's sentiment is the way everybody feels, though." That seemed to settle it. Marshall would go out with praise but not playing time. Case closed.

And then, just as they would for the rest of the season, the Jayhawks conspired to find a way to make the impossible happen. Marshall did "play" in his last home game, and few who were there will ever forget it.

The Marshall plan

8

No one is quite sure how many basketball fans have crowded into Allen Fieldhouse at any one time. When the big limestone structure — "The Monarch of the Midlands" it was dubbed — opened in 1956, Kansas coach Phog Allen pegged the seating capacity at 17,000. Every time the fieldhouse was sold out for a game, the announced crowd was 17,000. But after the legendary Allen died in 1974 at the age of 88, officials conceded that the fieldhouse, named for the only man who had ever guided KU to an NCAA championship, held only a few more than 16,000 fans. Later, when the dirt floor was covered and new bleachers installed on the lower level, the capacity was downsized again, to 15,800.

So on the night of March 5, at least 15,800 fans were on hand. That was obvious from the packed rows of seats. But how many more shoehorned in? People stood in the upper reaches, squeezed together on bleachers and pigeon-holed into all four corners. Hundreds more wanted in but were turned away.

"I'd say," remarked Richard Konzem, a KU assistant athletic director, "that this is the hottest game we've had." Why not? It was

Danny Manning's last home game, and fans wanted to be able to tell their grandchildren they were there. "We'll have 600,000 people saying they were here," predicted Larry Brown. Manning wasn't the only one bowing out. It was the final home outing for fellow seniors Chris Piper and Archie Marshall. Just before the game, all three were introduced with their parents.

Lawrence residents could forgive the 23-year-old Piper for squeezing the hands of his mother, Bonnie Stephenson, and father, Gary Piper — Chris' parents were divorced when he was 5 — extra hard. The Lawrence High School graduate was finally winning accolades for bringing his game further along than many had thought possible during the days when he'd heard catcalls from the stands.

Piper moved to Lawrence in 1974, at the end of his third grade year. He took up basketball in the sixth grade. "I was too skinny for football and I didn't like track," Piper recalled after the season. "I think I expected to be cut in the seventh grade — (he was) — but I thought I had a chance as an eighth grader. It was a little embarrassing. Fifteen guys made it and I didn't. In the

"We'll have 600,000 people saying they were here."

— LARRY BROWN

Chris Piper, in his final home game for the Jayhawks, was becoming a clutch performer. The win over Oklahoma State was the Allen Fieldhouse finale for seniors Piper, Danny Manning and Archie Marshall.

Ben Bigler

ninth grade, it was down to me and another guy."

By then Piper stood 6-3. "They'd set up a drill where you'd go around two pylons and make a layup. I'd dribble the ball off my knee and miss the layup. I had a terrible left hand. In fact, I still don't have one," he said. As a high school junior, "Coach (Ted) Juneau didn't know who I was." But Piper blossomed in

his senior year. He averaged 14.4 points for the Lions, who went 20-4 and won their first state title since 1948. He then became a late KU recruit on the recommendation of then-athletic director Monte Johnson, whose son Jeff was a junior on that LHS team. Piper started slowly at KU too. But as a junior, he averaged 6.6 points and 4.7 rebounds, starting all 36 games. For the 1987-88 season, despite injuries, he averaged 5.1 points and 3.8 rebounds. Mainly he became known for his defense. "I don't think defense was ever a big thing with me, but I really don't like to be scored on," he said. "It's pretty personal."

His senior season had been painful. Piper suffered a groin pull over the summer, and a small piece of bone pulled away from the pelvis. "I took quite a bit of stuff like Cortisone once every two weeks," he recalled. "That wasn't a pleasant experience. And I took an anti-inflammatory drug — all this stuff was legal — that made me sick to my stomach so I quit. But after the OU game (in Norman) I started again. It didn't sit well on my stomach, but I kept taking it. I really didn't feel it in the Final Four with so much adrenalin going."

The cheers for Piper before the OSU game were soon to be eclipsed. When Manning walked on the floor with his mother, Darnelle, the KU pep band — dressed in tuxedos and formals — played "Oh, Danny Boy" while fans tossed roses on the court. "I got a couple . . . I gave them to my sister," Manning said with a grin. And everything came up roses for Marshall and his parents, Archie and Laverne.

The game was almost an afterthought. Oklahoma State took a 5-2 lead before the Jayhawks went to work. "I thought we'd come out slow because our emotions were so high," Piper said. Manning agreed. "I think I wanted to do too much too fast," he said. Fortunately, there was plenty of time. Manning went on to score 31 points, snatch 10 rebounds and dish out six assists as the Jayhawks caught fire, posting a 75-57 win.

With victory assured, Brown orchestrated the most memorable moment in an evening few would have forgotten anyway. With 1:33 on the clock and Kansas ahead, 69-53, he called time and inserted Marshall into the game. Stepping onto the court from in front of the Jayhawk bench, the 6-6 senior, out of action since he injured his knee on Dec. 30, took two or three limping steps

forward — he was wearing an awkward leg brace — as the crowd roared. Seconds later, Manning flipped Marshall the ball. Loosely guarded, Marshall launched a 40-foot shot from the left side that connected with the glass backboard, if nothing else. Clint Normore rebounded the miss and was fouled. The clock stopped and, to another deafening roar, Marshall went back to the bench. He had played the final seven seconds of his college career.

Richard Gwin

Marshall walked onto the court twice on March 5: Once with his mother, Laverne, before the game, and once on his own at the end, when the limping senior unleashed a three-point try.

MARCH 5 AT LAWRENCE

Oklahoma State (57)

	MIN	FG m-a	FT m-a	REB o-t	PF	TP
Richard Dumas	32	9-15	3-5	2-9	5	21
William Woods	28	0-3	2-2	1-3	4	2
Sylvester Kincheon . .	31	3-6	4-4	1-3	1	10
John Starks	40	6-15	3-5	2-4	3	16
Derrick Davis	32	1-1	0-0	0-1	1	2
Royce Jeffries	18	1-6	2-2	2-7	3	4
Robert Smith	8	1-2	0-0	1-1	2	2
Chuck Davis	8	0-1	0-0	0-0	0	0
Chris Gafney	2	0-1	0-0	0-0	0	0
Bryan Fowler	1	0-0	0-0	0-0	0	0
Totals		21-50	14-18	9-28	19	57

Three-point goals: 1-7 (Starks 1-5, Woods 0-1, Gafney 0-1). Assists: 11 (Starks 4, D. Davis 4, Kincheon, Smith, Gafney). Turnovers: 20 (Dumas 8, D. Davis 4, Starks 3, Woods 2, Jeffries, Smith, Fowler). Blocked shots: 1 (Gafney). Steals: 6 (Dumas 2, Starks 2, Woods, Kincheon).

Kansas (75)

	MIN	FG m-a	FT m-a	REB o-t	PF	TP
Milt Newton	30	6-11	1-3	1-4	2	13
Chris Piper	27	5-7	0-2	1-6	2	10
Danny Manning	37	14-20	3-4	4-10	3	31
Kevin Pritchard	24	0-3	2-2	0-5	5	2
Jeff Gueldner	27	4-8	2-2	3-4	1	10
Scooter Barry	19	1-2	0-0	0-0	1	2
Keith Harris	16	2-3	1-2	2-4	1	5
Mike Masucci	8	0-3	0-0	0-1	2	0
Clint Normore	8	0-0	2-2	1-1	0	2
Otis Livingston	2	0-0	0-0	0-0	0	0
Archie Marshall	0	0-1	0-0	0-0	0	0
Mike Maddox	1	0-1	0-0	0-0	0	0
Marvin Mattox	1	0-2	0-0	1-2	0	0
Totals		32-61	11-17	13-37	17	75

Three-point goals: 0-4 (Newton 0-1, Gueldner 0-1, Marshall 0-1, Maddox 0-1). Assists: 23 (Manning 6, Gueldner 5, Newton 2, Piper 2, Pritchard 2, Harris 2, Masucci 2, Barry, Normore). Turnovers: 15 (Manning 4, Newton 2, Pritchard 2, Barry 2, Normore 2, Piper, Masucci, Livingston). Blocked shots: 2 (Piper, Manning). Steals: 10 (Manning 4, Newton 2, Gueldner 2, Piper, Barry).

Oklahoma State	20	37	— 57
Kansas	30	45	— 75

Officials: Stan Reynolds, Meryl Wilson, Rick Wulkow. Attendance: 15,800.

In Manning's final fieldhouse performance, it was all roses for Darnelle Manning and her son.

Richard Gwin

Kevin Pritchard and the Jayhawks put the defensive clamps on the Cowboys, who scored only 57 points.

"I wanted to be a part of it," a smiling Marshall said afterward. "The way the fans reacted, it's something I'll remember the rest of my life." Piper, who hit five of seven shots and matched his season high with 10 points, called Marshall's appearance the highlight of the season. "That's what we all wanted," he said — even if the Marshall Plan didn't go exactly as planned. "We were going to throw him the ball, then call time out," Brown said. "But he was wide open, so we figured why not shoot it?" The coach later revealed that he had "stayed up all night trying to figure out a way to get him in the game."

Leonard Hamilton, the Cowboys' second-year coach, was all too aware that his players were in the wrong place at the wrong time that night. But Hamilton also knew that KU's performance was sparked by more than the electric atmosphere. "Obviously, Manning's a great player," the former Kentucky assistant said. "He has a lot of class and represented Kansas well. I know how Kansas will miss him, but I can't say I will."

The loss gave Hamilton's Cowboys a 4-10 record, tying Nebraska for sixth place in the Big Eight race. Just as Ricky Grace had predicted, the other team from Oklahoma, the Sooners, wound up on top in the conference, with a 12-2 record. OU was followed by Kansas State, 11-3; Kansas, 9-5; Missouri 7-7; Iowa State 6-8; OSU and Nebraska at 4-10; and Colorado, 3-11. With the regular season at a close, Hamilton would have one more date with Manning and Company, this time in the first round of the conference tournament in Kansas City's Kemper Arena.

First there was time for the Jayhawks to reflect on their

recovery. Despite injuries and the schedule, they had clawed back from a 12-8 record on Feb. 3 to a 20-10 mark on March 5. "We've gone through some tough times. Nobody thought we'd finish in the top four in the conference," Manning said. "When we were down and out and people said we might not make the (NCAA) Tournament, Pipe and I talked for maybe five minutes. We said we had to do whatever it takes to make it."

"This," Piper added, "is probably the closest team we've had in the past four years. We realize we have to be close. Except for Danny, we don't have great talent. We finally realized we had to be one unit, to play defense as well as possible and get the ball to Danny." Manning returned the compliment. "Pipe is the heart and soul of this team," he said.

Brown realized how far his team had come from its disjointed play in Hawaii, from Marshall's injury, from Marvin Branch's departure, from the four-game losing streak. "I'm thrilled the way the kids are playing," he said. "We're playing as well as we can expect right now." It was in that frame of mind that the Jayhawks made their first short journey over to Kemper Arena for post-season play.

Brown, however, also announced that Otis Livingston had been suspended. At first the move was temporary; it would soon become permanent. The junior college transfer had seen little action in recent weeks, and there had been another confrontation. "There was a lot of things about my personality . . . I get down on myself when things aren't going so well, and he doesn't like that," Livingston said after the season. "I think that's what it was. I think something happened in prac-

"This is probably the closest team we've had in the past four years. We realize we have to be close."

— CHRIS PIPER

MARCH 11 AT KANSAS CITY, MO.

Oklahoma State (58)

	MIN	FG m-a	FT m-a	REB o-t	PF	TP
Richard Dumas	38	8-18	5-7	4-8	4	21
William Woods	29	2-6	2-4	1-3	2	6
S. Kincheon	11	0-7	0-0	5-7	0	0
Derrick Davis	13	0-1	0-0	1-2	0	0
John Starks	38	3-10	2-2	1-5	5	9
Robert Smith	25	1-4	6-7	3-7	5	8
Todd Christian	27	3-10	2-2	0-1	5	8
Royce Jeffries	15	1-3	2-4	1-1	5	4
Chuck Davis	1	1-1	0-0	0-1	0	2
Chris Gafney	2	0-0	0-0	0-0	0	0
Bryan Fowler	1	0-0	0-0	0-0	0	0
Totals		19-60	19-26	16-35	26	58

Three-point goals: 1-8 (Starks 1-4, Christian 0-3, Woods 0-1). Assists: 6 (Woods 2, Starks 2, Christian, Dumas). Turnovers: 21 (Dumas 5, Woods 5, Christian 4, Starks 3, D. Davis 2, Jeffries, C. Davis). Blocked shots: 0. Steals: 8 (Christian 4, Dumas 3, Starks).

Kansas (74)

	MIN	FG m-a	FT m-a	REB o-t	PF	TP
Milt Newton	35	11-17	5-6	2-9	3	29
Chris Piper	32	1-2	2-2	0-3	2	4
Danny Manning	31	5-10	2-6	3-11	4	12
Kevin Pritchard	15	2-4	0-0	0-1	1	5
Jeff Gueldner	22	2-7	1-1	1-1	1	6
Mike Masucci	4	1-1	2-6	0-1	1	4
Keith Harris	16	2-3	0-0	1-4	4	4
Scooter Barry	17	1-2	1-3	1-1	4	3
Lincoln Minor	10	2-3	0-0	0-0	4	4
Clint Normore	15	1-3	1-1	0-0	1	3
Mike Maddox	2	0-0	0-1	0-1	0	0
Marvin Mattox	1	0-0	0-0	0-0	0	0
Totals		28-52	14-26	8-32	21	74

Three-point goals: 4-13 (Newton 2-4, Gueldner 1-3, Normore 0-2, Pritchard 1-2, Manning 0-1, Barry 0-1). Assists: 18 (Manning 4, Newton 3, Pritchard 3, Barry 3, Piper, Gueldner, Harris, Minor, Normore). Turnovers: 18 (Newton 5, Manning 5, Harris 3, Barry, Minor, Normore, Gueldner, Masucci). Blocked shots: 4 (Manning 2, Piper, Pritchard). Steals: 14 (Piper 3, Manning 3, Harris 2, Maddox, Normore, Minor, Barry, Gueldner, Pritchard).

Oklahoma State	25	33 — 58
Kansas	27	47 — 74

Officials: Ron Spitler, Ed Schumer, Charles Greene. Attendance: 16,478.

Ben Bigler

In the Big Eight Tournament, Milt Newton was hardly all-thumbs against Oklahoma State, scoring a career-high 29 points on 11-of-17 shooting.

tice." The junior guard said he would transfer, although he wasn't sure where. Livingston played in 27 of the 30 KU games, starting eight. He averaged six points a game and was second on the team in assists.

KU followed its 75-57 win over OSU in Allen Fieldhouse with a very similar 74-58 victory over the Cowboys in Kemper. The sum was the same, but not the parts. Two unusual things happened. Milt Newton was the good news. The 6-4 junior scored a career-high 29 points, making 11 of 17 shots — in-cluding a couple of three-pointers — and five of six free throws. He also had nine rebounds. But point guard Kevin Pritchard pulled up lame, spraining his right knee with 5:44 left in the first half. "I came down wrong," the sophomore said about the first serious injury of his KU career. "It happened so fast." Trainer Mark Cairns was optimistic about Pritchard's chances of playing in the NCAA Tournament, which would start the next week, but Cairns declared the team's third-leading scorer out for the rest of the conference tourney.

Still, Newton had come through when the Jayhawks needed him most. Hamilton had devised a box-and-one zone defense. The box was on Manning, the one was on everybody else. Manning settled for

Pritchard's rebounding and leadership would survive for only 15 minutes against the Cowboys in Kemper Arena. He sprained his right knee, the first serious injury of his KU career.

12 points, tying his season low. He'd also had a dozen points in the home opener against Pomona-Pitzer, but that was in just 19 minutes. Against the Cowboys in Kemper, Manning played 31 minutes. Eleven Jayhawks scored at least three points apiece. Newton reacted mildly to his best game of the season. "The career high doesn't mean anything to me," he said. "I just try

to play consistently."

Brown wasn't quite sure what to think. "I've never been through anything like this." he said. "I feel real fortunate we won, considering they did such a great job on Danny. He gets 12 and we lose Kevin early in the game. But this team has been able to bounce back from problems all year."

Springing back in a rubber match against Kansas State wouldn't be easy. KSU had defeated Nebraska in its first-round game and now the intrastate rivals faced each other in the tournament semifinals. So far the two teams had engineered an odd split: Kansas had won in Manhattan and K-State in Lawrence. Now they would settle the series — or so it seemed — on a neutral court. With Pritchard missing his first college game ever, Manning was the only Jayhawk starting against the Wildcats who had also started the season opener in Hawaii. Scooter Barry, opening a game for the first time since Dec. 12, replaced Pritchard.

It wasn't even close. The Wildcats bolted to a 10-0 lead after 4½ minutes, led 17-4 with 13:49 remaining and went on to hand the Jayhawks a 69-54 defeat—their second worst of the season. Only the 100-81 November loss to Iowa in Hawaii had been by a wider margin. KU's 54 points were a season low.

"We remembered the loss in Manhattan and we felt really bad about it," the Wildcats' Mitch Richmond said. "I felt really really bad because I didn't have a good game, and I wanted to get that taste out of my mouth." Richmond, held to 11 points during the Jayhawks' 64-63 victory in Manhattan, netted 21 this time. He was eight of 11 from the floor. "We didn't have the answer for Richmond until Danny started

Ben Bigler

Kansas State's Lon Kruger had the right plan for the Jayhawks.

". . . this team has been able to bounce back from problems all year."

— LARRY BROWN

Mike Yoder

With Pritchard out with an injured knee, Kansas State's William Scott and Mitch Richmond were able to bottle up Newton, who scored 29 points in the Big Eight tourney's first round but only seven against the Wildcats. The 69-54 loss sent KU limping into the NCAA Tournament.

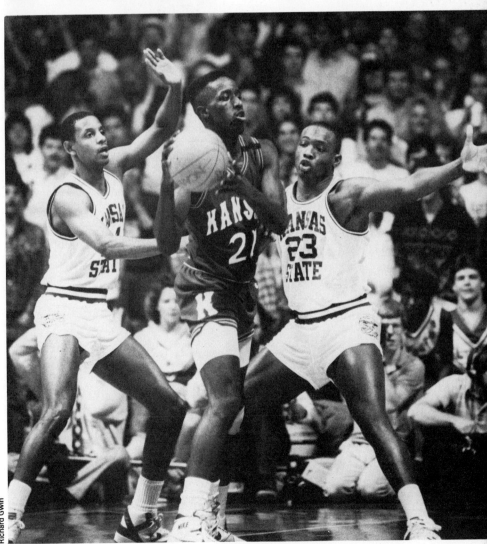

Richard Gwin

guarding him with eight minutes left," Brown said. By then it was too late. Steve Henson added 18 points and Will Scott 17 for K-State.

With the Wildcats running wild, Brown hopped on the officiating. He drew a technical foul after protesting a charging call against Manning early in the first half, his first technical since the St. John's game on Dec. 30. When the game ended he even ran off the floor sounding off to one of the referees, J.C. Leimbach, all the way up the tun-

84

The boards don't always tell the story: KU enjoyed a 28-22 rebounding edge against KSU. Keith Harris was able to take this one away from Newton and Richmond.

Mike Yoder

nel. Still, Brown stressed that the officiating was "not an excuse" for the lopsided defeat. KU lost because it shot 41.5 percent; the 'Cats 56.1 percent. K-State, in fact, was the first team to shoot over 50 percent against the Jayhawks in 14 games.

Manning took 16 shots and missed as many as he made, finishing with 18 points and 10 rebounds. Yesterday's hero, Newton, was just two of seven. The only bright spot was freshman Mike Maddox, who contributed 12 points and five rebounds, both career highs. Almost as an afterthought, Manning became the all-time leading scorer in

MARCH 12 AT KANSAS CITY, MO.

Kansas (54)

	MIN	FG m-a	FT m-a	REB o-t	PF	TP
Milt Newton	25	2-7	2-3	0-2	4	7
Chris Piper	19	2-3	0-0	1-1	0	4
Danny Manning	37	8-16	2-2	6-10	3	18
Scooter Barry	28	0-2	2-2	0-2	3	2
Jeff Gueldner	21	0-4	0-0	1-1	2	0
Clint Normore	16	1-4	0-0	1-2	1	2
Lincoln Minor	16	3-6	0-0	1-2	2	6
Keith Harris	23	1-5	1-1	1-3	0	3
Mike Maddox	14	5-6	0-0	3-5	0	12
Mike Masucci	1	0-0	0-0	0	0	0
Totals		22-53	7-8	14-28	15	54

Three-point goals: 3-13 (Maddox 2-2, Harris 0-1, Newton 1-4, Gueldner 0-4, Normore 0-2). **Assists:** 12 (Harris 3, Normore 3, Barry 2, Piper, Manning, Minor, Gueldner). **Turnovers:** 11 (Newton 2, Manning 2, Minor 2, Harris 2, Piper, Barry, Normore). **Blocked shots:** 2 (Normore, Harris). **Steals:** 4 (Manning 2, Barry, Harris).

Kansas State (69)

	MIN	FG m-a	FT m-a	REB o-t	PF	TP
Mitch Richmond	38	8-11	2-2	0-2	1	21
Charles Bledsoe	30	2-5	1-2	0-5	2	5
Ron Meyer	31	3-4	0-1	3-6	4	6
Steve Henson	39	4-7	9-9	0-1	2	18
Will Scott	30	5-11	4-4	0-4	2	17
Carlos Diggins	2	1-1	0-0	0-0	1	2
Fred McCoy	8	0-0	0-0	0-2	2	0
Buster Glover	10	0-1	0-0	0-0	0	0
Mark Dobbins	10	0-1	0-0	2-2	2	0
Mark Nelson	1	0-0	0-0	0-0	0	0
Todd Stanfield	1	0-0	0-0	0-0	0	0
Totals		23-41	16-18	5-22	16	69

Three-point goals: 7-13 (Scott 3-5, Richmond 3-5, Henson 1-3). **Assists:** 10 (Henson 4, Richmond 2, Scott 2, Meyer, Glover). **Turnovers:** 10 (Henson 4, McCoy 2, Richmond, Bledsoe, Meyer, Dobbins). **Blocked shots:** 1 (Richmond). **Steals:** 9 (Scott 3, Meyer 2, Richmond, Bledsoe, Henson, Dobbins).

Kansas	23	31 — 54
Kansas State	34	35 — 69

Technical foul: Kansas bench. **Officials:** Rick Wulkow, J.C. Leimbach, Bill Westbrooks. **Attendance:** 16,904.

Big Eight Tournament history, with 203 points. But he didn't make the all-tournament team. No Jayhawk did.

It was March 12. The Jayhawks, with 21 wins and 11 losses, waited for the NCAA to announce its 64-team tournament field the next day. It wasn't a matter of whether KU would make the field. Instead, players, coaches and fans wanted to know how high their team would be seeded, and where it would play. There was also the matter of how far the team would go in the tournament. With KU's lowly ranking in the polls, double-digit losses and the disappointing conference tournament, few would have bet the Jayhawks had just suffered their only defeat in March or April.

Meanwhile, there was a basketball game to be played. The Big Eight tourney's championship turned out to be more than a footnote. A crowd of 16,243 watched as Oklahoma outlasted Kansas State, 88-83. OU's Stacey King erupted for 34 points, leading the Sooners to their 30th win against three losses. "It's an outstanding thing to win the championship in the tournament and the conference," said coach Billy Tubbs. "A 20-win season is a heck of a season, but a 30-win season is special."

King, named the tourney's most valuable player, scored 10 points down the stretch, squelching a KSU rally. The Wildcats, led by the balance of Henson (20 points), Richmond (19) and Scott (17), rallied from a 13-point deficit to cut OU's lead to 72-66 before falling short. "We hung in there and kept fighting until the end," said Scott. "We've been fighting all year. We'll be back, no doubt about it."

So would Oklahoma. So would Kansas.

Staying alive

9

Xavier University coach Pete Gillen couldn't believe it. His Musketeers were 26-3 — 22-1 since Christmas — and had won 15 straight. They ranked 18th in the latest AP weekly poll. Yet they were seeded only No. 11 in the NCAA Midwest Regional.

"A lot of it is politics. These analysts . . . they're from the Big East, the Big Eight, the Big Ten, all the hierarchy," Gillen complained. "We hoped we'd be a little more highly seeded. But we're not analysts." Actually, the nine-person NCAA selection committee contained not a single member from the Big Eight or the Big East, and only one from the Big Ten. Gillen was simply frustrated that his team was seeded 11th while Kansas, with nearly four times as many losses and unranked in the AP poll, had the No. 6 seed. That, however, could be traced less to "politics" than to the committee's concern with schedule quality. Xavier hadn't played a Top Twenty team all season.

Nevertheless, backers of the Jesuit school in Cincinnati went into the NCAA Tournament decidedly unhappy. Nor were the Muskies overjoyed about their assignment to Lincoln, Neb. Xavier players made

snide remarks about Nebraska's capital, and some showed up in the Lincoln papers. In addition, Cincinnati sportswriters called Lincoln a "forlorn" place and "a Siberia with 7-Elevens."

While the Musketeers and the sportswriters groused, Kansas coach Larry Brown had one major concern — the health of sophomore point guard Kevin Pritchard. For that reason alone, Brown couldn't have been happier about the regional. True, Lincoln was only about a 200-mile road trip from Lawrence, but there was a bigger bonus. This regional was scheduled as a Friday-Sunday tournament, not a Thursday-Saturday affair. "I'm happy we got an extra day of rest for Kevin's sake," Brown said. And he realized his whole team was tired. After more than a month of hard work that had rescued the season and salvaged an NCAA berth, the Jayhawks had faltered without their point guard in the semifinals of the Big Eight Tournament. Pritchard didn't practice on Monday. Instead, he soaked his sprained right knee in a whirlpool for about three hours. "I'm going to play," he vowed, "even if they put me in a cast."

Increasingly, the Jayhawks' ability

Richard Gwin

Larry Brown knew that the Jayhawks' chances hinged on how quickly point guard Kevin Pritchard recovered.

"That's all they've got is Manning. I'm guarding him. No problem."

— DEREK STRONG

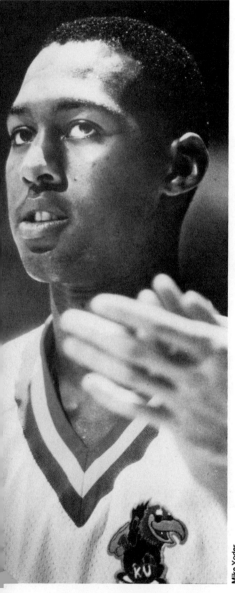

Xavier and five other NCAA Tournament teams would have an impossible time with the soft-spoken but increasingly assertive Danny Manning.

to move the ball effectively hinged on Pritchard's knee. On Thursday, Brown announced that reserve point guard Otis Livingston, temporarily suspended the previous week, had been dropped. Now, of the four junior college transfers Brown had counted on before the season began, only one, Lincoln Minor, was still available. Joe Young hadn't enrolled; Marvin Branch hadn't made his grades; and now Livingston was out. Even Minor wasn't getting much playing time.

On Tuesday, trainer Mark Cairns had fitted Pritchard for a knee brace. Again the 6-3 guard didn't practice, undergoing three hours of treatment instead. "I can bend it 90 degrees," Pritchard said, optimistically.

In the meantime, more gaffes came out of Cincinnati. Xavier center Derek Strong was quoted as saying: "That's all they've got is Manning. I'm guarding him. No problem." His coach, Gillen, rushed in to point out that Strong "has no idea what he's up against. Manning's No. 1 in the country. He's a lock as the first pick in the NBA draft." On that very day Danny was named Big Eight player-of-the-year for the third straight time by the Associated Press, and an AP All-American for the second year in a row.

Finally, on Wednesday, Pritchard practiced, wearing the knee brace. Brown didn't like what he saw. The next day in Lincoln — one day before the Xavier game — Brown told a press conference: "I don't anticipate Kevin playing at all. If he's healthy, he'll play. If he's not, he won't." Pritchard stressed that he would play, and without a brace. "I won't be 100 percent; hopefully I'll be 85," he said.

Brown also announced that freshman center Mike Masucci, who

had played in 23 games (averaging 2.2 points and 1.6 rebounds), had, like Livingston, been dismissed from the team. Brown said Masucci had failed to show up for a Sunday team meeting and was late to Monday's meeting. "He's missed practices more than once," Brown added.

So on the eve of the NCAA Tournament, the Kansas roster consisted of nine scholarship players — one with a gimpy knee — and two walk-on football players, Marvin Mattox and Clint Normore. Eleven players, eleven losses: it wasn't the strongest way to start the final stretch. But now the team was down to its core. Manning sensed his responsibilities and every other player had learned his own role. Archie Marshall was there on the bench for inspiration. If another dose of adversity wasn't enough to spur the Jayhawks in their NCAA opener, there was the extra incentive of knowing that Xavier had surprised Missouri, 70-69, in the tournament's first round the year before. "Hopefully we'll go into the tournament with a better frame of mind than Missouri did," said Milt Newton. "Last year, in the papers it said Missouri took the attitude of 'Who are these guys?'"

Xavier got no respect in Lincoln, that's for sure. A sellout crowd of 14,425 — made up mostly of hometown folk — booed the Musketeers and cheered the Jayhawks during introductions and afterward. "It was almost like playing at home," Brown said.

True to his word, Pritchard started the game, and he gave the Jayhawks a quick lift. With his knee taped — he decided against the cumbersome brace — he opened Kansas' scoring with a breakaway dunk before 10 seconds had elapsed. Playing 16 minutes the first half, he scored six points and ran the of-

Mike Yoder

In the NCAA Tournament, Milt Newton emerged as a potent scorer for the Jayhawks over defenders like Xavier's Tyrone Hill.

Richard Gwin

Manning (24 points, 12 rebounds, three blocked shots and three assists) passed up few opportunities to put KU's offense in gear against the Musketeers.

Scooter Barry filled in at guard for 21 minutes against Xavier and passed out five assists.

Mike Yoder

fense as KU sprinted to a 48-29 lead. During the blitz, Manning scored 12 points and Newton 10. Chris Piper had seven assists and nine rebounds.

KU's man-to-man pressure bothered the Muskies badly. Standout guard Byron Larkin hit just two of seven shots. The Muskies shot only 32 percent for the half. Kansas hit 50 percent, and the Jayhawks totaled 12 assists at the half to Xavier's four. "Kansas just came out on fire," said Gillen. "They came out . . . boom, shot out of a cannon, and we got knocked on our goolies and we were stunned. They scratched and clawed and outplayed us."

Two minutes into the second half, after Newton had hit three straight shots, the advantage ballooned to 25. Then the game changed abruptly. Xavier, pressing all over the floor, started to force turnovers. The Muskies quickly made up 10 points. Then they made up 17 points. Kansas' lead, once 54-29, shrank to 74-66 with 2:50 left. Finally KU put on the brakes. The Jayhawks made six of nine free throws in the final 1½ minutes while the Muskies, desperate now, missed 10 shots in a row. Kansas had overcome a staggering 30 turnovers — 19 in the second half — to post a 85-72 victory. "I almost had a heart attack in the second half," said Brown.

Manning and Newton, the only Jayhawks in double figures, finished with 24 and 21 points respectively. Each also collected a dozen rebounds, powering KU to an overall 47-27 advantage on the boards. And Pritchard? He logged 33 minutes with eight points, four rebounds, three assists and a steal. He even blocked a shot. "I was proud of him," Brown said. "I don't know how much of an emotional lift it was

MARCH 18 AT LINCOLN, NEB.

Xavier (72)

	MIN	FG m-a	FT m-a	REB o-t	PF	TP
J.D. Barnett........	29	2-6	0-0	1-3	4	5
Tyrone Hill	24	1-5	2-4	2-4	5	4
Tyrone Strong......	27	4-5	6-7	2-10	4	14
Byron Larkin	37	6-18	4-10	0-1	5	16
Stan Kimbrough	37	5-13	6-6	0-2	4	18
Jamal Walker.......	20	3-10	1-2	1-1	5	7
John Kennedy......	1	0-1	0-0	0-0	0	0
Michael Davenport ..	2	0-0	0-0	0-0	2	0
Jerry Butler	1	1-2	0-0	1-1	0	2
Mike Rainey........	0	0-0	0-0	1-1	0	0
Colin Parker	1	0-2	0-0	1-2	0	0
Dexter Campbell	20	2-2	2-3	0-2	3	6
Bob Koester.......	1	0-0	0-0	0-0	0	0
Totals		24-64	21-32	9-27	32	72

Three-point goals: 3-14 (Kimbrough 2-6, Barnett 1-3, Larkin 0-3, Walker 0-2). Assists: 13 (Kimbrough 4, Walker 3, Larkin 3, Barnett 2, Kennedy). Turnovers: 15 (Hill 3, Walker 3, Campbell 2, Kimbrough 2, Barnett 2, Larkin 2, Davenport). Blocked shots: 2 (Campbell 2). Steals: 18 (Kimbrough 4, Barnett 3, Strong 3, Larkin 3, Walker 3, Kennedy, Campbell).

Kansas (85)

	MIN	FG m-a	FT m-a	REB o-t	PF	TP
Chris Piper	29	2-3	5-7	2-9	3	9
Milt Newton........	34	9-14	3-4	4-12	2	21
Danny Manning.....	37	8-14	8-9	3-12	4	24
Kevin Pritchard	33	2-5	4-5	1-4	3	8
Jeff Gueldner	18	3-4	1-2	0-5	2	8
Clint Normore	8	0-3	0-1	0-1	2	0
Scooter Barry	21	1-2	3-4	1-2	3	5
Lincoln Minor	6	0-1	0-0	0-0	0	0
Mike Maddox	5	2-4	0-0	1-2	1	4
Keith Harris	8	2-3	2-2	0-0	3	6
Marvin Mattox......	1	0-0	0-0	0-0	0	0
Totals		29-53	26-34	12-47	23	85

Three-point goals: 1-5 (Gueldner 1-1, Newton 0-2, Normore 0-2). Assists: 22 (Piper 7, Barry 5, Newton 3, Manning 3, Pritchard 3, Gueldner). Turnovers: 30 (Piper 8, Manning 5, Newton 4, Gueldner 4, Pritchard 3, Normore 3, Minor 2, Harris). Blocked shots: 4 (Manning 3, Pritchard). Steals: 3 (Piper, Manning, Pritchard).

Xavier............................. 29 43 — 72
Kansas............................ 48 37 — 85
Officials: Booker Turner, Joe Mingle, John Bonder. Attendance: 14,425.

for the team to have him back, but it was an emotional lift for me, I'll tell you that."

It was for Manning, too. "I think the emotion of having Kevin back was the big thing," he said. "Seeing Kevin on the court made us come out and play hard." For his part, Pritchard shrugged off his injured knee. "It was fine," he said. "I came down on it wrong once and felt a twinge. There were a couple of sharp pains, but I expected that. I was going to play no matter what."

Mike Yoder

With Newton and Manning combining for 45 points against the Musketeers, KU was happy to move on to the tournament's second round.

Xavier coach Gillen, whose team had shot only 37.5 percent, complimented KU profusely. "We were stunned. We were outcoached, no question about it," Gillen said. "Their kids had a little more fire than us, and I'll take the blame for that. Kansas is the best team we played all year. They have an excellent supporting cast that's underrated. They don't get headlines, but they have an excellent cast. We lost to one of the top 10 programs in America."

The season's final AP poll, however, hadn't offered much support for Gillen's assessment. KU received only six votes. Thirty-two teams had more, but Murray State assuredly wasn't one of them. The unranked Racers, from Murray,

Ky., were champions of the Ohio Valley Conference. They went to Lincoln as the No. 14 seed in the regional, and promptly shocked the No. 3 team, North Carolina State, 78-75, in the game before the Kansas-Xavier contest. In beating the Wolfpack, forward Jeff Martin scored 23 points, and guard Don Mann added 16, including two free throws in the final 19 seconds. "We were the underdogs, but our guys

"Kansas is the best team we played all year. They have an excellent supporting cast that's underrated. They don't get headlines, but they have an excellent cast. We lost to one of the top 10 programs in America."

— PETE GILLEN

Richard Gwin

The Kansas Basketball Band made joyful noises in Lincoln and throughout the NCAA Tournament.

"I'm not 100 percent now. I don't know what percent I am."

— KEVIN PRITCHARD

Hard-driving Murray State and guard Don Mann threw a scare into the Jayhawks.

never believed it," said Racers' coach Steve Newton.

And so Murray, a school doomed to play in the shadows of Louisville and Kentucky in its home state, became the first of three straight dragonslayers to stand between KU and the Final Four. "It's a fairy tale year, and we're enjoying it," said coach Newton. According to USA Today, Murray State, 26-8, was rated a 250,000-to-1 shot to win the NCAA title. But Brown was genuinely concerned. In the 6-6 Martin, a 26-plus points-per-game scorer, the Racers had the Ohio Valley Conference's player-of-the-year, and point guard Mann, a 5-8 lefthander, was a threat too. "If I was Murray State, after watching the first half (of the Xavier game), I'd be scared," Brown remarked. "After watching the second half, I'd want to throw the ball up right away."

As usual, the KU coach was more concerned about how his own team would play, and a good part of that centered on Pritchard. Could he go again on a tender knee with less than two days rest? "I'm not 100 percent now," Pritchard said Saturday, a day before the game. "I don't know what percent I am." He still had some doubts, too, about his position. "I still feel I'm a two-guard," he said, referring to the shooting guard spot he'd held in his freshman year and earlier in the season. "I've worked hard the last two months to be a point guard. I'm getting better as far as confidence goes, but I don't know if I'm getting better."

All the skills of his demanding position would be tested against Murray State — and his shooting touch too. If he hadn't made four out of six three-point goals against

Ben Bigler

the Racers, KU's season might well have ended in Lincoln. An eight-point flurry by Pritchard — two three-pointers and two free throws — turned a 34-32 Kansas deficit into a 40-34 lead at 12:16. "I thought the most critical part of the game was when Kevin hit those shots," Brown said. "That opens it up for Danny."

KU, as it had so often, enjoyed a double-digit lead in the first half — this time 12 points (25-13) after an 11-0 run — and then watched the lead dwindle. At the half, Kansas led by five, 28-23. Manning and Newton had scored nine points apiece for the Jayhawks. Martin had eight points and Mann six for the cold-shooting Racers, who made eight of 24 first-half shots for just 33.3 percent.

"Give Kansas credit for a great defensive effort early," said the Racers' Newton. "We shot poorly the first half and had nine turnovers and still were down by five at half. We felt we were still in the hunt."

Down the stretch, the game tightened even more. Martin, who was to score 22 points, hit two free throws at :51 to give Murray a 58-57 lead. Then at :38, Manning's six-footer put KU ahead, 59-58. But Murray State had the ball now, and the 45-second shot clock was off. The Racers were about a basket away from chalking up another big upset. Surely, Martin or Mann would take the shot — and sure enough, with only three seconds left in the game Mann wheeled toward the goal and, bothered by Manning, who came up to assist defender Scooter Barry, tossed an off-balance four-footer while going to his right. It hit the rim and bounced off. Manning rebounded at :01, was fouled and hit two free throws to make the final score 61-58.

"I think I got a pretty good shot,"

Manning played all but five minutes against Murray State, and he stayed in the game even on the sidelines.

Mann said. "I was looking to pitch off, but they had everybody covered. So I shot. I tried to bank it off the glass. I thought I had good balance. It just didn't fall."

Manning led the Jayhawks with 25 points. He was credited with only five rebounds, but that was better than four. "Danny got a big, big rebound," Brown said of the last-second grab of Mann's miss. "I've been on his back about that. He goes and gets the biggest rebound of the year." Pritchard wound up with 16 points, and Keith Harris came off the bench for a team-high eight re-

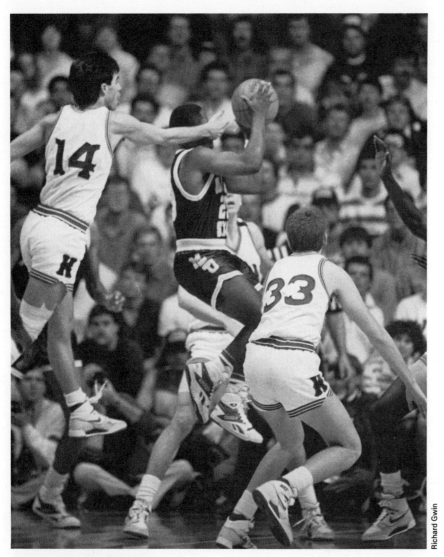

Richard Gwin

Pritchard and the KU defense gave Murray State few uncontested shots. It showed in the Racers's 37.3 percent shooting.

MARCH 20 AT LINCOLN, NEB.

Murray State (58)

	MIN	FG	FT	REB	PF	TP
		m-a	m-a	o-t		
Jeff Martin	40	7-16	7-7	2-7	2	22
Chris Ogden	31	1-4	0-0	2-4	1	2
Carl Sias	26	1-3	0-0	1-4	5	2
Don Mann	39	4-15	6-7	0-4	1	16
Paul King	32	3-7	0-0	0-1	1	9
R. McClatchey	14	1-1	0-2	0-0	1	2
Linzie Foster	9	0-0	0-0	0-3	1	0
Terence Brooks	9	2-5	0-0	0-0	0	5
Totals		19-51	13-16	5-23	12	58

Three-point goals: 7-18 (King 3-6, Mann 2-9, Martin 1-2, Brooks 1-1). **Assists:** 10 (Mann 6, Martin 3, Ogden). **Turnovers:** 13 (Martin 2, Ogden 2, Mann 2, McClatchey 2, Foster 2, Sias, Brooks, King). **Blocked shots:** 1 (McClatchey). **Steals:** 5 (Mann 3, Brooks, Ogden).

Kansas (61)

	MIN	FG	FT	REB	PF	TP
		m-a	m-a	o-t		
Milt Newton	29	5-10	1-2	2-3	3	11
Chris Piper	21	1-3	0-2	1-5	5	2
Danny Manning	35	10-19	5-7	3-5	2	25
Kevin Pritchard	38	4-9	4-4	0-4	2	16
Jeff Gueldner	23	1-4	0-0	1-4	0	3
Scooter Barry	17	0-0	0-0	0-0	2	0
Mike Maddox	12	0-1	0-0	1-3	0	0
Keith Harris	22	2-3	0-0	1-8	1	4
Clint Normore	2	0-0	0-0	0-0	1	0
Lincoln Minor	1	0-0	0-0	0-0	0	0
Totals		23-49	10-15	9-32	16	61

Three-point goals: 5-11 (Pritchard 4-6, Gueldner 1-2, Newton 0-2, Manning 0-1). **Assists:** 17 (Barry 4, Harris 3, Piper 3, Gueldner 2, Newton 2, Pritchard 2, Manning). **Turnovers:** 15 (Manning 3, Piper 3, Harris 3, Newton 2, Gueldner 2, Maddox 2). **Blocked shots:** 3 (Newton, Piper, Manning). **Steals:** 12 (Harris 3, Gueldner 2, Barry 2, Newton, Piper, Manning, Pritchard, Maddox).

Murray State	23	35 — 58
Kansas	28	33 — 61

Officials: Tim Higgins, Hank Armstrong, Terry Tackett. **Attendance:** 14,453.

bounds, along with four points.

"Defense was the key," Brown stressed. "It just wasn't meant to be," said Murray State's Newton. He had a point. Kansas must have set a record by winning twice in Lincoln despite 45 turnovers. But KU's defense had done the job: Xavier shot 37.5 percent and Murray 37.3 percent.

Reflecting on the game later, Brown noted that former Marquette coach Al McGuire says a team has to have one "lucky game" to win the NCAA Tournament. "I never thought we'd lose it, but it was close," Brown said. "I thought we got over the hump the first game.

Xavier was very underrated. The way we jumped on them early set the tone for the rest of the tournament."

Before the Jayhawks left town, Brown was visited by George Shinn, majority owner of the NBA expansion Charlotte Hornets, and club general manager Carl Scheer. Shinn reportedly dangled a lucrative multi-year contract offer. The KU coach said little about it. If Brown was going to leave Kansas, he wasn't going to talk about it before the season was over, and if another job truly tempted him, it would be in the college ranks, in California.

Despite all the adversity, KU had

made the tournament's final 16 for the third year in a row. "That's something I want the kids to reflect on and be proud of," Brown said. "We had some kids this year who didn't hear me. Now our kids who play listen. They win in spite of me. I think they've rallied around that cause."

Manning hit two free throws to make the final score 61-58. But the Racers had given the Jayhawks their closest NCAA Tournament game.

Richard Gwin

"We had some kids this year who didn't hear me. Now our kids who play listen. They win in spite of me. I think they've rallied around that cause."

— LARRY BROWN

Ben Bigler

Pritchard and Manning were happy to tell the world that the Jayhawks were No. 1 in Lincoln. For the third year in a row KU had advanced to the NCAA Tournament's final 16. The next stop was the Pontiac Silverdome.

Sunflower power

10

"You look at Danny. He's not even considering it will end."

— LARRY BROWN

Over in one corner under the massive fabric roof of the Pontiac Silverdome waited the basketball court that would be a testing ground for Kansas, Kansas State, Purdue and Perdue — make that Vanderbilt. Will Perdue was only the Commodores' 7-foot senior center, not the whole team. He was, however, the Southeastern Conference player of the year as well as a man renowned for his shoe size — 21½ AAAAAAA.

Perdue was the leading scorer for one of the few giant-killer teams left in the NCAA Tournament, now down to its Sweet 16. In Lincoln, the seventh-seeded Commodores had upset Pittsburgh, the No. 2 seed, in an overtime game as dramatic as any played so far. With 17 seconds left, Pitt led by six points, but Vanderbilt guard Barry Goheen hit a pair of three-point baskets, one of them at the buzzer, to force overtime. Goheen then added five free throws in the extra period and the Commodores won, 80-74,

Kansas advanced from Lincoln with its shaky 61-58 win over Murray State. Big Ten champion Purdue, the top seed in the Midwest Region, and No. 4 Kansas State won their way to Pontiac, a Detroit suburb, in

the sub-regional at South Bend, Ind. With Kansas and Kansas State both in the regional, a Kansas City-to-Detroit airline reservation became a hot ticket. Still harder to find was anyone outside the Sunflower State who thought KU and K-State would play in the regional's championship game. The Wildcats would have to upset Purdue, and Kansas, with more losses than any team left in the field, would have to neutralize Perdue and Vanderbilt.

"If you'd asked me on Oct. 15, I'd be disappointed if we didn't get this far," Kansas coach Larry Brown said in the week before the game. "After all the things that happened to us, I had no idea this would happen. It's a strange year when you consider all the different peaks and valleys we've had. We'd adjust to one problem, then another would come up. Our kids would adjust, then it's something else. I've seen kids like Danny grow from all this. You look at Danny. He's not even considering it will end. It's been great for him."

A victory over Vandy would make it even greater, and Manning rose to the challenge early in the game. The semifinal was hardly a minute old when he fired up a 20-

Mike Yoder

"I kept saying, 'When's this man going to miss?'"

— FRANK KORNET

Danny Manning drove past Will Perdue and the Vanderbilt defense for 33 points, 25 of them in the first half.

footer for three points. He kept shooting. Scoring on jump shots, soft hooks, breakaways and slams, the 6-10 senior amassed 25 points by halftime, hitting 12 of 17 shots. It was the most Manning had ever scored in a half.

Vanderbilt coach C.M. Newton didn't have an answer. He tried zones and he tried man-to-man, using 6-8 sophomore Frank Kornet and Perdue as cover men. "It seemed like everything he shot was going in," Kornet said. "I kept saying, 'When's this man going to miss?'"

The KU defense chipped in too. With the Commodores missing 10 of their first 12 shots, Kansas led 19-4 after less than nine minutes. "We got some easy hoops because of our defense," said Brown. Hounded by Kevin Pritchard, Goheen scored just one point in the half. Perdue, guarded by Manning, had only eight. By halftime, the Jayhawk lead was 41-29. Vanderbilt's best

With his right knee feeling better, Kevin Pritchard hurt the Commodores with five-for-six shooting that included a layup over Perdue.

Mike Yoder

"We needed Manning to have a so-so night, and he didn't."

— C.M. NEWTON

hope for the second half was that Manning would lose his touch. And he did: A series of shots fell short. Manning recalled later what happened: "The second half, when I cooled off, coach Brown said, 'Danny, why are you taking those long jumpers?' I said, 'Coach, I've got the feeling.' He said, 'Danny get rid of the feeling and get back in the paint.'"

Despite Manning's misses, Vanderbilt couldn't get closer than nine points in the second half, and Kansas cruised to a 77-64 victory. Manning finished with 38 points and

MARCH 25 AT PONTIAC, MICH.

Vanderbilt (64)

	MIN	FG m-a	FT m-a	REB o-t	PF	TP
Frank Kornet	29	2-5	0-0	3-7	2	4
Eric Reid	23	1-5	0-0	3-5	0	2
Will Perdue	36	7-13	2-3	1-8	5	16
Barry Booker	33	8-16	0-0	0-3	1	22
Barry Goheen	31	1-7	1-2	0-0	3	3
Scott Draud	13	1-3	1-2	0-0	4	4
Charles Mayes	9	0-1	0-0	0-0	0	0
Derrick Wilcox	11	3-4	0-0	1-2	2	7
Steve Grant	14	1-2	2-2	0-0	1	4
Fred Benjamin	1	1-1	0-0	0-1	0	2
Totals		25-57	6-9	8-26	18	64

Three-point goals: 8-20 (Booker 6-13, Draud 1-3, Wilcox 1-1, Goheen 0-2, Mayes 0-1). Assists: 17 (Kornet 4, Goheen 4, Booker 3, Draud 2, Mayes 2, Reid, Perdue). Turnovers: 15 (Kornet 5, Wilcox 3, Booker 2, Goheen 2, Perdue, Draud, Grant). Blocked shots: 3 (Perdue 2, Booker). Steals: 6 (Kornet 2, Wilcox 2, Goheen, Draud).

Kansas (77)

	MIN	FG m-a	FT m-a	REB o-t	PF	TP
Chris Piper	33	3-5	2-2	2-10	2	8
Jeff Gueldner.......	22	1-2	0-0	0-2	2	2
Danny Manning.....	29	16-29	4-7	2-5	2	38
Kevin Pritchard	33	5-6	0-2	0-1	3	11
Milt Newton........	23	2-7	0-0	1-7	2	4
Scooter Barry	26	2-4	4-6	0-3	0	8
Mike Maddox.......	7	0-0	4-4	0-0	2	4
Keith Harris	22	0-3	0-0	4-6	0	0
Clint Normore	3	0-0	0-0	0-1	0	0
Lincoln Minor	1	0-0	0-0	0-0	1	0
Marvin Mattox......	1	1-1	0-0	0-0	0	2
Totals		30-57	14-21	9-35	14	77

Three-point goals: 3-5 (Manning 2-3, Pritchard 1-1, Barry 0-1). Assists: 21 (Gueldner 7, Pritchard 5, Barry 3, Piper 2, Manning, Newton, Maddox, Harris). Turnovers: 12 (Manning 5, Piper 2, Pritchard 2, Gueldner, Newton, Maddox). Blocked shots: 3 (Manning, Pritchard, Newton). Steals: 6 (Piper, Gueldner, Manning, Pritchard, Harris, Mattox).

Vanderbilt	29	35 — 64
Kansas	41	36 — 77

Technical foul: Vanderbilt bench. Officials: Jim Burr, Tom O'Neill, Terry Tackett. Attendance: 31,309.

might have surpassed his career-high of 42 if he hadn't missed eight of 12 shots after intermission. Vanderbilt's Newton put his finger on it: "It was a case of a great player rising to the occasion," he said. "We needed Manning to have a so-so night, and he didn't." In addition to Manning's first half outburst — the most impressive half turned in by any player in the tournament — Manning set an NCAA record against Vanderbilt by playing in his 144th game. The previous record-holder, Georgetown's Patrick Ewing, had played in 143. Manning also moved past Larry Bird into eighth place on the NCAA career scoring chart, with 2,875 points.

The win was tonic for the Jayhawks and their fans. "We've gone through a lot of hard times this year," said Manning. "That's why it's so rewarding to make it this far. It's 'Go-For-It time.'" Added Chris Piper: "There were a lot of times I even wondered if we'd make the NCAAs. Now we're one game from the Final Four. It's unbelievable."

Equally incredible was what had happened in the stands. In the vast arena, Sunflower State loyalties and Big Eight pride combined to bank the fires of one of the nation's oldest rivalries. Purple-clad Kansas State backers among the throng of 31,309 found themselves cheering for the Jayhawks against Vanderbilt, and the KU fans stayed to give equally vocal support to the Wildcats when they met Purdue in the second game. Andy Galyardt of Lawrence was an example of the crossovers taking place. A Kansas State alumnus, he wore a Jayhawk pin on his purple-and-white shirt. "I even wore it to the K-State alumni reception here," Galyardt said. "This is great for the Big Eight Conference and for the State of Kansas," he added.

Mike Yoder

Mike Yoder

Vanderbilt's Barry Goheen had upset Pittsburgh with his three-point shooting, but Jayhawk defenders like Chris Piper and Jeff Gueldner held him to three points for the entire game.

Assistant coach Alvin Gentry and Larry Brown eagerly embraced victory over Vanderbilt. The Jayhawks had made the NCAA Tournament's final eight.

In the first game the two old rivals had ever played outside of Lawrence, Manhattan or Kansas City, KU and Kansas State tangled in Pontiac for a spot in the Final Four. Chris Piper, shooting over Will Scott, logged 36 minutes.

Mike Yoder

"One of us is in the Final Four. As far as I'm concerned, there's no way we can lose." KU fan Tom Grey took the same approach. "When they broke our streak, they were so decent," he said, referring to KSU's Allen Fieldhouse victory that snapped the 55-game homecourt winning streak. "They congratulated us and then walked off the court. And besides, they beat the Evil Empire."

The Evil Empire? "Yeah," he said, "Oklahoma."

Kansas State gave its freshly minted fans plenty to cheer about against Purdue — but not right away. The Boilermakers jumped to a 10-0 lead as Everette Stephens hit a pair of three-pointers. KSU coach Lon Kruger was forced to call a timeout just 2:01 into the game. The Wildcats responded by scoring the next five points. "We didn't even wait for coach at the bench," said center Ron Meyer. "We were talking among ourselves about what we had to do to come back."

"I thought we could put them away," said Purdue coach Gene Keady, a Kansas State alumnus. "We wanted to get up 15, but do it gradually, but it wasn't to be and they came back." K-State inched within one twice in the first half, the last time at 24-23 at 9:33 on a driving hoop by Fred McCoy. But Purdue kept its composure and opened a 43-34 halftime lead. Then the Wildcats, led by Mitch Richmond, who finished with a game-high 27 points, put together a 12-1 run.

"We talked at halftime," Kruger said, "primarily about that we didn't do the things we do every day in practice. We went out, regained the pace and gained control of the game." The score was tied at 54 when Kansas State went on another

run — this one 12-3 — to take its largest lead. Richmond later confirmed that he even called "glass" on a bank shot from about 23 feet. "Yeah, I called that," he said with a grin. "Right then I felt that if it was close, we'd win." Purdue answered with a 7-2 streak and crept within 68-64 with 3:32 left. Then, with 1:29 to go, the Boilermakers were within two points. But with effective foul shooting and two Purdue turnovers the Wildcats held on and won, 73-70. Will Scott had scored 17 for KSU, all but two on three-pointers — he was five of five from long range. Afterward, Richmond thanked the KU supporters. "When we came on the court for warmups," he said. "KU's fans and cheerleaders were out there yelling for us. It made me feel good. We're all part of Kansas."

And so an unusual stage was set for the season's fourth meeting of Kansas and Kansas State. In a massive domed stadium in Michigan the two old rivals — Kansas led the series 130-84 — would play for the first time ever outside of Lawrence, Manhattan or Kansas City, Mo. "I don't know what takes precedence, the rivalry or the regional," said KSU's Kruger. "It's a great rivalry. A healthy rivalry." Kansas pride filled the stadium, even if the crowd, listed at 31,632, fell short of the Silverdome's 50,000 "supermax" capacity for basketball. This time, however, KSU's purple-clad followers would cheer only for their Wildcats; wearers of the red and blue would root exclusively for the Jayhawks.

"It's remarkable," Brown said. "When I first saw the bracket I never thought of the possibility of writing in KU and K-State. To be honest, I didn't think there was any way we could get to this point. I thought K-State was good enough, but I didn't think other people realized it."

KU's Pritchard had missed the last meeting, the 69-54 KSU blowout in the Big Eight semifinals two weeks earlier. Only now had his right knee fully recovered. "That was the worst feeling sitting on the bench. I felt I had no control," Pritchard said of the K-State game in Kemper. "But my knee is 100 percent now. I'm only using tape on it as a precautionary measure."

This time, with Pritchard starting, KU avoided falling behind early. Neither team led by more than a basket in the first 12 minutes; the score was 20-20 with 8:09 left. K-State put on the first rally. Richmond hit a three-pointer and Buster Glover a short jumper in the lane, giving the Wildcats a 25-20 lead with 5:34 left. Kansas State led by as many as five, 29-24, following Scott's three-point goal with 47 seconds left before halftime. Then Scooter Barry, who would break Wildcat hearts this day, narrowed that gap to two, 29-27, with a three-pointer — just his second of the season — right before halftime. The Jayhawks went into the locker room on an upbeat note. The Silverdome wasn't going to see a replay of the Kemper disaster.

Kansas State's 3-2 zone defense had been effective, holding the Jayhawks to 13 of 28 first-half shooting, or 46.4 percent. The Wildcats, led by Scott's 13 (three of five three-pointers) hit 55 percent, 11 of 20. Manning was able to free himself for 10 points on five of 10 shooting, but he wasn't dominating the game.

Early in the second half, K-State went up by seven. But Kansas, sparked by six points from Manning, four from Piper, two apiece from Barry and Milt Newton, fought back to cut the lead to a one at 42-41. Then the KU defense began to take control. Keith Harris and Lincoln Minor swiped the ball from Richmond on back-to-back possessions. Harris' dunk after his steal gave KU a 43-42 lead. Brown later singled out the plays: "The turning point in my mind was Lincoln and Keith making those steals."

"When I first saw the bracket I never thought of the possibility of writing in KU and K-State. To be honest, I didn't think there was any way we could get to this point."

— LARRY BROWN

Keith Harris and fellow KU defenders fought Mitch Richmond to a Silverdome standoff, holding the Kansas State star to 11 points on 4-of-14 shooting.

Mike Yoder

Facing KU's intense man-to-man pressure, K-State's shooters went cold, missing 18 of their final 22 shots. In the last 10 minutes KU turned a one-point game into runaway and went on to win, 71-58. There were plenty of Jayhawk heroes. All too aware of his breakout against Vanderbilt, the Wildcats had concentrated on keeping Manning in check. They had done so in the three previous games, holding the KU senior to 18 points twice and 21 once. This time, Manning did about as well as he could against KSU's zone, scoring 20 points. Newton added 18 points and nine rebounds, including a key rebound and stickback of a missed free throw by Piper. Coming with 2:53 left, it gave KU a 59-52 lead. But when it came time to cut down the Silverdome nets — Archie Marshall limped up a ladder to do the first honors — every Jayhawk got a cut except Barry. He was too busy

A determined Milt Newton went up for 18 points (on seven-of-10 shooting) against Scott and the Wildcats. The KU junior also pulled down nine rebounds, four of them on the offensive boards.

Mike Yoder

MARCH 27 AT PONTIAC, MICH.

Kansas (71)

	MIN	FG m-a	FT m-a	REB o-t	PF	TP
Milt Newton........	29	7-10	2-2	4-9	3	18
Chris Piper.........	36	3-6	0-2	2-4	2	6
Danny Manning.....	39	10-18	0-1	2-6	3	20
Kevin Pritchard.....	38	2-7	3-4	0-3	3	8
Jeff Gueldner.......	11	0-3	0-0	0-0	1	0
Scooter Barry	25	5-6	4-4	0-5	1	15
Keith Harris	15	2-3	0-0	0-1	0	4
Lincoln Minor	4	0-1	0-0	0-0	0	0
Mike Maddox.......	1	0-0	0-0	0-0	0	0
Clint Normore	1	0-0	0-0	0-0	0	0
Marvin Mattox......	1	0-0	0-1	0-0	0	0
Totals		29-54	9-14	8-28	13	71

Three-point goals: 4-11 (Newton 2-3, Barry 1-1, Pritchard 1-4, Piper 0-1, Manning 0-1, Gueldner 0-1). **Assists:** 22 (Newton 7, Pritchard 7, Barry 3, Gueldner 2, Piper, Manning, Minor). **Turnovers:** 10 (Barry 3, Newton 2, Pritchard 2, Piper, Gueldner, Minor). **Blocked shots:** 1 (Manning). **Steals:** 6 (Pritchard 2, Harris 2, Newton, Barry).

Kansas State (58)

	MIN	FG m-a	FT m-a	REB o-t	PF	TP
Mitch Richmond	37	4-14	2-4	2-4	3	11
Charles Bledsoe.....	33	5-6	0-4	4-9	4	10
Ron Meyer.........	26	1-3	0-0	1-2	0	2
Steve Henson	40	2-8	0-0	1-3	4	6
Will Scott..........	30	6-15	2-2	0-0	0	18
Fred McCoy........	18	3-5	3-4	3-5	2	9
Buster Glover.......	9	1-3	0-0	0-1	0	2
Carlos Diggins	3	0-0	0-0	0-0	1	0
Mark Dobbins	3	0-0	0-0	0-1	0	0
Todd Stanfield......	1	0-0	0-0	0-1	0	0
Totals		22-54	7-14	11-26	14	58

Three-point goals: 7-22 (Scott 4-10, Henson 2-6, Richmond 1-5, Glover 0-1). **Assists:** 15 (Richmond 5, Henson 5, Meyer 2, Bledsoe, Scott, Glover). **Turnovers:** 12 (Richmond 6, Bledsoe 4, Henson 2). **Blocked shots:** 3 (Bledsoe, Henson, Scott). **Steals:** 4 (Scott 2, Meyer, Henson).

Kansas............................	27	44	— 71
Kansas State.......................	29	29	— 58

Officials: Booker Turner, Dick Paparo, Wilson Tanner. **Attendance:** 31,632.

being interviewed on national television. Rick Barry's son had finally shaken the shadow of his father, the former NBA great and Hall of Famer, by scoring a career-high 15 points.

"I was open today," said Barry, who made five of six shots. "They were so worried about Danny there was nobody within five feet of me." KSU's Kruger called Barry ". . .a big key to the game. He's a great kid, too, and you like to see a great kid who works hard do things like that." Barry was ecstatic. "Who haven't I

hugged?" he bellowed in the jubilant KU locker room. "This is so sweet, it's honey. We've shown so much character the entire tournament. We deserve this." Noting that reporters were comparing him to his father, he added, "There haven't been any comparisons since high school — because I've never scored more than 10 points until today."

On the Wildcat side of the floor, Richmond had missed 10 of 14 shots and settled for 11 points, as he had when KU won in Manhattan. Scott, whose outside shooting boosted the Wildcats into the Silverdome, was only six of 15, and fellow guard Steve Henson two for eight. Kansas State, one of the best three-point shooting teams in the country, had attempted 22 from beyond the line and made only seven. Overall, the Wildcats shot just 41 percent from the field.

Kansas had now played four teams in the NCAA Tournament, and the four had shot a combined 39.8 percent (90 of 226). Offense sells tickets, but defense was winning games for the Jayhawks. Essentially, KU played a straightforward man-to-man, with emphasis on overplaying the man with the ball. "We're not very complicated," Brown explained. "What we've tried to do is be really solid fundamentally, keep our man in front of us, play the ball, block out, push them to the places where we could help without being burned. So much of defense is a willingness to go out and do it for

Mike Yoder

Even with a taped knee, Kevin Pritchard was up for a supporting role in KU's 29-of-54 shooting performance against KSU.

Mike Yoder

Against Charles Bledsoe and the Kansas State zone, Manning was held to 20 points, but the Wildcats' concentration on Manning enabled Scooter Barry to break free for a career-high 15 points.

"I was open today. They were so worried about Danny there was nobody within five feet of me."

— SCOOTER BARRY

40 minutes. The kids have taken a lot of pride and accepted that."

Barry offered a player's view. "Defense is almost a lost art," he said. "Everybody reads about the guys who score the most. Like I've said before, our defense has saved us all year. Teams that haven't played us aren't used to it. Teams that have played us have talked about it being one of our strong points. The trick is sustaining it an entire game."

Kansas sustained it in Pontiac,

KU players regretted that both teams from Kansas couldn't advance to the Final Four, but that didn't dampen the net-cutting festivities as the Jayhawks gloried in winning the NCAA's Midwest Regional. Among those doing the honors were Newton, left, Piper and Manning, below left, and Archie Marshall, below, who made the first cut.

winning twice by 13 points. Now the Jayhawks were goin' to Kansas City.

"You have highs and lows as a coach, but I don't think anybody is experiencing what I am now," Brown said after the net-cutting ceremonies. "We know what Danny can do," he said, "but the other kids played so well. Scooter's been reluctant to shoot and he gets 15. We have so many unlikely kids that I wasn't smart enough to play earlier, and I think that's been the key."

So Kansas, an unlikely choice for a tournament berth a month and a half earlier, qualified for its second Final Four appearance in three years. Despite outstanding tournament performances, Kansas State had failed to make the championship round for the 24th straight year. "K-State is a great team," said Piper. "It's too bad just one of us can go." "I like that team. Now I wish we both could go," added Harris. "K-State had a great year too," said Manning.

In Kansas, where everyday activity had virtually ceased during the hours the game was on radio and television, there was heartbreak and triumph. In the state's 105 counties,

KU alumni cheered, K-Staters groaned. Manhattan was gloomy, Lawrence overjoyed.

On campus, the win over the Wildcats touched off an impromptu horn-honking parade on Jayhawk Boulevard. Two lines of cars jam-packed with celebrating fans inched their way along Mount Oread. As they passed, cars darted toward each other so their occupants could exchange high fives. Then, as word came that the team would arrive home that night, the faithful began pouring into Allen Fieldhouse.

First, though, about 1,500 people gathered at Topeka's Forbes Field to greet the Jayhawks' charter flight. Then more than 7,000 showed up in the fieldhouse for an uproarious welcome-home session at which Brown and his players called KU fans the best in the country. Finally, everybody went home. It had been a happy day but a long one, and for many it was time to dream about the coming weekend's Final Four in Kansas City.

About 500 fans didn't go home,

Mike Yoder

however. They were dreaming of actually being inside Kemper Arena, and so they waited through the night outside the fieldhouse until the next morning, when 230 or so tickets would go on sale to students. For thousands more of the Jayhawk faithful, Kemper Arena, a mere 40 miles down the road from Lawrence, was suddenly so near and yet — when it came to obtaining a ticket — so far.

KU fans were flying high in Pontiac, above, and in Lawrence, where victory over Kansas State and a ticket to the Final Four sparked a horn-honking, high-fiving motorized celebration along Jayhawk Boulevard.

Ben Bigler

Duke's up

11

"It's not easy to say no to somebody who donated $2,000 to the program last year. But we just have no choice."

— BOB FREDERICK

As soon as the Big Eight Conference became the King Midas of college basketball, Bob Frederick wished somebody would give him King Solomon's phone number. For the first time ever, two Big Eight schools — Kansas and Oklahoma — had qualified for the NCAA Final Four. Athletic directors around the league were calculating how they'd spend their shares of the projected $3,691,200 windfall. All except Frederick. He had other things on his mind — including how to dole out the 1,625 Kemper Arena tickets the Jayhawks had been allotted. After the 230 student tickets were gone, and approximately 600 faculty, staff, players and coaches taken care of, Frederick had only about 800 tickets left. He felt he had but one choice — offer them to athletic department donors in descending order of contributions. As it turned out, if you hadn't given nearly $2,500 to the Williams Fund, you didn't make the cut.

"It's just a terrible situation to be in," Frederick lamented. "It's not easy to say no to somebody who donated $2,000 to the program last year. But we just have no choice. We had a nightmare of a ticket problem at the Final Four in Dallas two

years ago, and this is much, much worse. I wish we had 10,000 more tickets."

Oddsmakers and sportswriters didn't need calculators to decide which Final Four entrant was least likely to succeed. Arizona was 35-2 and ranked No. 2 in the final AP Poll. Oklahoma was 34-3 and ranked No. 4. Duke was 28-6 and ranked No. 5. Kansas was 25-11 and unranked. No team with as many as 11 losses had ever won the championship.

Then there was this: Arizona won the West Regional, beating, among others, Iowa and North Carolina. Oklahoma won in the Southeast, defeating Auburn, Louisville and Villanova. Duke had taken the East Regional by beating Temple, the No. 1 team in the final AP poll. KU, in contrast, had reached Kansas City with victories over Xavier, Murray State, Vanderbilt and Kansas State — hardly murderer's row, even if they had knocked off some big names.

For KU fans on their heady tournament run, sobering facts meant little. To be part of a quartet that began with 291 Division I schools was the ultimate accomplishment. What did it matter that Kansas had lost six straight games in Final Four competition over the years, or that both Duke and Oklahoma had handled the Jayhawks earlier in the season? The 1987-88 Jayhawks already ranked as notable overachievers. And there was always the underdog's hope, and the example of Villanova. Three years earlier the Wildcats from Philadelphia, with 10 defeats, weren't given a wisp of chance in the championship game against powerful Big East rival Georgetown. Yet, in a brilliantly staged upset, Villanova had won, 66-64.

"I've thought of some similarities between us and Villanova," Larry Brown said. "Going in, Georgetown had beat Villanova handily. All of a sudden, they win the national championship. It's dumb of me to think that way. We've got to worry about Duke."

If the Jayhawks couldn't get past the Blue Devils, there would be no chance for an upset in the championship game. Facing the nation's fifth-ranked team, KU at least had a stong motive: Revenge. A highly talented Kansas team — Calvin Thompson, Ron Kellogg, Greg Dreiling, Cedric Hunter and Danny Manning were the starters, with Mark Turgeon and Archie Marshall coming off the bench — had met Duke in the 1986 Final Four semifinal and lost, 71-67. The Blue Devils had also defeated KU, 92-86, in the finals of the Big Apple NIT in New York that year. And of course Duke had beaten the current KU team, 74-70, in overtime a month earlier in Allen Fieldhouse.

"We look at it like we want to pay them back," said Chris Piper. "We had a chance to pay back Kansas State and we did. Now we have a

"We look at it like we want to pay them back. We had a chance to pay back Kansas State and we did. Now we have a chance against Duke, and hopefully Oklahoma."

— CHRIS PIPER

Final Four fever spread rapidly through Kansas, striking young and old. These youthful Jayhawk fans displayed all the symptoms at a rally before the Duke game.

chance against Duke, and hopefully Oklahoma." The 1986 game was on Manning's mind too, because it was often described as the worst game of his career — a four-point performance that had given him an unwarranted national reputation, in some quarters, as overrated. Manning said he used the experience as ". . . a motivational factor. I never want to play that bad a game again."

It wasn't that simple, Brown pointed out. "Danny says he played poorly but he never was truly allowed to play, he was in such foul trouble. The thing that bothers me is so many people judge Danny off that

"They say we're a one-man team, but it's not a one-man sport."

— DANNY MANNING

Danny Manning had scored 31 points in the overtime loss to Duke in Lawrence and he didn't have anything to prove against the Blue Devils this time. But with 25 points, 10 rebounds, four steals and six blocked shots, he found ways to strengthen Duke coach Mike Krzyzewski's feeling that Manning was the nation's player-of-the-year.

Mike Yoder

performance." Manning had a retrial in the game in Lawrence and was more than acquitted, scoring 31 points and grabbing a dozen rebounds. He really had nothing to prove against the Blue Devils. Besides, as he pointed out, "They say we're a one-man team, but it's not a one-man sport."

Manning was, however, one man on the Kansas team that other coaches, including Duke's Mike Krzyzewski, always noticed. "What I remember most about Manning is how hard he worked," Krzyzewski said of the Feb. 22 game. "I was impressed by that. I knew he had great skills, but I think I underestimated him a bit. After that, he had my vote for player-of-the-year in the country." The vote must have counted. The day Krzyzewski made that statement Manning received the Eastman Award, the player-of-the-year award presented by the National Association of Basketball Coaches.

"Danny and Pipe have pretty much taken over the team," Brown said. "Danny sees me yelling at kids like Scooter, and doesn't like it. I can see it in his face. Chemistry is such a factor. Right now we have it. Danny is so relaxed. Of all the times I've seen him the past four years, the last two months I've never seen him as relaxed. It's obvious what he's done. Where we are is a tribute to him."

It was almost time to head to Kansas City. But first the *Los Angeles Times* reported that Brown was a leading candidate for the UCLA head coaching job that had opened with the firing of Walt Hazzard. "I can't talk about anything like that now. I'm busy coaching KU and trying to win the national championship," Brown told the *Times*. "But I love UCLA, and I'm concerned

about whatever happens there." Later, that concern would lead to one of the closest calls KU would experience in five years of Brown's coaching regime. For now, the coach and the Jayhawks focused on the task at hand. Ever superstitious, Brown found another way to give his team an edge. Back in Detroit, the team had been driven to and from the Silverdome in a Greyhound bus by a driver named Jimmy Dunlap. Dunlap and the team hit it off. When KU beat Vanderbilt and Kansas State, Dunlap became a good-luck symbol, but it was more than that. As Brown would explain later, Dunlap won his affection by the way he'd treated Ryan Gray, the Lawrence teen-ager who, with his inoperable brain tumor and cheerful courage, had become an inspiration to the Jayhawks. So Brown had the bus driver flown in from Detroit, and in Kansas City it was Dunlap who ferried the team from its headquarters at the Marriott Plaza to Kemper Arena and to practice at Rockhurst High.

In addition, John Erickson, former head basketball coach at Wisconsin and former director of the Fellowship of Christian Athletes, provided further inspiration by speaking to the team before each tournament game. Erickson, who had interviewed for the KU athletic director's post following the resignation of Monte Johnson, told the Jayhawks they were on a six-step journey to the national crown.

On the Friday morning before the showdown with Duke, the trip took a short detour. Dunlap drove the team to Rockhurst for practice because Brown suspected he wouldn't get much done during the mandatory practice session — more or less a dunk-a-thon — that after-

Mike Yoder

Larry Brown directed the Jayhawks to high-pitched performances in Kemper Arena.

"Danny and Pipe have pretty much taken over the team."

— LARRY BROWN

"Usually when you get to the Final Four it's a new tournament. But to us it was like Game Five, not the first game of the Final Four and we were pretty loose."

— CHRIS PIPER

Milt Newton made his case for national recognition with strong Final Four performances. He started with 20 points and seven rebounds against Duke. Newton, who began his basketball year playing for the Virgin Islands at the Pan American Games, ended up on the NCAA all-tournament squad.

noon in Kemper. Indeed, so many people showed up that the fire marshal had to order the doors closed with many fans still clamoring to get in.

Duke, working out before the Jayhawks, was roundly booed. When the Kansas players ran onto the floor they heard a thunderous ovation. "I had a feeling it would be special," Brown said later with a smile. "I had a feeling this would top it all, and it did."

The players were ready for Duke. "Usually when you get to the Final Four it's a new tournament. But to

us it was like Game Five, not the first game of the Final Four, and we were pretty loose," Piper said after the season. "Danny and I would say silly stuff like, 'It's just another game' to try to relax everybody. I don't think Danny and I were nervous." He recalled a big difference from 1986 in Dallas. "Everybody was scared (then). There was a lot of apprehension. We were happy to be there, but we didn't know what to expect."

At last, the tipoff. Or was it the kickoff? Before five minutes had elapsed, Kansas was ahead by two touchdowns. Flustered by KU's intense interior defense, Duke wasted its first nine trips down the floor — five turnovers, four missed shots — while Kansas scored 14 points, eight by Milt Newton. The Jayhawks weren't finished, either. At 13:44, Kansas led 18-2. At 10:54, it looked like a football score again: Kansas 24, Duke 6.

But hadn't Kansas bolted to a 23-8 lead against the Blue Devils in Lawrence? There was a difference this time. In Allen Fieldhouse, KU's lead dwindled to 28-27 at halftime. In Kemper, Kansas was 10 points better. The halftime lead was 38-27. At the break, Manning had scored 15 points on seven of 11 shooting, and Newton added 14. In all, KU had hit 55.2 percent of its shots to Duke's 45.8. The Devils' leading scorers, Danny Ferry and Kevin Strickland, had just six points apiece.

Yet Duke had staged a monumental comeback in Lawrence and was about to do it again. First, though, Newton's three-pointer at 14:06 boosted KU's lead to 49-33, a 16-point bulge. Then — as had happened so often during the season, most recently against Xavier — the Jayhawks lost momentum in a hurry. KU scored three points in the next 10 minutes; Duke chalked up 19.

With 4:17 to go, KU's lead was down to just three points, 55-52. Two minutes later, the scoreboard read 57-54. Kevin Pritchard drove the baseline and flipped up a shot that rolled off and . . . seemingly from nowhere, Manning grabbed the ball, whirled and stuck it back in. KU led by five with 2:11 to go. "I thought the biggest play of the game was when Danny tipped in Kevin's missed layup," Brown said later. "I don't know where he came from."

Those were to be Manning's last points, but down the stretch he rebounded, blocked shots and defended. At :21, KU was ahead 64-56, after hitting seven of nine free throws in the last 1:43. Duke, desperate, missed seven straight three-point shots. Kansas won, 66-59. The earlier losses had been avenged; a tired KU team stood one game away from the school's first NCAA championship in 36 years.

"The atmosphere on this team is, 'Let's go home and get some sleep and worry about the championship game tomorrow,'" Piper said, red-faced and fatigued. "We're tremendously excited, but we don't show it because we're so darned tired. We're so tired it's hard to realize

No matter how Danny Ferry and Quin Snyder lined up, Duke's defense was never too deep for Chris Piper and the Jayhawks.

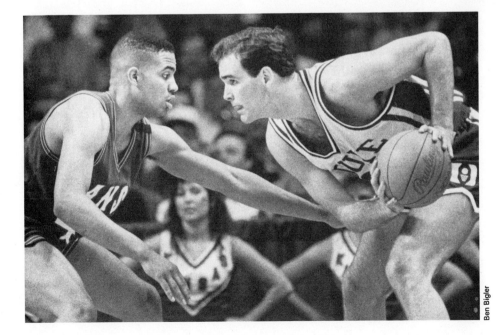

Keith Harris stretched to help hold Ferry to seven-of-22 shooting. KU's defense had emerged as a powerful weapon: Overall, the Blue Devils shot just 34.3 percent.

we're actually in the title game." So tired was Pritchard that he almost fell over walking down the hallway. "I'm dizzy I'm so tired," he said. "It's as exhausted as I've ever been after any game."

Kansas had shot 55.2 percent in the second half, but only 43.5 percent in the second. Duke was worse. For the game, the Blue Devils shot 34.3 percent. "I think a lot of shots didn't go down because the kids on both teams had no legs," Brown said of the fatigue factor. Manning deserved to be tired. He had collected 25 points and 10 rebounds. He also had six blocked shots, the most ever in a Final Four game, and he made four steals, a

record for a national semifinal game.

Newton wound up with 20 points and seven rebounds. In all, only five KU players scored. After Manning and Newton, Piper matched his

Ball-hawking Jayhawks like Manning, Kevin Pritchard and Piper had Duke outnumbered as they scrambled for loose balls and steals.

Robert Brickey was shorthanded when it came to stopping Manning, who was 12-of-21 from the floor. "When it started getting close, I thought he was the difference," said Duke's Krzyzewski.

season high with 10; Pritchard had six; and Scooter Barry five off the bench.

"They were terrific," said Krzyzewski. "I think it's a credit to Larry Brown and his staff . . . what

they've done to turn this season around. I just wish we'd gotten off to a better start. I think we did turn it around, though. If we kept going like we were, it could have been maybe 82-20." For Duke, Danny Ferry had 19 points and 12 re-

In Lawrence, KU let a lead over Duke slip away. In Kansas City, the Jayhawks kept it together.

APRIL 2 AT KANSAS CITY, MO.

Kansas (66)

	MIN	FG m-a	FT m-a	REB o-t	PF	TP
Milt Newton........	32	8-14	2-3	1-7	3	20
Chris Piper.........	29	3-4	4-4	0-6	2	10
Danny Manning......	39	12-21	1-2	4-10	3	25
Kevin Pritchard.....	36	2-6	2-2	1-7	2	6
Jeff Gueldner.......	9	0-1	0-0	0-1	2	0
Scooter Barry......	27	1-2	3-4	0-1	4	5
Clint Normore......	11	0-0	0-0	0-1	0	0
Keith Harris.......	15	0-4	0-0	2-3	0	0
Lincoln Minor	1	0-0	0-0	0-0	0	0
Mike Maddox.......	1	0-0	0-0	0-0	0	0
Marvin Mattox......	1	0-0	0-0	0-0	0	0
Totals		26-52	12-15	8-36	16	66

Three-point goals: 2-4 (Newton 2-3, Pritchard 0-1). Assists: 16 (Pritchard 5, Newton 3, Piper 3, Manning 2, Gueldner, Barry, Normore). Turnovers: 21 (Manning 7, Barry 3, Newton 2, Piper 2, Pritchard 2, Gueldner 2, Normore 2, Harris). Blocked shots: 9 (Manning 6, Newton, Piper, Pritchard). Steals: 9 (Manning 4, Pritchard 2, Newton, Piper, Normore).

Duke (59)

	MIN	FG m-a	FT m-a	REB o-t	PF	TP
Danny Ferry........	36	7-22	4-4	8-12	4	19
Billy King..........	26	1-4	1-2	0-1	4	3
Robert Brickey......	27	2-9	2-5	4-6	1	6
Quin Snyder.......	28	4-10	1-2	0-3	4	9
Kevin Strickland	35	5-13	0-0	3-6	2	10
John Smith	4	0-0	0-0	0-0	0	0
Phil Henderson	16	0-2	0-0	1-3	0	0
Alaa Abdelnaby.....	12	1-2	2-4	0-0	2	4
Greg Koubek.......	16	3-5	0-0	1-4	2	8
Joe Cook..........	1	0-0	0-0	0-0	0	0
Totals		23-67	10-17	17-35	19	59

Three-point goals: 3-14 (Koubek 2-3, Ferry 1-5, Snyder 0-3, Strickland 0-3). Assists: 13 (Snyder 5, Ferry 4, King 2, Strickland, Henderson). Turnovers: 16 (Snyder 5, King 3, Brickey 3, Ferry 2, Henderson 2, Koubek). Blocked shots: 5 (Strickland 2, King, Brickey, Abdelnaby). Steals: 8 (Ferry 3, Snyder 2, Brickey, Strickland, Smith).

Kansas............................	38	28 — 66
Duke..............................	27	32 — 59

Officials: Booker Turner, Larry Lembo, Jim Burr. Attendance: 16,392.

Mike Yoder

Mike Yoder

The Duke bench was a picture of intensity as the highly seeded Blue Devils trailed unranked Kansas. "They were terrific," Krzyzewski, right, said of the Jayhawks.

"I thought the biggest play of the game was when Danny tipped in Kevin's missed layup."

— LARRY BROWN

With the clock ticking down, right, Manning was all business while Newton pointed to Piper as a smiling example of KU's defensive excellence against Duke. At the buzzer, KU coaches and players erupted from the bench in a victory salute.

bounds, but made only seven of 22 shots. Guard Quin Snyder, who had scored a career-high 21 in Lawrence, wound up with nine points. Like the fans in the Allen Fieldhouse finale, Krzyzewski tossed a rose to Manning. "When it started getting close, I thought he was the difference," the Duke coach said. "Manning played like the player-of-the-year he is."

Ferry stressed the role played by

Mike Yoder

Mike Yoder

Manning's supporting cast. "I think everybody underestimates them," the Blue Devils' 6-9 junior center said. "It's a smart team and Milt Newton is a great player. If you could have three players guarding Danny Manning, he'd have a tough game, but you can't because of players like Newton."

Then there was the defense. Tired or not, for the fifth straight tournament game a Kansas opponent had shot poorly. Barry, for one, thought it was time the Jayhawks' strength was recognized. "Everybody was talking about how great Duke plays defense. Nobody mentioned our defense," he said. "That's the story of us in this tournament. Kansas is not praised. Kansas is not expected to win. That's helped us. We're so loose."

In the second game, Oklahoma, perhaps the nation's loosest team, set up the first all-Big Eight championship game in NCAA history by knocking off Arizona, 86-78. The Sooners fell behind 9-2 in the opening minutes but steals by Mookie Blaylock and Ricky Grace helped bring OU within one at 9-8. Oklahoma took the lead for good at 14-13 on a bank shot by Stacey King. In all, the Sooners forced Arizona into nine first-half turnovers and led 39-27 at intermission. Arizona cut the gap to 51-48 in the second half on a three-pointer by Sean Elliott. But the Sooners went on a 7-2 run with 10:42 left to take a 58-49 lead. It was still 58-49 at 9:16, when King left the game with his fourth foul. Substitute center Andre Wiley did more than hold his own, finishing with 11 points in 17 minutes. "I wasn't worried that we would get the job done," said Wiley. "I've learned a lot this year and I was ready to help our team show the

Brenda Steele

world what Oklahoma basketball is all about." Aided by Harvey Grant's 21 points and a zone defense that the Sooners had rarely used, Oklahoma basketball put on an impressive show indeed. "We'll play any way it takes to get the job done," Tubbs warned.

Even with OU looming, KU fans were overjoyed. Impromptu celebrations broke out all over the state. Brown came quickly back to earth when a California sportswriter asked him if he was going to take the UCLA job. "Why did you ask me that now?" he replied. "I just want to do what's right here."

Less than a week later, Brown would struggle to do what was right regarding UCLA. But first he had to plot all the right moves against Oklahoma. Otherwise, the Jayhawks had come a very long way to end the season on a losing note.

After the game in Kansas City, the Jayhawk players were worn out; in Lawrence, the celebration flowed along Jayhawk Boulevard.

Danny and the Miracles

12

"People will be talking about Kansas being 'dogs like Villanova and NC State, but we won't overlook them a bit."

— RICKY GRACE

The Big Eight Conference's 14th floor offices in Kansas City, Mo., command a lofty view of the skyline, and in early April the conference headquarters seemed even closer to the clouds. Two Big Eight teams were about to play for the national championship in basketball, and in Kansas City at that.

The conference had made its bid to host the 1988 Final Four three years earlier. Kansas City, the Big Eight pointed out, should be a sentimental favorite for the 50th anniversary tournament. It had hosted more Final Fours — nine — than any other city, and was the site of the NCAA's own offices. The first Final Four conducted by the NCAA, in 1940, had been at Kansas City's Municipal Auditorium. The city had also hosted the championship in 1941, 1942, 1953, 1954, 1955, 1957, 1961 and 1964. The historical connection paid off: The Big Eight's bid was accepted even though Kemper Arena, with fewer than 17,000 seats, was small by the standards of the hugely popular and lucrative tournament.

Certainly Kansas and Oklahoma were appropriate finalists, but improbable ones, too. Someone asked Bill Hancock, a Big Eight assistant commissioner, who might have written such a script? "Well," Hancock said, pausing to think, "Pollyanna would be close."

The hundreds of sportswriters who flocked to Kansas City didn't have to dream up an angle. Oklahoma had defeated Kansas twice during the regular season; the powerful Sooners were about to be crowned college champions. End of story. The betting line also told the tale: The Jayhawks were an eight-point underdog. KU players and coaches said little to change the storyline. "They're great, an NBA caliber team," point guard Kevin Pritchard said of the Sooners. "They are truly the best team in the country," said Larry Brown. "But the thing I remember," he added, "is in both games we had a chance to win and our kids understand that."

Oklahoma coach Billy Tubbs professed to recall little, if anything, about those previous meetings. "They're a blur," he said. "It seems like a long time since we played them." It had, in fact, been 38 days since the game in Norman and 59 since OU's win in Lawrence. Oklahoma went into the title game with 35 wins and only three losses, all on the road — to LSU, Kansas

State and Missouri. Kansas had 11 defeats. With Stacey King, Harvey Grant and Company piling up nearly 104 points a game, Oklahoma was second in the nation in scoring. The Sooners had scored 100 or more points in 20 games; KU had hit the century mark only once — against Rider (110-72).

Everybody knew the favorite, but they also knew the underdog had won in 1985 (Villanova) and in 1983 (North Carolina State). "People will be talking about Kansas being 'dogs like Villanova and NC State, but we won't overlook them a bit," said OU guard Ricky Grace. "Oh, man, it'll be tough," said King. "That team knows us inside and out. We want it bad, though. We want to show a big ring to our football players, because they say we've choked the last two or three years."

More than a few of Oklahoma's opponents wanted to choke the Sooners during the 1987-88 season. Given a decent opportunity — any opportunity, really — they would run up the score. "I always believed you score every chance you get and you try to stop the other team from scoring. That's the way it was when I played, and it's not going to change," Tubbs said. "He likes to beat you and beat you bad, because of his kids," Brown said. "You've got to accept that."

The championship game would be played two months and one day after the Jayhawks had bottomed out in the home loss to Oklahoma. At that time, KU had lost four straight and five of its last six. The Jayhawks stood 12-8 and were out of the AP poll after being ranked No. 7 in the preseason. "Things were real bleak then," Danny Manning recalled. Since that night, Kansas had won 14 of 17 games. Why the turnaround? "There's no one

answer, but the word *team* is more important than anything," Chris Piper said. Along the way, the Jayhawks had regained confidence and maintained a relaxed attitude. "We had nothing to lose, nobody expected us to get that far," Piper recalled after the season. "There were no doubts about getting blown out. We might have questioned deep down if we could win. I thought everybody believed we could."

Oklahoma had never won the NCAA title, and the Sooners hadn't been in the title game since 1947. Kansas had captured its only NCAA title in 1952, and was making its first championship appearance since 1957. Finally, after all the hoopla that surrounds the Final Four, it was Monday evening and time for one of the two teams to erase years of frustration. A capacity crowd of 16,392 was waiting in Kemper, but a capacity national television audience wasn't. Figures later showed that the game drew the lowest Nielsen rating since the championship contest was moved to prime time in 1973. Nevertheless, nearly 17 million households were tuned in, and the nation was treated to a first-half track meet, a second-half chess match and, ultimately, a down-to-the-wire thriller. It was one of those rare times when the game itself outstripped the hype of a major sporting event.

Don't run with the Sooners. That was the first warning on every team's scouting report, and the first words on every announcer's lips. So the Jayhawks ran. They ran because when they did their shots found the mark. KU made 17 of its first 20 field goal tries and 22 of 31 overall in a madcap first half. "We shot 71 percent and we were tied," Brown said. "We wondered what

"There were no doubts about getting blown out. We might have questioned deep down if we could win. I thought everybody believed we could."

— CHRIS PIPER

When times are golden for the Jayhawks, KU fans wave the wheat.

Ben Bigler

"Sometimes our kids are selective in what they hear."

— LARRY BROWN

Mike Yoder

The word was out: Don't run with Oklahoma. But that's what the Jayhawks did, until Larry Brown's signals, right, eventually slowed them down. Meanwhile, it was off to the races for Kevin Pritchard. KU and the Sooners split 100 points in the first half.

Ben Bigler

the heck we had to do to get the lead. We were concerned because we couldn't get ourselves slowed down." He said the KU players "wouldn't listen to me. I jumped up a number of times." Piper also stressed that a fast pace wasn't in the game plan: "We wanted to control the tempo and not get in a running game."

"Sometimes," Brown said, "our kids are selective in what they hear." Nevertheless, "the fact we played them 50-50, playing their style, helped us a great deal. When we went in the dressing room, their kids, I feel, felt we were for real. But we didn't try to run with them."

Kansas had scored 50 points, but so had Oklahoma, despite shooting only 48.7 percent. It was the highest scoring half in NCAA championship game history, and it left everyone limp. "When I saw it was 50-50, I thought, 'Can you imagine the 50th anniversary of the game and it's 50-50?'" Brown said. "That blew my mind." Ed Steitz, chairman of NCAA basketball rules committee, called it "the most exciting half of college basketball I've seen in 36 years." Said Hank Nichols, the NCAA's director of referees, "Maybe I better get a replacement crew for the second half. I don't know if these guys can take another half like that."

Milt Newton made all five shots he tried, including a pair of three-pointers, for 12 points. Yet the player he was guarding was even hotter. OU's Dave Sieger launched eight three-pointers and made six. "He was on fire," Newton said. "Believe it or not, I tipped a couple of them and they still went in." Manning had a solid half, with 14 points. The surprise was reserve guard Clint Normore, who was three for three

Ben Bigler

"Maybe I better get a replacement crew (of referees) for the second half. I don't know if these guys can take another half like that."

— HANK NICHOLS

Harvey Grant took a swipe but Milt Newton defied Grant and gravity on an acrobatic layup, one of the six shots he tried — and hit — against the Sooners.

from the floor, including a three-pointer, for seven points. In the first five games of the tournament Normore hadn't scored. "I'm a role player and that's what I did," he said. "It was great because our role players played a big part." Normore, the starting free safety on KU's football team, would wind up with half of KU's bench points. And after the game, few would dispute that the benches had made a big difference.

Brown made 42 substitutions. He used 10 players — everyone he had except Marvin Mattox, another football player. Tubbs made just a dozen substitutions, using six players in all. In the first half, the only OU starter Tubbs rested was Grace, and the senior guard was spelled for just three minutes.

The Jayhawks had played Oklahoma's game and had survived. It gave them a boost. "At halftime we thought we'd win, no doubt," Piper

Clint Normore hadn't scored in the NCAA Tournament until his numbers — three-of-three shooting, including a three-pointer — came up against Oklahoma in the first half. At right, Chris Piper, playing defense that later won raves from North Carolina coach Dean Smith, was a handful for OU's Stacey King under the basket.

recalled. Now it was time for Oklahoma to play KU's game. By breaking OU's fullcourt press, KU was able to slow the pace. "The biggest concern I had," Brown reflected, "was to try to utilize the clock and get our big people to handle the ball. Their guards are so quick, and I thought if our big people handled the ball, Stacey and Harvey would have trouble defending us."

In the meantime, King and Grant — perhaps the best post tandem in the country — had increasing difficulty with the Kansas defense. King had scored 13 in the first half; Grant 10. In the second half, they managed four points apiece. In the final 12 minutes, Grant would make one basket, King none. "Chris Piper really worked hard on denying us the ball and when I did get open Danny Manning would come over and help out," King said. "You have to commend them on their inside defense. That was the toughest defense we faced this year." Later, Brown would mention that North Carolina's Dean Smith, his former coach, had called to say he'd "never seen anyone play post defense like Chris Piper did. That's the ultimate compliment."

Despite the clampdown on King and Grant, the game wasn't decided until the final minute. The Sooners were ahead 65-60 — their biggest second-half lead — before Kansas forged a 65-65 tie at 11:13. For five more minutes, neither side gained an advantage. At 6:13, it was 71-71. But then Kansas spurted, outscoring the Sooners 6-0 during the next three minutes on baskets by Pritchard, Manning and Piper, who took a last-second pass from Normore and arched in a baseline jumper at 3:05 just before the 45-second clock ran out. Even that 77-71 lead wasn't safe, because KU missed four of its next five free throw attempts, and when Mookie Blaylock hit a 13-foot turnaround jumper at :41, KU's lead had slipped to 78-77. Tubbs called time out. Then Kansas successfully killed 24 seconds before Blaylock fouled Barry. Barry made the first free throw — "I concentrated hard on that first one because it was so important" — and missed the second — "I relaxed too much on the next one." Kansas fans groaned, but the game's biggest play was at hand. Somehow Manning had captured the rebound of Barry's errant free throw, and, before falling to the floor, he drew a foul from King at :14.

Manning stepped to the line. At :52, he had missed the front end of a one-and-one opportunity with KU ahead 78-75. Now he had a chance to redeem that miss and put KU into a commanding position. What was he thinking as went to the line? "That it's over. It's over," he said later. Manning hit the first free throw. Then the second slipped through the net. KU held an 81-77 advantage; Oklahoma would need two possessions to tie or go ahead. Grace took the ball and wormed through the lane under the Kansas basket for what amounted to an uncontested layup. Tubbs called his last timeout at :07. Down 81-79, Oklahoma, the national leader in steals, needed one desperately. Piper, who was to make the inbounds pass for KU, called time when he wasn't sure he could make the play. After that timeout, Piper flipped a pass to Manning, who dribbled for only two seconds before Grant fouled him. So at :05, Manning stepped to the line again. If he missed the first free throw, Oklahoma still had time to tie, or

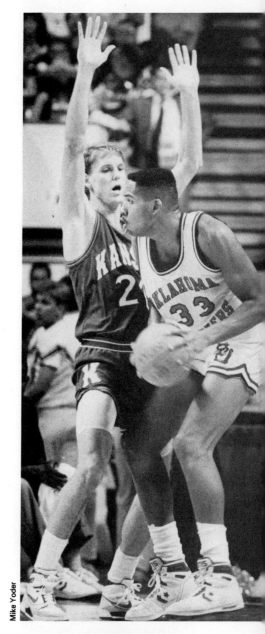

Mike Yoder

Larry Brown said Piper and Danny Manning would have to play great post defense against OU's Grant and King. They did. "You have to commend them on their inside defense," King said after the game. "That was the toughest defense we faced this year."

Manning shot his jump hooks so quickly that King and the Sooners were too late.

even win with a three-pointer. If Manning made just one, a Sooner three-pointer could still tie it. But if he made both, Oklahoma was finished.

Manning's 30th point of the night flew through the net. Then his 31st. Kansas 83, Oklahoma 79.

Three seconds later, when Grace's desperation 25-footer went clanging off the rim at :02, there was Manning again, snatching his 18th rebound, a career-high in his 147th and last college game. As the buzzer sounded Manning raced toward midcourt to join a jubilant celebration.

"Danny was a skinny kid the last time we played in the Final Four," Brown said later. "He was a man tonight."

Oklahoma's big men, Grant and King, had combined for 31 points and 12 rebounds. Manning alone had 31 points and 18 rebounds. He had played 36 minutes. Grant had

gone the route, and King rested only for about a minute toward the end. "I did feel Oklahoma got tired. I could sense it," Brown said. "He played his inside people for 40 minutes. I looked at Stacey and Harvey and they were exhausted." In the Sooners' victory over Arizona in the semifinals, Tubbs had brought Andre Wiley off the bench. The 6-7 junior college transfer had collected 11 points and four rebounds in 17 minutes. Why hadn't Wiley been used against Kansas? "I went into the game planning on getting him in during the first half, and it never really happened," Tubbs said. "It just didn't materialize." Neither did the Sooners' national championship. Was Tubbs outcoached? "I don't know," Piper said. "I don't think you could say anybody was outcoached in a national championship game. Just getting that far means you were well coached."

Brown, whose own coaching job

KANSAS CITY

Mike Yoder

was drawing instant praise, was fulfilled. "I can't imagine anyone having a high like I have now," he said, smiling. "I'm not happy, I'm ecstatic," said KU Chancellor Gene Budig. "I've consumed three packages of Rolaids since 3 o'clock. I take this very seriously." Mattox put it more boldly. "This is better than anything," he said. "This is better than birth."

"How do you like us now?" Manning proclaimed at the postgame press conference. "People said we were lucky. This wasn't a gift. What's luck? It's preparation and opportunity."

"I kept telling the kids," Brown said, "that if we get it to the last five minutes we have a chance. That's

because we have the best player I've been associated with, and he'd lead us." Manning, who was named the tournament's outstanding performer, met the challenge. So did Newton, who wound up with 15 points despite suffering a slightly twisted ankle in the second half. The junior forward, who didn't start for the Jayhawks until the 12th game, also made the all-tournament team.

The Sooners were gracious — mostly. Manning had picked up his

As KU clamped down, Mookie Blaylock found major obstacles in defenders like Lincoln Minor.

APRIL 4 AT KANSAS CITY, MO.

Kansas (83)

	MIN	FG m-a	FT m-a	REB o-t	PF	TP
Milt Newton	32	6-6	1-2	0-4	1	15
Chris Piper	37	4-6	0-0	1-7	3	8
Danny Manning	36	13-24	5-7	7-18	3	31
Kevin Pritchard	31	6-7	0-0	0-1	1	13
Jeff Gueldner	15	1-2	0-0	0-2	0	2
Scooter Barry	9	0-2	1-2	0-0	1	1
Clint Normore	16	3-3	0-1	0-1	3	7
Keith Harris	13	1-1	0-0	0-1	2	2
Lincoln Minor	11	1-4	2-2	0-1	1	4
Mike Maddox	1	0-0	0-0	0-0	1	0
Totals		35-55	9-14	8-35	16	83

Three-point goals: 4-6 (Newton 2-2, Pritchard 1-1, Normore 1-1, Manning 0-1, Gueldner 0-1). Assists: 17 (Pritchard 4, Normore 4, Piper 2, Manning 2, Barry 2, Newton, Gueldner, Minor). Turnovers: 23 (Piper 5, Pritchard 5, Manning 4, Harris 4, Barry 2, Normore 2, Minor). Blocked shots: 4 (Newton 2, Manning 2). Steals: 11 (Manning 5, Piper 3, Pritchard, Gueldner, Minor).

Oklahoma (79)

	MIN	FG m-a	FT m-a	REB o-t	PF	TP
Harvey Grant	40	6-14	2-3	3-5	4	14
Dave Sieger	40	7-15	1-2	3-5	2	22
Stacey King	39	7-14	3-3	2-7	3	17
Mookie Blaylock	40	6-13	0-1	3-5	4	14
Ricky Grace	34	4-14	3-4	3-7	4	12
Terrence Mullins	7	0-0	0-0	0-1	1	0
Totals		30-70	9-13	14-30	18	79

Three-point goals: 10-24 (Sieger 7-13, Blaylock 2-4, Grace 1-7). Assists: 19 (Sieger 7, Grace 7, Blaylock 4, Grant). Turnovers: 15 (Sieger 6, King 3, Grace 3, Blaylock 2, Mullins). Blocked shots: 3 (King 2, Grant). Steals: 13 (Blaylock 7, Sieger 3, Grant, King, Grace).

Kansas	50 33 —	83
Oklahoma	50 29 —	79

Officials: John Clougherty, Tim Higgins, Ed Hightower. Attendance: 16,392.

Mike Yoder

With the game going KU's way, Scooter Barry and the bench were highly pleased.

Ben Bigler

Manning found a way under King's arm for a foul and two more of his 31 points.

Ben Bigler

third foul, a charge, 25 seconds into the second half, but didn't foul again, and that prompted a bittersweet remark from OU's King. "It seemed like the officials let Manning do whatever he wanted to do," King said. "He's a great player and the player-of-the-year and I'm happy for that, but in his heart, he knows he should have fouled out." Tubbs praised the Jayhawks. "The first half I don't think you could have shot any better. Maybe our defense was lacking, but they were hitting both inside and out. Our hat's off to them. It's a bitter defeat because we thought we could win it all. Yet we have to accept it."

Everyone could point to a different reason why KU won — Manning's dominance, Newton's shooting, Piper's defense — but a

key to the Jayhawks' edge was clear. After an 11-of-31 second half, OU had made just 42.9 percent of its shots for the game. "We've come so far defensively and play team defense so well," said Brown. "That was a great game. I'd look at the refs and they were shaking their heads. It had all the drama. It was a close ballgame with great individual plays."

Still, in the midst of celebrating the biggest victory of his coaching career, Brown was asked again about UCLA. "Man, this is . . . I don't know what to say," he answered. "I'm part of a national championship and I'm going to enjoy it with these guys. That's not fair." Fair or not, three nights later, Brown was in Los Angeles being interviewed by UCLA officials.

Ben Bigler

"*That was a great game. I'd look at the refs and they were shaking their heads. It had all the drama. It was a close ballgame with great individual plays.*"

— LARRY BROWN

Mike Yoder

Amid the bustle of the postgame celebration, Brown saluted the KU crowd.

Ben Bigler

The slipper fits

13

"When you put it in the perspective of it being the largest spontaneous gathering on campus, we should be very proud of their behavior."

— DAVID AMBLER

The sound of Danny Manning's final free throw slipping through the net in Kemper Arena echoed in Lawrence for days. Almost from the moment Kansas shocked the basketball world by upending Oklahoma, celebrations rang out all over town. Bob Frederick's phone began to ring, too. "I guess you could divide them into thirds," the KU athletic director said later. "One-third congratulations, one-third questions about Larry and the other third people who have a deal for us." Frederick would soon add a fourth category — phone calls from Larry Brown, troubling phone calls. But first came the celebrating.

Mount Oread erupted in a festival that lured thousands of people and touched off horn-honking and high-fiving until 3 a.m. "It looked like a typical parking-lot fraternity party with 27,000 kids," said Tom Anderson, the man in charge of cleaning up. "All in all it came off very well," said David Ambler, vice chancellor for student affairs. There were some injuries and damage but, "when you put it in the perspective of it being the largest spontaneous gathering on campus, we should be very proud of their behavior."

The fans were only warming up.

Round 2 was in Memorial Stadium on Tuesday. The Jayhawks rode back to Lawrence around midday, and the stadium was the only place big enough for the welcoming party. Soon an estimated 30,000 people were enjoying themselves in the west stands.

"You've been our sixth man all year," Chris Piper told the crowd. Archie Marshall, holding the NCAA championship trophy, announced, "This is for you as much as it is for us." When Danny Manning's turn came, the crowd shouted "Dan-ny, Dan-ny." Manning said: "The first question I want to ask is, 'Does this feel good?'" That prompted another roar. "You've supported us through all the hard times, the good times and especially the great times. Thanks a lot. I love you all." Even Jimmy Dunlap, the bus driver from Detroit, was there. "If anybody's ever had a dream come true before, then they can understand how I'm feeling," he said. "Only in America. You can be a nobody today, and tomorrow everybody will recognize you."

Brown had his turn, too. "I always imagined what it would be like," he said of the championship, "but I never thought I'd experience

The Jayhawk was flying high as 30,000 fans flocked to Memorial Stadium.

Ben Bigler

The NCAA championship and the stadium crowd put smiles on the faces of Archie Marshall and Danny Manning.

Richard Gwin

Richard Gwin

Marshall had a hand in showing the KU fans the trophy they all shared.

Students had learned Newton's first law: The KU team was more than Manning.

Marvin Mattox got more than a T-shirt. As he told the stadium crowd, he didn't get to play against Oklahoma, but he wound up with a championship ring.

those rumors throughout the Final Four. He addressed them again after the Memorial Stadium gathering. "In the last 24 hours, I've heard six places I'm supposed to be coaching next year," he said. "I don't think it's fair. I just want to enjoy this. I wish people would focus on the team and their accomplishments."

Wednesday passed quietly. Danny and Ed Manning went to Los Angeles where the KU senior accepted the Wooden Award. Brown stayed home, but a cloud appeared on the horizon. "UCLA has contacted me and they've contacted Larry, but he hasn't talked to them at this point," Frederick, the KU athletic director, reported. Meanwhile, plans were made for the Jayhawks to be honored at the Kansas City-Detroit baseball game on Sunday in Royals Stadium, then to fly to Washington, D.C., for a ceremony with President Ronald Reagan the next day. Two days after that, all the hoopla was scheduled to end with a downtown Lawrence parade and the annual KU basketball awards dinner.

On Thursday, Brown was supposed to go with Danny Manning to Atlanta, where he and the 6-10 All-American were to receive Naismith Awards for coach and player-of-the-year respectively. Manning went; Brown didn't. Quietly, with no public word, UCLA officials had sent a jet to fly Brown to Los Angeles. There, on Thursday night, he was offered what was later reported to be the best contract proposal the Bruins ever had made to a coach. Brown, who had frequently said leaving UCLA was the greatest mistake he'd ever made, accepted — verbally. On Friday morning, CBS sportscaster Jim Lampley, tipped off by Brown, announced that

it." Chancellor Gene Budig made a public bid for continuing the Brown era in KU basketball. "Do we want Larry Brown to stay forever?" he asked. So loud and long was the reaction that Brown eventually stood and waved in acknowledgment. "I believe he got the message," Budig said. He did — but its impact would take time to be fully felt. In the meantime there was only turmoil, because approximately 72 hours after Brown coached Kansas to the top of the college basketball world, he decided he would coach at Kansas no more.

Rumors linking Brown to UCLA, where he had coached from 1979-81, cropped up as soon as the Bruins fired head coach Walt Hazzard during the tournament. Brown, to his chagrin, was asked about the KU coach had accepted the UCLA job and would return to Lawrence that day to inform Frederick and the players. Gloom descended over the KU athletic department. "I assume from everything I've heard it's a done deal, but I haven't heard that from coach," Frederick said early in the afternoon.

Hours later, a haggard-looking Brown walked into Allen Fieldhouse, sat down before a battery of microphones and stunned just about everybody.

"I came back and after thinking about it, I've decided to stay at the University of Kansas," he said wearily. "I apologize at this time for these things to be coming out. I think it's a time everybody ought to be celebrating the accomplishments of our team. Right now I'm just going to meet with the our team and leave it at that." He stood and left.

Counted among those most surprised was Peter Dalis, UCLA's athletic director. "When coach Brown left Los Angeles this morning, we had every reason to believe

that he had accepted UCLA's offer," Dalis said. KU players were more pleasantly shocked. "It was tense on campus today," said junior Clint Normore. "It's great, great he's staying." Said Scooter Barry: "I'm just glad coach made a decision he's comfortable with."

The only trouble was that Brown wasn't entirely comfortable, and Frederick sensed it. "I had a feeling Friday night after dinner," he said later. "My wife showed me a tape of the press conference, and I realized he'd had a difficult time saying that." Frederick's feeling was confirmed on Saturday afternoon, when Brown asked him over to his house. They met for about an hour. Frederick went home feeling more confident.

"I still thought we were OK," he recalled. "I was really surprised when I got the call at 1:45 in the morning." Frederick dressed and drove over to Brown's house again. He found the coach "struggling."

"It was tough," Brown remembered. "I had a real empty feeling. I sat down and said I didn't

"I was going through a personal hell from the time we won the championship until the morning when we were in the White House."

— LARRY BROWN

The small crowd of students gathered in Allen Fieldhouse to hear Brown announce his departure got a great surprise, but Brown would suffer second thoughts for days.

Mike Yoder

Some 60,000 people narrowed Massachusetts Street to a one-lane road as Lawrence celebrated. Brown rode in style while a squad of Dick Vitale imitators cleaned up.

know if I did the right thing. It was always my dream to coach at UCLA. I wanted to prove something to them." Frederick soon realized that Brown was still "having a lot of personal anxiety. I could understand because he and I have talked over the years about his feelings about UCLA." Time was running out if Brown was to reconsider. UCLA had to have his final word.

Frederick left the house about 3:15 a.m. Sunday. "I had suggested Larry take some time and not talk to anybody," he said. "We were supposed to go to the Royals game that afternoon, but I suggested he skip that and just go to the airport (for the trip to Washington) that evening." In the meantime, both Brown and Frederick talked by phone with Joe Glass, Brown's financial adviser in New York. Then Brown, Frederick and the team flew to Washington.

On Monday morning Brown's private struggle became public news. The *Los Angeles Times* reported that the KU coach might not be out of the UCLA picture after all. Sources close to Brown "were making calls saying he might be reconsidering a hasty decision." But

for Frederick, the uncertainty was ending. "On Monday morning I called Mr. Glass from Washington about 9 a.m. and he was on the phone talking to Larry in the room across the hall," Frederick said. "He (Glass) told me to relax and smile at the President, because Larry was going to stay."

"As I look back," Brown said later, "I was going through a personal hell from the time we won the championship until the morning when we were in the White House. The timing was terrible," he continued. "There was nothing wrong with UCLA. They were great to me, maybe too nice. They gave me anything I asked for. I accepted the job, but on the way back I thought 'How am I going to tell the kids?' We had our banquet coming up, and a parade, and then we were going to the White House to meet President Reagan. How was I supposed to go through with all these things and then become the UCLA coach? I just felt like I was deceiving people. I couldn't handle it."

If he couldn't handle that, he finally decided, he couldn't handle recanting the decision to stay. "Can I tell the kids I made a mistake? Can I deal with the media ridicule for changing my mind again? All the things I've asked the kids to stand for, I have to stand for, too."

At the White House, Reagan praised the Jayhawks' ability to bounce back from adversity as a "testament to determination." Reagan also joked that, with Brown turning UCLA down, he'd be the only one returning to California. "Perhaps nothing exemplifies the true meaning of teamwork than the support you've all given to Archie Marshall and the untiring support Archie Marshall has given you," the

President said. "In my opinion, that's just the way it should be." Manning gave the president a Kansas athletic letter jacket, and one for Nancy Reagan, too. Brown quipped softly that, unlike the second-term President, he'd never stayed anywhere for eight years. He said the Jayhawks had "a real difficult time getting here, but I think the difficulties made it all that more meaningful."

The complex emotions surrounding Brown's changes of heart gave way to simple feelings of celebration as the scene shifted back to Lawrence. Along Massachusetts Street early on Wednesday morning pickup trucks began parking in anticipation of the 4 p.m. parade. They were there for a reason: What better way to get a clear view than from the back of a truck? Police later estimated that 60,000 people — equivalent to the city's entire population — turned out. Onlookers stood eight-deep along the 1½-mile route as Brown and his

players paraded through town in convertibles. Many parade-goers said they wanted to cheer the team one more time for what they'd accomplished and for what the championship meant to the city and state.

There were more ovations to come. Athletic department officials had sold about 1,200 tickets to the evening's banquet but the crowd was probably closer to 1,500. More fans listened on the radio. To no one's surprise, Manning earned the Phog Allen Most Valuable Player trophy. Manning's next act was unexpected: He performed a side-splitting impersonation of Brown, complete with horned-rim glasses, a rolled-up program and a limp. He couldn't have won a louder hand if he'd slam-dunked over Oklahoma's Stacey King.

Frederick, who knew best how close KU had come to losing Brown and how proud Kansans were of the Jayhawks, summed it all up. "They proved to 80 million people," he said, "that nice guys can finish first."

"They proved to 80 million people that nice guys can finish first."

— BOB FREDERICK

Jayhawk seniors Marshall, Piper and Manning rode into the sunset together.

Richard Gwin

The Manning watch

After the season, Danny Manning revealed that the Jayhawks' NCAA championship was part of a personal plan. "When I was younger," he said, "I set four goals for myself. One was a high school championship. One was a national championship. One was an Olympic gold medal, and one was an NBA championship. So far I'm on course."

Manning also gave a postseason assessment of the hard times the KU team had struggled through: "The things, all the adversity we went through, helped me mentally and physically. I'm a lot stronger and more flexible in dealing with things when they don't go my way."

In hindsight, Manning certainly had the kind of senior season he dreamed about when he decided not to turn professional at the end of his junior year. Yet his standing in pro scouts' eyes was already so high that the championship season may not have enhanced his NBA draft status.

"What's to enhance? I mean, he's the No. 1 pick in the country from the git-go," Marty Blake, director of NBA scouting, remarked after the season. "He certainly played great, but I expected him to. He quieted a lot of critics who were not pro people, but he was No. 1 last fall and he still is. There's nothing to embellish. When I put out my sheet, he's the top player in the draft and that's it. He's a multi-faceted player."

Manning was so multi-faceted that he set school records in 17 season and career categories. No Kansas player has ever scored more points (2,951), and Manning ended

up No. 6 on the NCAA career scoring chart, behind Pete Maravich of LSU (3,667), Freeman Williams of Portland State (3,249), Harry Kelly of Texas Southern (3,066), Hersey Hawkins of Bradley (3,008) and Oscar Robertson of Cincinnati (2,973). Manning played in 147 games, more than any NCAA Division I player ever, and started 146. That's right. Manning failed to start only one college game. Displeased with Manning's performance against South Dakota State in the fifth game of his freshman season, coach Larry Brown brought Manning off the bench the next time out against Abilene Christian. It was Dec. 8, 1984. Manning responded with eight assists, a career high, and never began a KU game on the bench again.

Mike Yoder

"The thing I remember most is when he came in his freshman year, we were a senior-oriented team," teammate Chris Piper said. "He sacrificed his game for the seniors. He wanted them to score." Manning handed out more assists as a freshman — 108 — than in any of his three other seasons.

He was also the best shooter in KU history, making 1,216 field goals in 2,049 attempts — both school records — for a 59.3 percentage. Greg Dreiling, who wrapped up his career after the 1985-86 season, had held the record with 57.2 percent.

Manning didn't arrive in Lawrence unnoticed, and he never left the spotlight. Before his senior year in high school, his father Ed, a former pro player then working as a long-haul truck driver, was hired as an assistant coach by Brown, who had known him well in the pros. So Manning, after helping Greensboro Page High win the North Carolina state title as a junior, moved to Lawrence with Ed, his mother Darnelle and his younger — by three years — sister Dawn. That November, he signed a national letter of intent to play at KU. As a senior at Lawrence High, he averaged 22.7 points and 9.2 rebounds a game but the LHS team fell just short of winning the state championship.

As a KU freshman, Manning averaged 14.6 points and 7.6 rebounds a game. As a sophomore, he helped the Jayhawks go to the Final Four in Dallas while averaging 16.7 points and 6.3 rebounds. He also compiled his career high in steals, 80. As a junior and one of only two returning starters — point guard Cedric Hunter was the other — Manning was called upon to

score more. He boosted his average to 23.9 points per game, shooting a school record 61.7 percent. He also averaged 9.5 rebounds a game, his best at KU. While leading the Jayhawks to the NCAA championship as a senior, he averaged 24.8 points and 9.0 rebounds. His shooting percentage dipped slightly, to 58.3 percent. His blocked shot total climbed dramatically, to 73; his previous best had been 47. For his four years at KU, Manning averaged 20.1 points and 8.1 rebounds a game. He was also a 74 percent foul shooter.

What kind of a player will he be in the NBA?

"Danny will be a good player. He could start and help a team right away," Blake said. "But there are no more impact players. The league is just too good. The last impact player was Michael Jordan. Manning can play a lot of positions. He can play small forward and big forward, but he's not a center."

Manning, did, however, take on more of a center's build during his KU years. When he reported for pre-season drills in 1984 he logged in at 6-10, 205 pounds. As he senior, he played at 230 pounds. "I think he's matured physically, obviously, since he was a senior in high school," said Ron Grinker, who became Manning's agent after the college season ended. "He's really filled out. You look at his shoulders from behind the bench and they remind you of Ed's. And he has a backside that's a useful tool in pro basketball." Grinker had been Ed Manning's agent and is a longtime family friend. "I've known Danny as long as there's been a Danny," he said. "I feel like he's my own kid. I watched him play when

"The things, all the adversity we went through, helped me mentally and physically. I'm a lot stronger and more flexible in dealing with things when they don't go my way."

— DANNY MANNING

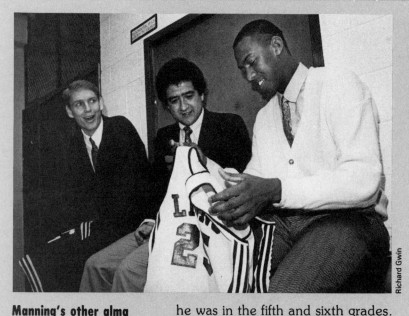

Manning's other alma mater — Lawrence High School — retired his number, and Piper's. LHS coach Ted Juneau did the honors near the end of KU's championship season.

"He's really filled out. You look at his shoulders from behind the bench and they remind you of Ed's. And he has a backside that's a useful tool in pro basketball."
— RON GRINKER

he was in the fifth and sixth grades. He was always a man playing with boys."

Although Manning turned 22 on May 17 — two days after walking down The Hill at commencement — only in the last couple of years has his mother considered him a man among boys. Darnelle Manning, a kindergarten special education teacher in Lawrence, said she started calling her son Dan when she realized he could take criticism from his father and not let it bother him. "He prefers Danny, but Danny and Billy and Bobby are boys' names. He isn't a Danny anymore. He's a Dan. When he came to KU he was a boy. He isn't anymore," she said.

Off the court, Manning has earned as much respect as he has on the floor. "When I talk about Danny Manning, I talk about him as a person," Grinker said. "He has charisma, charm, he's bright and he's eloquent. And he made the decision to go back to school (for his senior year at KU) for all the right reasons."

"He's a lot of fun to be around.

He keeps me laughing all the time," his mother said with a smile. "Everybody knows he's an All-American on the court," teammate Milt Newton said. "What a lot of people don't know is he's an All-American off the court, too."

Mrs. Manning likes to tell the story of the day she brought Dawn home from the hospital amid concern that Danny might be jealous. Hardly. "Dan was 3 at the time and when I put the baby in the cradle, he went to his room and got every pair of shoes he had and put them under her baby bed."

As the No. 1 draft choice, Manning will command a multi-million-dollar contract. But Grinker doesn't think wealth will alter his personality. "You have to consider that Danny has grown up in a comfortable environment," he said. "Ed made a very handsome living and Darnelle has taught school. They've had two incomes. Ed always drove a nice car and had a nice house — actually they've always had a home not a house — and I don't see where that's going to affect Danny. He's used to nice things."

On the other hand, Manning has never lived far from home, and his mother worried about the temptations and outside influences he'd run into as a wealthy young man out on his own.

"I just hope the way we've raised him he won't get into things he shouldn't," she said. "I worry about athletes, especially black athletes, who suddenly come into money and get involved in drugs. He has to have good enough sense to know better." Manning has done anti-drug promotions for the NCAA, and he was a booster of the No Drugs patch worn on the Kansas warmups during the championship season.

"He's what college athletics is all about. He deserves every single thing he's gotten," said KU coach Larry Brown, who time and again has called Manning "the best player I've ever been associated with."

Praise for Manning also comes from the NBA ranks. "He embodies everything you strive for in the game of basketball," said Al Menendez, director of player personnel for the New Jersey Nets. "Manning is an outstanding player and a young man that everyone can be proud of. He'll be a perfect ambassador for our youth."

DANNY MANNING RECORDS

School Season
Points: 942 (1987-88)
Games: 39 (1985-86)
Minutes: 1,336 (1987-88)
Field goals: 381 (1987-88)
Field goal attempts: 653 (1987-88)
Field goal percentage: 61.7 (1986-87)
Blocked shots: 73 (1987-88)
School Career
Points: 2,951
Minutes: 4,961
Field goals: 1,216
Field goal attempts: 2,049
Games: 147
Games started: 146
Rebounds: 1,187

Blocked shots: 200
Fouls: 473

Big Eight Records
Career Big Eight Tournament points: 203.
Single Big Eight Tournament points: 89 (1987).
Single Big Eight Tournament free throw percentage: .958, 23 of 24 (1987).
Consecutive Shots Made in a Half Without a Miss: 8 vs. Oklahoma State (1985-86).
Highest Field Goal Percentage in Game (minimum 15 attempts): .938, 15 of 16 vs. Oklahoma State (1985-86).
Highest Field Goal Percentage in a Conference Season (minimum 130 attempts): .667, 98 of 147 (1986-87).
Consecutive Games Started: 141.
Consecutive Games Played: 147.
Career Games Started: 146.
Career Games Played: 147.
Career Minutes: 4,961.
Career Field Goals: 1,216.
Career Points: 2,951.
Career Points Conference Games: 1,250.
Career Field Goals Made Conference Games: 505.
Career Field Goal Percentage Conference Games (minimum 500 attempts): .617 (505-815).
Average Percentage of Team's Points Conference Career (four seasons): .286 (1,250 of 4,366).
Scoring Average Conference Career: 22.3 (56 games).
Career Games Conference: 56 (tied with several others).
Career Games Started Conference: 56 (tied with several others).

NCAA Record
Games played: 147.

"Everybody knows he's an All-American on the court. What a lot of people don't know is he's an All-American off the court, too."

— MILT NEWTON

Epilogue

"These kids probably played our basic defense better than any I've had."

— LARRY BROWN

Until Kansas in 1988, no team had won the NCAA championship with more than 10 losses. Yet a look at KU's 11 defeats offers an insight into why the Jayhawks were able to win. Five of the losses were to teams that wound up in the Final Eight: Kansas State and Oklahoma (twice each) and Duke. Five others were against other teams that made the NCAA Tournament: Iowa, Illinois, St. John's, Notre Dame and Iowa State. Only one school with a losing record, 13-18 Nebraska, beat KU, and that came in Lincoln on Beau Reid's jumper at the buzzer. Nebraska and St. John's (17 wins) were the only teams with fewer than 20 victories to defeat KU.

Anyone who dismisses Kansas' championship as a fluke should check that schedule. Statistics offer further proof that the Jayhawks weren't as out of place as they seemed in the Final Four. Exhibit A: Kansas ranked No. 3 nationally in field goal percentage defense, holding opponents to 41.2 percent. Only Temple (39.2), ranked No. 1 in the polls most of the season, and Marist (40.1) compiled better numbers. Add the fact that KU ranked No. 11 in field goal percentage at 52.1, and the Jayhawks achieved a

10.9 percentage-point spread between their shooting and that of their opponents. Only Arizona, another Final Four team, had a better spread than Kansas — 11.7. What's more, KU improved the figure during the tournament. In six games the Jayhawks shot 53.8 percent while holding foes to 39.4 percent, a difference of 14.4 percentage points, the best by a champion since Michigan State in 1979. In its two Final Four games, Kansas boosted the spread to 18.3 (57.0 to 38.3), also the largest gap since 1979. In the championship game against Oklahoma, Kansas shot 63.6 percent — the fourth highest mark in the 50 NCAA title games — and allowed 42.9 percent.

In fact, good shooting and dogged defense have been hallmarks of Larry Brown's coaching career, including his five seasons at Kansas. The 10.9 offense-defense spread of the 1987-88 squad matched that of the 1985-86 team, which finished with a 35-4 record. "So much of our defense is a willingness to go out and do it for 40 minutes," Brown said after the season. "These kids probably played our basic defense better than any I've had."

True. They compiled the best

Ben Bigler

As Danny Manning spread his wings in the NCAA Tournament, the Jayhawks soared to the peak of college basketball.

"I was as impressed with Kansas and the coaching job Larry Brown did as any team I've ever watched. It may have been the finest post-season charge as a unit I've seen."

— STEVE NEWTON

Jayhawks like Keith Harris and Milt Newton stretched their abilities to the limit.

Brenda Steele

field goal percentage defense of any of Brown's five Kansas teams. Here's a look at KU's shooting, its defense against shooting and the percentage-point difference during Brown's tenure:

1983-84 — 52.2 to 44.7 (7.5)
1984-85 — 53.7 to 44.4 (9.3)
1985-86 — 55.6 to 44.7 (10.9)
1986-87 — 51.1 to 42.6 (8.5)
1987-88 — 52.1 to 41.2 (10.9)

How good was KU's defense dur-

"We all hung together."

— LARRY BROWN

The 1987-88 Jayhawks developed a winning camaraderie. Manning, at the postseason basketball banquet, offered an affectionate spoof of coach Larry Brown, complete with glasses, rolled-up program and some of the mannerisms he'd observed for four years.

Richard Gwin

ing the championship year? "I feel Kansas defended as well as anyone we played or watched," Murray State coach Steve Newton said after the season. "They took away so many things we were trying to do."

Kansas eluded Murray State, 61-58, in the second round mainly because the Jayhawks held the Racers to 37.3 percent shooting, typified by guard Don Mann's off-balance, against-the-grain shot with five seconds remaining. Murray State's Newton was also impressed by KU's defensive work against Oklahoma's Stacey King and Harvey Grant. "They did as good a job as I've seen in 10 years of defending in the post. Technically, they

were very sound," he said. He added that Brown's game plan "was definitely a beautiful piece of work. It was a master plan. I was as impressed with Kansas and the coaching job Larry Brown did as any team I've ever watched. It may have been the finest post-season charge as a unit I've seen. If Larry Brown is not coach-of-the-year, then I'm a Chinese aviator."

"They made very few mistakes," said Oklahoma State's Leonard Hamilton. "You had to make the play to hurt them, and they denied the ball to the post." Added Nebraska's Danny Nee: "They were really fundamentally sound. Larry's whole game plan was not to give up easy shots." Example: The Jayhawks surrendered only 15 stuff shots — or one about every 3½ games — while jamming the ball 56 times themselves.

Kansas had a disappointing 12-8 record during its first 20 games, then went 15-3 in its last 18. But the Jayhawks didn't struggle during the early going because they weren't playing defense. In the first 20 games, opponents shot 41.5 percent. In the second 18 the figure was 40.7 percent. Not much difference there. What about the Jayhawks' own shooting? In the first 20 games, KU actually shot better than it did later — 52.2 percent to 51.9 percent. Dramatic improvements occurred, however, in three-point shooting and at the free-throw line.

KU's early season three-point shooting was dreadful. After the first 20 games the Jayhawks had hit only 25 percent (24 of 96). In the last 18 they shot a respectable 39.4 percent (54 of 137). Still, their final three-point percentage of 33.5 tied with Colorado's — the Buffs finished 7-21 — for last in the Big Eight. A sidelight was KU's inability to make three-pointers in Allen Fieldhouse. KU players hit only 12 of 64 three-point attempts in the 14 games on their home floor, or 18.8 percent. On the road, Kansas shot 39.1 percent (66 of 169). In foul shooting, the Jayhawks' improved from 66 percent after 20 games to 72.8 percent over the final 18.

Combined, KU's opponents had a higher three-point percentage (35.2 to 33.5) and percentage from the foul line (70.6 to 69.0). Opponents made 161 three-pointers to KU's 78, and 595 free-throw shots to KU's 562. And Kansas had 643 turnovers to its foes' 637. On the other hand, KU posted sizable advantages in assists (670 to 494) and blocked shots (137-70). The Jayhawks also had a 325-to-293 edge in steals. KU averaged 75.3 points a game; opponents 67.9.

As Clyde Lovellette was to KU's 1952 national championship team, so was Danny Manning to the Jayhawks' 1988 title squad. Lovellette was the last man both to lead the nation in scoring (28.4 points a game) and lead his team to the NCAA crown. Manning didn't lead the nation in scoring — he was 12th with a 24.8 average — but he was the first player since North Carolina State's David Thompson in 1974 to combine a national player-of-the-year award with the NCAA Tournament's most outstanding performer honor and a national championship in the same year.

Numbers and awards, however, don't win basketball games. It takes something intangible. "I think the first word is determination," said Nebraska's Nee. "Larry had the kids believing in themselves. And Danny Manning had the attitude 'I'm not going to let us lose.'" Manning

definitely set the tone in Kemper Arena. "He was at the peak of intensity," said OSU's Hamilton. "He had a never-say-die attitude and it was contagious." Hamilton also gave high marks to Brown for his handling of the pressure of being so near and yet so far from a national title. "He had a real good understanding of the mental and emotional part of the Final Four," Hamilton said, "and he did an outstanding job of keeping his players fresh by rotating them in the championship game."

In the end, the Jayhawks won because adversity and 11 losses toughened them, because Ryan Gray, Jimmy Dunlap, John Erickson and Archie Marshall inspired them, because Brown's defensive drills gave them a tool for overcoming Oklahoma. At one point, Brown admitted after the season, he'd hoped KU could win as many as 17 games. Then, he thought, "with a player of Danny's stature, we hoped we could make the NCAAs. We all hung together." Because they did, another championship banner will hang in Allen Fieldhouse.

"Larry had the kids believing in themselves. And Danny Manning had the attitude 'I'm not going to let us lose.'"

— DANNY NEE

Jayhawk fans young and old would have something special to remember.

Cumulative statistics

The Jayhawks

	Games	Games Started	Minutes	Average Minutes	Field Goals Made	Field Goals Attempted	Field Goal Percentage	3-Point Goals Made	3-Point Goals Attempted	3-Point Goal Percentage	Free Throws	Free Throws Attempted	Free Throw Percentage	Rebounds	Rebound Average	Personal Fouls	Disqualifications	Assists	Turnovers	Blocked Shots	Steals	Dunks	Points	Average
Danny Manning	38	38	1336	35.2	381	653	58.3	9	26	34.6	171	233	73.4	342	9.0	114	5	77	115	73	70	16	942	24.8
Milt Newton	35	27	805	23.0	166	299	55.5	29	64	45.3	44	78	56.4	175	5.0	80	2	60	67	13	20	14	405	11.6
Kevin Pritchard	37	36	1100	29.7	144	296	48.6	17	54	31.5	88	119	73.9	95	2.6	100	5	113	84	7	52	5	393	10.6
Archie Marshall	12	11	247	20.6	45	90	50.0	6	11	54.5	9	16	56.3	48	4.0	24	-	17	8	2	5	5	105	8.8
Marvin Branch	14	14	305	21.8	38	78	48.7	-	-	-	41	59	69.5	86	6.1	34	2	12	32	11	7	6	117	8.4
Chris Piper	34	23	877	25.8	66	123	53.7	-	1	-	43	61	70.5	130	3.8	79	3	57	56	9	27	-	175	5.1
Lincoln Minor	34	12	510	15.0	72	172	41.9	-	17	-	18	27	66.7	48	1.4	47	1	65	65	6	39	3	162	4.8
Jeff Gueldner	34	16	562	16.5	46	109	42.2	7	27	25.9	32	47	68.1	67	2.0	55	1	61	37	1	17	-	131	3.9
Scooter Barry	35	3	481	13.7	31	65	47.7	2	8	25.0	53	65	81.5	46	1.3	50	-	70	40	-	20	1	117	3.3
Keith Harris	27	-	371	13.7	32	71	45.1	-	1	-	19	30	63.3	69	2.6	32	-	22	31	3	16	1	83	3.1
Otis Livingston	27	8	388	14.4	26	40	65.0	-	2	-	19	31	61.3	38	1.4	51	1	74	58	2	31	1	71	2.6
Mike Maddox	24	-	183	7.6	25	47	53.2	3	6	50.0	8	17	47.1	36	1.5	28	-	7	10	3	5	2	61	2.5
Mike Masucci	24	1	226	9.4	22	51	43.1	-	-	-	7	15	46.7	36	1.5	40	-	10	12	3	7	2	51	2.1
Clint Normore	25	1	225	9.0	16	36	44.4	5	16	31.3	10	15	66.7	23	.9	29	-	25	26	4	8	-	47	1.9
Marvin Mattox	8	-	9	1.1	1	4	25.0	-	-	-	-	1	-	6	.8	-	-	-	-	-	1	-	2	.3
Kansas	38	-	7625	200.	1111	2134	52.1	78	233	33.5	562	814	69.0	1351	35.6	763	20	670	643	137	325	56	2862	75.3
Opponents	38	-	7625	200.	912	2215	41.2	161	458	35.2	595	843	70.6	1274	33.5	781	28	494	637	70	293	15	2580	67.9

ALL GAMES: WON 27, LOST 11

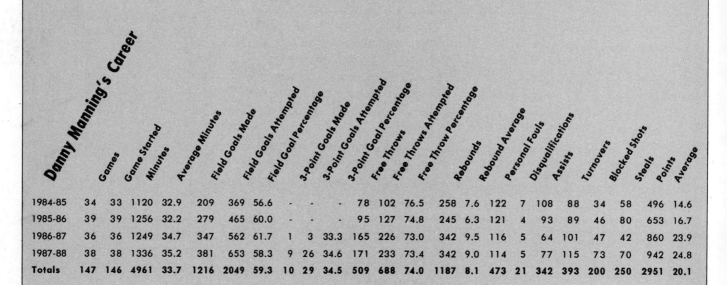

Danny Manning's Career

	Games	Game Started	Minutes	Average Minutes	Field Goals Made	Field Goals Attempted	Field Goal Percentage	3-Point Goals Made	3-Point Goals Attempted	3-Point Goal Percentage	Free Throws	Free Throws Attempted	Free Throw Percentage	Rebounds	Rebound Average	Personal Fouls	Disqualifications	Assists	Turnovers	Blocked Shots	Steals	Points	Average
1984-85	34	33	1120	32.9	209	369	56.6	-	-	-	78	102	76.5	258	7.6	122	7	108	88	34	58	496	14.6
1985-86	39	39	1256	32.2	279	465	60.0	-	-	-	95	127	74.8	245	6.3	121	4	93	89	46	80	653	16.7
1986-87	36	36	1249	34.7	347	562	61.7	1	3	33.3	165	226	73.0	342	9.5	116	5	64	101	47	42	860	23.9
1987-88	38	38	1336	35.2	381	653	58.3	9	26	34.6	171	233	73.4	342	9.0	114	5	77	115	73	70	942	24.8
Totals	147	146	4961	33.7	1216	2049	59.3	10	29	34.5	509	688	74.0	1187	8.1	473	21	342	393	200	250	2951	20.1